The Black Fire Reader

The Black Fire Reader

A Documentary Resource on
African American Pentecostalism

EDITED BY

Estrelda Alexander

FOREWORD BY

A. G. Miller

 CASCADE *Books* · Eugene, Oregon

THE BLACK FIRE READER
A Documentary Resource on African American Pentecostalism

Cascade Books
An Imprint of Wipf and Stock Publishers
199 W. 8th Ave., Suite 3
Eugene, OR 97401

www.wipfandstock.com

ISBN 13: 978-1-60899-562-2

Cataloging-in-Publication data:

The black fire reader : a documentary resource on African American Pentecostalism / edited by Estrelda Alexander ; Foreword by A. G. Miller.

+ p. 23 cm.—Includes bibliographical references and index.

ISBN 13: 978-1-60899-562-2

1. African American Pentecostals—History. 2. African American churches. 3. African Americans—Religion. 4. United States—Church History. I. Alexander, Estrelda, 1949-. II. Miller, A. G. (Albert George), 1951-. III. Title.

BR1644.3 A45 2013

Manufactured in the USA

Contents

Contents

six   Black Pentecostals in Majority-White Denominations | 127

seven   Women in African American Pentecostalism | 157

Contents

Foreword

As the first such collection of primary documents from men and women who have been or are the key players within the African American Pentecostal, Holiness, and Charismatic traditions, this volume of sermons, testimonies, theologies, prayers, and hymns is a watershed in the study of the movement. Professor Estrelda Alexander has provided students of the history, sociology, theology, and ethics of African American Pentecostalism with a great resource for teaching and research on the phenomenon of Pentecostalism worldwide.

Scholars might dispute whether American Pentecostalism emerged solely from the African American experience. Yet, this volume makes it clear that the African American religious experience is at its roots. It also makes clear that this experience helped to profoundly shape its contours from the early beginning at the Azusa Street Revival under William Joseph Seymour to the megachurch phenomenon that is bursting the seams of some once-dying black congregations. Consequently, that experience has continued to influence the phenomenal growth of worldwide Pentecostalism and its Charismatic and Neo-Pentecostal offshoots that is occurring today.

For too long, scholars have debated how to understand, interpret, analyze, contextualize and historicize the development of African American Pentecostalism without having access to materials that would help them with this process. Some have suggested that black Pentecostals left no written theology or record of their beliefs and practices from which to draw adequate inferences. Some have argued that these believers were so driven by otherworldly and heavenly passions that they gave no thought to how to engage the temporal world below. Proponents of the social deprivation theory have argued that "heavenly-minded" Holiness and Pentecostal believers sublimated the hard realities of this present world for the future comforts of a life in heaven, completely rejecting any involvement in social and political life in a way that made them "no earthly good."

It is true that historically, the largely oral tradition of African American Pentecostal produced few substantial theological resources. It is also true that many within the movement have resisted attachment to what they considered the worldliness of such social and political concerns, in search of sanctification, personal piety, and righteous living. As the materials in this volume show, however, a scattered record does exist, though it often must be ferreted out from divergent sources. These sources evidence that black Pentecostal have always shown concerned about this world and the impact of racism, sexism, and harsh economic and social realities with which many black Pentecostals have had to contend for much of the life of the movement.

Important is that through the documents in this collection, we hear African American Pentecostal individuals and leaders speak in their own voices. These voices tell us what *they* want us to hear about their beliefs, practices, theology, and basic understanding of the social and political realities that colored their existence. They share their hopes for a better life on this earth as well as their strong expectation of a good life in the beyond.

These voices come from the educated and the uneducated, Trinitarians and Oneness adherents, pre–Azusa Street Holiness adherents and post-Azusa Pentecostals, integrationists and nationalists, Word of Faith and Classical Pentecostals, historical and contemporary women and men. Their inclusion in this volume shows the variety of views within this diverse movement that has often been understood as a monolith; so this volume sheds light on the broad and far-reaching depth in its multiplicity. In doing so, the voices here give us a welcome new lens through which to engage the tradition at a deeper—indeed richer—level.

A. G. Miller

Preface

This project is a labor of love for a tradition that has been so significant in shaping my spirituality and forming me ethically and morally in ways that have sustained me through life.

As I read through the material, sometimes for the first time, I came to see more clearly how reductionist depictions of Pentecostalism as largely otherworldly had missed the intricacies of a movement that is more diverse than appears on first glance.

The essays—autobiographies, sermons, tracts, testimonies, and hymns—have been selected from a treasure chest of possible artifacts that have remained largely unexplored by those who have spoken so knowingly about the movement for one hundred years. They represent much more than a nostalgic look at a primitive, bygone past. Rather they are a way of linking the most salient values of that past to the issues that still face African American people, congregations, and communities today. They are a valuable, though largely neglected reminder, that even today our help comes from the Lord. The same God and communal solidarity that sustained our parents and grandparents, and empowered them to overcome the obstacles of rampant racism, economic hardship, and social dislocation are a vital resource for the struggle of the contemporary African American community.

I knew few of these people personally, but the stories of their lives and ministries have become an integral part of the communities of which I have been a part. They are told and retold, but often only as sketches with very little supplied substance to fill in the details of the struggle that they portray. This work is a way of tying into a vital African spirituality by venerating the black Holiness-Pentecostal ancestors who helped form and shape a movement and a spirituality that is the fastest-growing segment of the Christian church—not just in the United States but throughout the world.

Further, this project is, in a small way, vindication of the tireless work of these men and women—work that in many cases shortened their lives and gave them very little personal reward except the satisfaction of knowing that God was indeed pleased with them. It is also a word of encouragement to the children of the faith, that what was important to our parents and grandparents had both eternal significance and temporal value. It is an acknowledgment that neither their nor our labor is in vain, and we, as an African people, will "reap, if we faint not."

It is a special honor that the privilege of giving voice to the men and women who were the pioneers and backbone of this movement has fallen to me. For in many ways, the voices contained in this volume, crying out from the grave, are my voice. Their burdens are my burdens, their concerns my concerns. Their encounter with a living God has been my encounter. That I have been called to such a task is both humbling and daunting. So in the words of the saints, I make one request that as you read this volume, "those that know the words of prayer, pray my strength in the Lord!"

Estrelda Y. Alexander

Introduction

Contemporary scholarship on African American Pentecostalism has generally been undertaken by those standing intellectually, culturally, and spiritually outside of its purview. These investigations have known of Pentecostalism and the African American experience from a distance, drawing primarily—and often uncritically—on secondary sources. These scholars have not lived within the socio-historical reality out of which the movement arose or personally encountered the people who have shaped and embody its contours. Resultantly the monolithic portraits that sometimes evolve have been skewed in directions that do not accurately represent the movement.

A number of explorations have highlighted important contributions of African Americans to Pentecostal spirituality and the moral and practical life of the church, drawing attention to salient aspects of the movement that arrested the investigator's attention. Yet, many treatments have been largely caricatures, critiques, or polemics against the perceived otherworldliness of a movement populated by dysfunctional, "disinherited"[1] religious fanatics. Such depictions have been more focused on obvious failings of black Pentecostal believers than on any significant role they

have played, for over a century, in shaping a substantial movement within American and global Christianity.

Resultantly, the unfolding historiography of Pentecostalism has relegated African American contributions to a footnote, as if these contributions were inconsequential for the outworking of American Pentecostalism, or as if adherents could not adequately articulate their experience of the Spirit. Yet, through more than one hundred years, no segment of American Christian culture bears a more solid imprint from the black community than the Pentecostal movement. Further, African American Pentecostals have never ceased speaking to themselves (and to anyone else who would listen) about their experience of the Spirit. Though their voices often have been muted by inattentive and unready ears, for those who would listen voluminous tracts, sermons, hymns, testimonies (spiritual autobiographies), and other material speak volumes about this vital aspect of Pentecostalism and allow a much broader picture to emerge.

Such a portrait presents evidence that at their base, the concerns of African American Pentecostals mirror those of other Evangelical Christians—indeed, those common to all people. Yet black Pentecostals have also borne the onus of carving out an authentic existence in the

---

1. Robert Mapes Anderson used this characterization in his 1992 work *Vision of the Disinherited: The Making of American Pentecostalism.*

midst of American race politics. The voices within this volume peer into that often hostile world colored by the inescapable experience of discrimination, segregation, and disparity that has not left any segment of that community—including its religious life—untouched.

The testimonies that proceed from these pages speak of how a dynamic encounter with the Holy Spirit provided courage to survive being virtually locked out of the American political and economic mainstream during the first half of the twentieth century. They also speak of how the Holy Spirit also provided resources to navigate a place within a somewhat more open society in the latter half of that century. The voices in this volume speak of God's miraculous provision despite disparity; triumph over overwhelming adversity; and an unquenchable hope for a better life for themselves and their children—both in this world and in the world to come.

Their testimonies are echoed by reflections of some of those who, though never part of the movement, positioned themselves near enough to imbibe its unique spirituality in a manner that allowed them to see, firsthand, what they sensed was going on. Like other outsiders, however, what they reported was not always what practitioners saw themselves doing. One testimony comes from someone who once personally imbibed its spirituality but moved on to other traditions. His intimate knowledge of Pentecostal culture is coupled with a critical distance that allows them to speak honestly but no less lovingly of the movement. Interpretations from both of these groups provide a keener lens than the secondhand reporting often representing scholarship on African American Pentecostalism. Taken together, the writings of

the Pentecostal "saints" and their chroniclers challenge monolithic, reductionist characterizations.

The founders, bishops, pastors, and other leaders in this volume speak with a consuming passion for the church, demonstrated in work that ranges from simplistic, naïve biblicism and unashamed loyalty to verbal-plenary inspiration, to sophisticated theological explorations that engage philosophical and other intellectual resources. Such variety dispels misconceptions about the range of theological depth the movement exhibits. These pieces, instead, display the breadth of intellectual engagement of Pentecostal laypersons and leaders.

Yet, they knew the Bible well, as least as far as the plain meaning of the text. Some even showed a rudimentary facility with biblical languages. Some had been exposed to the classics and to prominent social and political thinkers, and drew on these resources in their arguments. For though the Bible has been the major text for these believers, it clearly has not their only text. A surprising number of contributors to this volume draw on the classics within the humanities to support what they consider biblical assertions. At the same time, they dispel characterizations of Pentecostal leaders as uneducated, ignorant "jacklegs" whose congregations are little more than resources for amassing personal gain. In reality, though many early black Pentecostals were undereducated, not all were untaught. Their compositions exhibit a degree of literacy that attests that many were at least well read and had attained some facility in writing.

Moreover, a historical deficit in formal theological training has not left the movement without at least a seminal theology. Surely, such theological insight is more aligned with African ways of thinking than mainline Greek or En-lightenment paradigms. And despite the recent emergence of promising scholars among African American Pentecostals, the movement still has yet to produce a theology that is in any way systematic. Rather, black Pentecostal theologies arose from elements at the center of worship. Sermons attested to reliance on Scripture as the major source and foundation of inspiration and theological reflection—whether delivered in the regular weekly meeting of storefront congregations with a dozen members, or in large camp-meeting style revivals with several hun-dred in attendance. Later, they became more sophisticated and were delivered in megachurch sanctuaries and televised with cutting-edge technology.

The most elaborate doctrinal treatis-es were developed as apologetics by those defending the doctrine of initial evidence, or by oneness leaders in response to the heavy criticism from other Pentecostals of their modalistic conceptions of the nature of the Godhead. Indeed, the respective denominations' doctrinal formulations represent attempts to develop under-standings of the Christian faith that could sustain a spiritual vitality. But even these have more often become measuring rods for determining authentic Christianity—who is or is not saved. Still, they point out what groups hold in common and where they differ, highlighting again the multi-faceted nature of the movement, and at-testing to the diversity that precludes any monolithic characterizations.

The inclusion of lyrics in this volume testifies that music—sung, danced, and played on instruments of every ilk—has always been integral to African life. From simple slave ditties through the spirituals to sophisticated contemporary stylings, African life throughout the Diaspora is permeated with music. Therefore music has been an important medium for car-rying the theology of African American Pentecostalism, and every era has pro-duced songwriters who have interwoven into their compositions the socio-theo-logical witness to both the challenges and the enduring faith of the community.

At the one-hundred-year milestone of the movement, Pentecostal individuals and congregations struggle with the same social, ethical, and spiritual concerns as does every other Christian—indeed every other human being. The issues of personal identity and value, justice, economic sur-vival, and social positioning are as real as spiritual concerns. Such engagement is often couched in what some consider the hyperspiritual Pentecostal language that identifies all social ills as demonic, and credits God with every human victory. Yet, that engagement represents an au-thentic attempt to conceptualize the Holy Spirit's power as an aid in confronting and resisting elements that seek to deny one's humanity and limit one's ability to live a holistic existence.

Finally, this volume demonstrates that there is no one African American Pentecostal movement. Instead, within the black community, more than one hundred bodies self-identify as classically Pentecostal. Further, with the advent of the Charismatic and Neo-Pentecostal movement, several dozen additional groups align themselves in some way with Pentecostal spirituality, and several hun-dred thousand African American Pen-tecostals are members of predominantly white bodies.

As we enter further into the twenty-first century, these several iterations of Pentecostalism have allowed this spiri-tuality to become a predominant force among African American Christians.

Whether as classical Pentecostals (who have dominated most of the movement's one-hundred-year history) or as Charismatics (who emerged in at mid-twentieth century within mainline denominations, or as those who profess Neo-Pentecostal spirituality (that came to prominence throughout much of the previously resistant Black Church near the end of the twentieth century), the movement's influence is undeniable. It is important, then, to let those within it inform us of their self-understanding—their spirituality and the issues that shape their reality. We must hear their message of struggle—no matter how crudely their message is articulated—and let it speak for them.

At the end of the day, the people represented in this volume understood three important truths: they were black in a society—and sometimes in a movement—that had no regard for blackness; they were empowered by the indwelling Holy Spirit to live an authentic human existence in the midst of such disregard; and there had been an unfortunate failure within the movement to appropriate that Holy Spirit empowerment to dismantle the sinful structures and attitudes that perpetuated this state of affairs. These believers were disappointed that a opportunity was missed for the Spirit to accomplish God's purposes for the unity of the church.

I hope the insertion of these voices into the ongoing scholarly conversation regarding the contemporary Pentecostal movement will spur deeper exploration of the faction that has previously received only scant consideration. It is further hoped that such exploration will spark an interest in promoting full social justice within a movement and a society that has not always been aware of the need to do so.

chapter one

Pentecostal Retentions from African Spirituality and Slave Religion

Every Time I Feel the Spirit
(Negro Spiritual)

Chorus:
Every time I feel the spirit
Movin' in my heart I will pray
Every time I feel the spirit
Movin' in my heart I will pray

Up on the mountains my Lord spoke
Out of His mouth came fire and smoke
Looked all around me, it looked so fine
I asked the Lord could it be mine

The Jordan river is chilly and cold.
It chills the body but not the soul.
There aint but one train upon this track.
It runs to heaven and then right back.

Oh, I have sorrow and I have woe
I have heartaches here below
But while God leads me I'll never fear
For I know that He is near

WILLIAM F. ALLEN
(1830–1889)

William Allen, an American classical scholar, wrote prolifically for journals, magazines, and school texts. The Harvard College graduate traveled and studied in Europe and considered a career as a Unitarian minister before deciding to pursue a literary career. In 1856, he became assistant principal at the English and Classical School in West Newton, Massachusetts. During the Civil War, he and his wife ran a school for newly emancipated slaves on the Sea Islands of South Carolina, and in 1864–1865 he worked as a sanitary agent among black war refugees in Arkansas. After the war, he taught at Antioch College before moving to the University of Wisconsin at Madison. Allen's *Slave Songs of the United States*, published in 1867, was the first published work on American slave songs.

The Ring Shout[1]

There is a ceremony which the white clergymen are inclined to discountenance, and even of the colored elders some of the more discreet try sometimes to put on a face of discouragement; and, although if pressed for Biblical warrant for the "shout," they generally seem to think, "he in de Book," or, "he dere-da in Matchew," still it is not considered blasphemous or improper if "de chillen" and "dem young gal" carry it on in the evening for amusement's sake, and with no well-defined intention of "praise." But the true "shout" takes place on Sundays, or on "praise" nights through the week, and either in the praise-house or in some cabin in which a regular religious meeting has been held. Very likely more than half the population of a plantation is gathered together. Let it be the evening, and a light wood fire burns red before the door of the house and on the hearth. For some time one can hear, though at a good distance, the vociferous exhortation or prayer of the presiding elder or of the brother who has a gift that way and is not "on the back seat"—a phrase the interpretation of which is "under the censure of the church authorities for bad behavior"—and at regular intervals one hears the elder "deaconing" a hymn book hymn, which is sung two lines at a time and whose wailing cadences, borne on the night air, are indescribably melancholy.

But the benches are pushed back to the wall when the formal meeting is over, and old and young, men and women, sprucely dressed young men, grotesquely half-clad field hands—the women generally with gay handkerchiefs twisted about their heads and with short skirts—boys with tattered shirts and men's trousers, young girls bare-footed, all stand up in the middle of the floor, and when the "sperichil" is struck up begin first walking and by and by shuffling around, one after the other, in a ring. The foot is hardly taken from the floor, and the progression is mainly due to a jerking, hitching motion which agitates the entire shouter and soon brings out streams of perspiration. Sometimes they dance silently, sometimes as they shuffle they sing the chorus of the spiritual, and sometimes the song itself is also sung by the dancers. But more frequently a band, composed of some of the best singers and of tired shouters, stand at the side of the room to "base" the

---

1. [Ed.] Allen, "The Ring Shout," *The Nation* [May 30, 1867]; reprinted in *Afro-American Folk-Songs*, 33.

others, singing the body of the song and clapping their hands together or on the knees. Song and dance are alike extremely energetic, and often, when the shout lasts into the middle of the night, the monotonous thud, thud of the feet prevents sleep within half a mile of the praise-house.

ZORA NEALE HURSTON
(1891?–1960)

Novelist, folklorist, and anthropologist Zora Neale Hurston was the daughter of a Baptist preacher, tenant farmer, and carpenter. Her mother, a schoolteacher, died when Zora was thirteen, and during her teenage years, Hurston worked at odds jobs, including as a domestic servant, before moving to Washington, DC, to study under Alain Locke at Howard University. She migrated to New York City around 1925 to involve herself in the Harlem Renaissance, and while there studied at Barnard College under famed anthropologist Franz Boas.

Hurston published her best-known work, *Their Eyes Were Watching God*, in 1937 and went on to produce numerous articles and short stories as well as several full-length manuscripts of both fiction and ethnography. Yet, in later life, Hurston suffered several setbacks that virtually destroyed her personally and professionally. By the end of her life, within a year of suffering a fatal stroke, she had become a penniless recluse. Though she was buried in the unmarked grave usually reserved for those of no acclaim, her work was later rediscovered, and she received renewed prominence.

From The Sanctified Church[2]

The rise of various groups of saints in America in the last twenty years is not the appearance of a new religion as has been reported. It is in fact the older forms of Negro religious expression asserting itself against a new.

Frequently they are confused with white protest Protestantism known as Holy Rollers. There are Negro Holy Rollers, but they are very sparse compared to other forms of sanctification. The branches of the sanctified church are: (a) Church of God in Christ, (b) Saints of God in Christ.

The sanctified church is a protest against the highbrow tendencies in Negro Protestant congregations as the Negroes gain more education and wealth. It is understandable that they take on the religious attitudes of the white man which are as a rule so staid and restrained that it seems unbearably dull to the more primitive Negro who associates the rhythm of sound and motion with religion. In fact, the Negro has not been Christianized as much as generally believed. The great masses are still standing by their pagan altars and calling old gods by new names. As evidence of this, note the drum-like rhythm of all Negro spirituals. All Negro-made church music is dance-possible. The mode and mood of the concert artists who do Negro spirituals is absolutely foreign to the Negro churches. It is a conservatory concept that has nothing to do with the actual renditions in the congregations who make the songs. They are twisted in concert from their barbaric rhythms into Gregorian chants and apocryphal appendages to Bach and Brahms. But go into the church and see the priest before the altar chanting his barbaric thunder-poem before the altar with the audience behaving like a Greek chorus in that they "pick him up" on every telling point and emphasize it. That is called "bearing him up" and it is not done just any old way. The chant that breaks out from time to time must grow out of

2. [Ed.] Hurston, *The Sanctified Church*, 103–5. Used with permission from the Zora Neale Hurston Trust.

what has been said and done. "Whatever point he come out on, honey you just bear him up on it." Mama Jane told the writer. So the service is really drama with music. And since music without motion is unnatural among Negroes there is always something that approaches dancing—in fact IS dancing—in such a ceremony. So the congregation is restored to its primitive altars under the new name of Christ. Then there is an expression known as "shouting" which is nothing more than an African possession by the gods. The gods possess the body of the worshipper and he or she is supposed to know nothing of their actions until the god decamps. This is still prevalent in most Negro Protestant churches and is universal in the Sanctified churches. They protest against the more highbrow churches' efforts to stop it. It must be noted that the sermon is not the set thing that it is in the other highbrow churches. It is loose and formless and is in reality merely a framework on which to hang more songs. Every opportunity to introduce new rhythm is eagerly seized upon. The whole movement of the Sanctified church is a rebirth of song-making. It has brought in a new era of spiritual-making.

These songs by their very beauty cross over from the little store-fronts and the like occupied by the "Saints" to the larger and more fashionable congregations and from there to the great world. These more conscious churchgoers, despising these humble tune-makers as they do always resist these songs as long as possible; but finally succumb to their charm, So that it is ridiculous to say that the spirituals are the Negro "sorrow songs." For just as many are being made in this post-slavery period as ever were made in slavery as far as anyone can find out. At any rate the people who are now

making spirituals are the same as those who made them in the past and not the self-conscious propagandist that our latter-day pity men would have us believe. They sang sorrowful phrases then as they do now because they sounded well and not because of the thought-content.

Examples of new spirituals that have become widely known:

He is a Lion of the House of David

Stand By Me

His Little Light I Got

I Want Two Wings

I'm Going Home On The Morning Train

I'm Your Child

There are some crude anthems made also among these singers.

O Lord, O Lord, let the words of my mouth, O Lord Let the words of my mouth, meditations of my heart Be accepted in thy sight. O Lord. (From the Psalm. "Let the words of my mouth and the meditation of my heart be accepted in thy sight, O Lord.")

Beloved, beloved, Now are we the sons of God

And it doth not yet appear what we shall be

But we know, but we know, but we know, but we know,

When He shall appear; when He shall appear,

When He shall appear, when He shall appear

We shall be like Him, we shall be like Him

We shall see Him as He is

(St. Paul: Beloved, now are we the sons of God but it does not yet appear what we shall be. But we know that when He shall appear we shall be like Him and we shall see Him as He is.)

The Saints, or the Sanctified Church is a revitalizing element in Negro music and religion. It is putting back into Negro religion those elements which were brought over from Africa and grafted onto Christianity as soon as the Negro came in contact with it, but which are being rooted out as the American Negro approaches white concepts. The people who make up the sanctified groups, while admiring the white brother in many ways, think him ridiculous in church . . .

The real singing Negro derides the Negro who adopts the white man's ways in the same manner. They say of that type of preacher, "Why he don't preach at all. He just lectures."

And the way they say the word "lecture" make[s] it sound like horse-stealing. "Why, he sound like a white man preaching." There is great respect for the white man as law-giver, banker, builder, and the like but the folk Negro do not crave his religion at all. They are not angry about it; they merely pity him because it is generally held that he just can't do any better

that way. But the Negro who imitates the whites comes in for spitting scorn. So they let him have his big solemn church all to himself while they go on making their songs and music and dance motions to go along with it and shooting new life into American music. I say American music because it has long been established that the tunes from the street and church change places often. So they go on unknowingly influencing American music and enjoying themselves hugely while doing so in spite of the derision from the outside.

It is to be noted the strong sympathy between the white "saints" and the Negro ones. They attend each other's meetings frequently, and it is interesting to see the white saint attempting the same rhythms and movements. Often the white preacher preaches the sermon (in the Negro manner) and the Negroes carry on the singing. Even the definite African "Possession" attitudes of dancing mostly on one foot and stumbling about to a loose rhythm is attempted. These same steps can be seen in Haiti when a man or a woman is "mounted" by a loa, or spirit.

The Holiness Meeting[3]
Anonymous

Once a year a group of 200 to 300 ne-groes give a religious Camp meeting in a field on the Canton Pike about one mile southeast of Hopkinsville. There is quite a settlement of negroes call themselves or their church the Holiness Church. They claim to be sanctified and cannot sin. A few nights ago, I was invited to attend one of these meetings, the negroes reserve some benches under the tent for white people.

. The night that I attended there were two preachers and it seems as though it is the duty of these preachers to bring; their discourse to such a point as to play on the emotions of their congregation.

The order of service begun with a hymn by the choir. The music for this consisted of a piano, banjo guitar and numerous tambourines. The negroes be-ing naturally born with a great sense of rhythm the songs were not in the same tempo as the songs or the whites but were of a jazz tempo and with the banjo and tambourines it makes one think of the stories of the African jungles. The services start around 7:30 P.M. and usually break up around midnight.

The negroes in about one hour after the services start [begin] to testify and then after each testimony someone offers

3. Rawick, ed., *The American Slave*, 16:71–72.

a prayer then by this time someone in the congregation will be worked up to the pitch of shouting; "Glory [Hallelujah.]" When this shout starts the tambourine players will begin shaking the tambou-rines and shortly the majority of the con-gregation would be shouting;. moaning or praying. The tambourines [*sic*] play-ers bounce around in time to the music. There were some excellent untrained voices in the choir and the congregation. The mourners bench was always full of mourners and when one of the Mourn-ers would begin to shout the "Workers" would then let the congregation know that this brother or sister had repented by saying "Let's pray for Bro. or Sister _____ for he or she had "Come Through." The congregation would begin clapping their hands while this prayer was in progress and general moanings with one or both of the preachers praying at the same time while the brother or sister is taken in to the flock to sin no more.

While the above is in progress there are other workers talking and singing to the rest of the mourners and when two or three "Come Through" at once there is great shouting, rejoicing, clapping of hands and the tambourines continue to clang and the choir members dance and this process continues for hours or until the preachers became so exhausted with their exhortations and contortions that the meeting is adjourned.

CHARLES HARRISON MASON
(1866–1961)

Church of God in Christ

Once Mason broke with his colleague, Charles Price Jones, he went on to recast the Church of God in Christ (COGIC) and head the body that would become the largest African American Pentecostal body in the world. As head of that body, the son of former slaves championed African spirituality and incorporated its elements and slave religion into COGIC's ritual and practices. He vigorously promoted African healing rituals, worship styles, and communal practices and sought to make them respectable within the African American Pentecostal community. The prominence of COGIC within that community lends a certain air of acceptability—if not respectability to these practices among black Pentecostals.

Is It Right for the Saints of God to Dance?[4]

Yes. The word of the Lord says: "Let them praise him in the dance" (Psa 149:3, also 150:4). "Then shall the virgin rejoice in the dance, both the young man and old together" (Jer 31:13). "When Israel's joy ceased her dance was turned to mourning" (Lam 5:15; Jdgs 21:21)."There is a time of dance or a time of dancing" (Eccl 3:4). "David danced before the Lord with all his might" (2 Sam 6:16). "We may sing and dance" (I Sam 21:1). "When God builds up his people as they are to be built up, then they shall go forth in the dance" (Jer 31:4). People may go and dance with the wrong purpose or object in view, as did Israel (Ex 32:19).

Dancing shows that we have victory (I Sam 18:6). Sometimes there may be only women in the dance (I Sam 18:6; Ex 15:20). God turned for me my mourning into dancing (Ps 30:11).

4. Originally published in *History and Formative Years of the Church of God in Christ with Excerpts from the Life and Work of Its Founder* (Memphis: Church of God in Christ Publishing House, 1969).

Dancing is mentioned four times in the New Testament. Christ himself making mention of it (Matt 11:17; Lk 7:32). In the 15th chapter, 25th verse of Luke, Christ's parable of the prodigal says he was received with music and dancing. Dancing here denotes or expresses joy. It is the parable of the heavenly joy over the repentance of one sinner. Dancing of the people of God is to be in the spirit of Jesus only, for as in Jesus only we rejoice and dance and praise God. We must have Jesus and all Jesus, Jesus in all things in the Church and His Saints.

The people of God do not dance as the world dances, but are moved by the Spirit of God. So you can see it is all in the Spirit of God and to the glory of God. It is not to satisfy the lust of the flesh, or the carnal appetite, as the world's dance, but only to glorify god and satisfy the soul. The world dances of the world, about the world and to the world. The children of god dance of God, for God and to the praise and glory of His name. They have the joy of the Spirit of the Lord in them. They are joyful in their King—the Christ. At times they may be dancing Christ is all, or none but Christ.

How sweet it is to dance in Him and about Him, for he that dances in the Spirit of the Lord expresses joy and victory. Amen.

chapter two

The Legacy of the Nineteenth-Century Black Holiness Movement

Deeper, Deeper

Charles Price Jones

(1865–1949)
Church of Christ (Holiness) USA

Deeper, deeper in the love of Jesus
Daily let me go;
Higher, higher in the school of wisdom,
More of grace to know.

Refrain:
   Oh, deeper yet, I pray,
   And higher every day,
   And wiser, blessed Lord,
   In Thy precious, holy Word.

Deeper, deeper, blessed Holy Spirit,
Take me deeper still,
Till my life is wholly lost in Jesus,
And His perfect will.

Deeper, deeper! though it cost hard trials,
Deeper let me go!
Rooted in the holy love of Jesus,
Let me fruitful grow.

Deeper, higher, every day in Jesus,
Till all conflict past,
Finds me conqu'ror, and in His own image
Perfected at last.

Deeper, deeper in the faith of Jesus,
Holy faith and true;
In His pow'r and soul exulting wisdom
Let me peace pursue.

WILLIAM CHRISTIAN
(1853?–1928)

Church of the Living God (Christian Workers for Fellowship)

The founder of the Church of the Living God (Christian Workers for Fellowship, CWFF), one of the oldest black Holiness bodies in America, was born in Mississippi several years before emancipation and was reared as a slave during his earliest years, an experience that left an indelible mark. This mark would be evidenced in the incorporation of tenets on racial equality into the structure of his new body. Prior to accepting the Holiness teachings on which his church was framed, Christian had been a Baptist pastor and colleague of Charles Harrison Mason. A former Freemason, after reportedly having a divine revelation in which God instructed him that the Baptist church taught an erroneous, sectarian gospel, Christian held that membership in secret societies such as the masons is incompatible with Holiness doctrine.

Christian served at the head of CWFF for almost forty years, crafting a unique identity for the body that distinguishes itself from other Holiness bodies, as a branch of black Judaism. Congregations are temples, not churches, members are black Jews, and the Church of the Living God originally celebrated the Sabbath and worshiped on Saturday rather than Sunday. Unlike their Holiness colleagues, Christian's group uses water and unleavened bread in the Lord's Supper. Further, these ordinances are administered to a believer only once. As with other Holiness groups, CWFF does not see speaking in tongues as the initial sign of Holy Spirit baptism, but only one of the several gifts that come with Holy Spirit baptism, and only permits speaking in tongues in recognizable languages in its worship.

Poor Pilgrim's Work

Chapter 6

Repent of your sins sinners, or you will be lost. I want to show you in this work that men have to repent, but they don't have to pray and repent. They have to repent and then pray. It repented the Lord and grieved him at his heart that he made man on the earth. Gen. 6:6.[1] This would show that repentance and sorrow are in close connection with each other. Read these note[s] on repentance closely and see that none of them says pray and repent, but they say: 'repent,' Deut. 32:36; I Sam. 15:11; II Sam. 24:16; I King[s] 8:47; Job 42:6; Jer 18:8; Ezek. 14:6; 18:30. This is the Old Testament scriptures, now we will go in the New Testament. John preached repentance, Matt. 3:1–2, but he never did say pray and repent, and Jesus Christ, our Savior, preached and taught repentance. Matt. 4:17. Read these notes closely on repentance and you will see that they say repent all right, but they don't say pray and repent. Matt 9:13; 12:4; Mark 1:4.

Jesus taught men to repent and believe the gospel. Mark 1:15, but if Jesus, our saviour taught men to repent and believe the gospel, . . . he never said pray and repent and believe the gospel. All this praying to repent and this mourners' bench business, and going out in the woods to hunt God is all a humbug and ignorance of the deepest dye. The

1. [Ed.] Placing Scripture references in the text without enclosing them in parentheses is a convention of William Christian.

apostles when they preached they taught men to repent. Mark 6:12. I don't know where this idea came from teaching men to pray and repent, unless it came from wine drinking preachers. Proverbs gives us to understand that those who drink wine and strong drink are not wise. Prov 20:1. Then the preachers who drink wine in the church and give it to their members must not be wise according to the Bible. John still preaches repentance, Luke 3:3. Friends at large, you all must repent or perish. Lk 13:3, 5. Notice friends Christ speaks of great rejoicing over one sinner that repents. Lk 5:7. Also when the apostles were sent out to preach they were told that they should preach repentance and remission of sins. Luke 24:47. And on the day of Pentecost the sinners asked the apostles what they must do, Peter said repent. Acts 2:38.

Now when sinners ask the preachers what they must do to be saved, they tell them to come to the mourners' bench and go rid get religion.[2] They are telling the poor sinners to do something they never saw in the Bible in their lives. Postle Peter still preaches repentance. Acts 3:19, 7:30; 20:21, 26:20; Rom. 2:4. Our preachers have been teaching that Godly sorrow was repentance. The Bible doesn't teach it. The Bible says Godly sorrow worketh repentance. II Cor. 7:9–10; II Peter 3:9; Rev. 2:4–5, 16, 21–22; 3:3,19; and the nearest we can connect praying and repentance together is when Postle Peter said repent and pray God. Acts 8:22. But understand this chapter and verse it is repent and pray which shows repentance comes first. It is not as most of the preachers have it: Pray and repent.

About sinners' prayers being heard: Job says God will not cast away a perfect

man neither will he help an evil doer. Job 8:20. I understand a perfect man to be righteous, and I understand the evil doer to be a sinner. Psalms shows that God would not hear somebody pray and we know he will hear the righteous, and those he would not hear must have been sinners. Ps. 4; 66 Ps. 18; Prv. 1:28;15:29; Isa 1:15, Jer 11:11; Ezek 8:18; Zach 7:13.

And the man that Christ healed his eyes said: Now we know that God heareth not sinners, but if any man be a worshipper of God him he heareth. St. John 9:31. Remember that Postle Peter says the eyes of the Lord are over the righteous and his ears are open to their prayers but his is against them that do evil. I Peter 3:12. If the Lord's face is against the wicked I don't think He will have much to do with them in prayer. Notice Christ never told the apostles to tell sinners to pray when he sent them out to preach. Christ when he sent the apostles out to preach told them to preach the gospel to every creature. He that believeth and is baptized shall be saved. Mark 6:16. Christ never said a word about telling sinners to pray or telling sinners to come to the mourners' bench. If you poor sinners want to be saved accept the word of God and believe in Jesus Christ. Remember friends the word is God. St. Jn 1:1 and the word was recommended to be Christ. St. Jn 1:14. And the word is the spirit also. St. John 6:63. Then those who accept the words, accept the Father, Son and Holy Spirit, because they all agree in one I Jn 5:7. Sinners, believe in Christ and obey him and he will save you. St. Jn 3:15–16; 36; 20:30–31. And if you sinners believe on Christ and confess him before men he will confess you before his father. Matt. 10:32; Acts 8:36–40, 16:30–36; Rom. 10:9–10. Sinners, poor sinners, if you will accept the word of God like he gave it through Christ he will

2. [Ed.] Christian's meaning is uncertain here.

save you. You don't need to have any fits and spasms, but just accept the word and he will save you. Matt. 7:24–25. And you who don't obey him need not expect to be saved. Matt. 7:26–27. Think: on judgment. Deut. 32:22; Mal. 4; Job 14:13; 39:19; Luke 17:29; II Thess 1:7–8. With this I will leave you all in the hands of the Lord . . .

Chapter 7

The first sin or disobedience I see is the angels fighting in heaven [The disobedient angels fell]. Then some one of these fallen or sinful angels or serpents went to Eve and persuaded her to eat the forbidden fruit. That, of course, made Eve a sinner if I understand it. Then Eve persuaded Adam to eat the fruit. Gen 3:1–6. What is sin? It is disobedience. God told Adam and Eve not to eat the fruit of a certain tree and as long as they obeyed God they were all right, but when they disobeyed God it was not long until God drove them out of the garden. Gen. 3:24. This is plain that sin is disobedience.

I trust that this will enable you all to see if any person wants to get rid of their sin they must get rid of disobedience and then they are rid of their sin and Jesus Christ will save those who forsake their evil way Isa. 1:16–17; 55:7; Zach. 8:16–17. The way that sinners or the wicked are to get rid of their sin, they must quit doing wrong, and here is the proof of it if the Bible is true. Ezek 18:21, 27–28. Friends don't wait on God to turn you, but turn yourself. Ezek 18:30–32. Friends there is no use to try to dodge it. We must lay aside our sins. Remember Postle Paul says, let us lay aside every weight and sin. Heb. 12:l. Poor sinners, look to Jesus Christ, our saviour, and he will save you all . . .

Chapter 8

Some preachers and members pretend that it is such a hard thing to obey the Lord, but it certainly ain't so. Christ, our saviour, said, my yoke is easy and my burden is light. Matt. 11:30. And if we can't be pure, we can't be Christians, because Christ, our saviour, taught us that the pure in heart shall see God Matt. 5:8. Someone may say, Brother Christian, that only means your heart being pure. Brothers and sisters don't be narrow minded on Christianity. Christ Jesus, our saviour taught us to be perfect even as our father which is in heaven is perfect. Matt 5:48. You remember that Christ said O righteous Father. Jn 17:25. Then if God the father is righteous, we ought to be sanctified. Jn 17:17. That would lead me to believe that Christ, the true vine is righteous, then if we are branches in the vine, we would have to be righteous as God and Christ is because God is the husbandman and Christ is the vine[,] and it is a fact we would have to get our substance from the vine and if Christ, the vine affords pure substance then there could not be another substance in the branches unless it is pure substance. Christ is the vine and God the husbandman. Jn 15:1. And here Christ says, I am the vine, ye are the branches. Jn 15:5–6. Then if the vine is pure the branches must be pure.

Remember Christian friends that Postle Paul says in Romans, if the first fruits be holy the lump is also holy and if the root be holy so are the branches. Rom. 11:16. Remember Christian friends that Postle Paul teaches us that we must live righteous and Godly in this world. Tit. 2:12. John teaches us to purify ourselves even as he is pure. I Jn 3:3. You must remember Christian that Christ was manifested to take away our sins and whosoever abideth in Christ sinneth not. I Jn 3:5–6. Notice what John says here in particular: Little children let no man deceive you. He that doeth righteousness, is righteous even as He is righteous. I Jn 3:7, 9–10.

You had better keep out of sin if you want to make heaven your home. And all of you that can't go to judgment in righteousness can prepare to be lost if I understand the Bible. We are taught in the Revelation, "Behold, I come quickly; and my reward is with me to give to everyman according as his work shall be. Rev 22:12. This goes to show just as we live just so God is going to settle with us in the judgment . . .

Chapter 13

God and Christ nor the apostles never told anybody to get religion, nor neither did they tell anybody that religion would get them. Yet we have got thousands of preachers all over this country telling people to get religion and no preacher has ever seen such doctrine in the Bible. It is awful funny that preachers will teach people to oar get something they have never seen in the Bible.[3] Ask most of our preachers and members what religion is and they will say the love of God is religion, and others will answer that the love of God in the heart is religion. Postle Paul spoke of the love of God in the heart, but he did not call it religion. St. James tells us what counterfeit religion is, if I understand it in these words: If any man among you seem to be religious and bridleth not his tongue, but deceive his own heart, this man's religion is in vain. James 1:26. Now James goes onto tell us what pure religion is. He don't stop at telling us that it is pure, but he tells us that it is pure before God and the father. Now let James tell us what this pure religion is, then we can soon tell whether it is to get or do pure religion and undefiled before God and the father is this: To visit the fatherless and widows in their affliction, and to keep himself unspotted from the world. James 1:27. Now dear readers, you can see if religion is what James says it is something to do and not to get, and if this is religion, there are a mighty few people who have begun to work at it yet. God grant that every human being may come to the idea of pure religion and the condition of the people will be so much better[.] Baptist preachers and Methodist bishops and preachers and all other preachers of any kind that are teaching people to get religion had better quit it.

---

3. [Ed.] Christian's meaning is uncertain here.

AMANDA BERRY SMITH
(1837–1915)

African Methodist Episcopal Church

Lay Holiness preacher Amanda Berry Smith addressed white camp meetings in the United States and England as often as she did black congregations. While in England in 1878, she made friends with prominent Keswick leaders Hannah Whitall Smith and Mary Broadman. These relationships opened an opportunity to attend the Keswick Conference for the Promotion of Higher Life, and invitations to preach throughout the United Kingdom, and made her the first black woman international evangelist. From England she travelled to India, spending two years holding revivals and working with churches in large cities and in numerous smaller towns and villages. After returning to England for a short time, she departed again and spent almost eight years (1881–1889) helping with churches and establishing temperance societies in Liberia and Sierra Leone. Despite being a member of the African Methodist Episcopal (AME) church, Smith's missionary work was financed by limited Methodist Episcopal Church (MEC) support and donations from individual supporters. There she not only preached but led temperance meetings for people such Bishop William Taylor, the famed Methodist missionary leader, who said that she "had done more for the cause of missions and temperance in Africa than the combined efforts of all missionaries before her."[4]

Throughout Smith's work in Africa, she championed the status of women and the need for education of children—male and female. As prolific as her work was, it drew criticism from mainline AME Church leaders who explicitly and regularly castigated her for supporting Holiness teaching on sanctification, for not contributing her gifts and talents to support the burgeoning AME women's effort in the church, and for focusing her attention on ministering to whites rather than to blacks.

From An Autobiography: The Story of the Lord's Dealings with Mrs. Amanda Smith[5]

My Last Call—How I Obeyed It, And What Was The Result

It was the third Sunday in November, 1890. Sister Scott, my band sister, and myself went to the Fleet street A. M. E. Church, Brooklyn. It was Communion Sunday. Before I left home I said to Sister Scott: "I wish I had not promised to go to Brooklyn." She said "Why?"

"Oh, I feel so dull and stupid."

We went early, and went into the Sabbath School. At the close of the Sabbath School the children sang a very pretty piece. I do not remember what it was, but the spirit of the Lord touched my heart and I was blessed. My bad feeiings had gone for a few moments, and I thought, "I guess the Lord wanted to bless me here." But when we went upstairs I began to feel the same burden and pressure as I had before. And I said, "Oh, Lord, help me, and teach me what this means." And just at that point the Tempter came with this supposition: "Now, if you are wholly sanctified, why is it that you have these dull feelings?"

4. Brown, *Homespun Heroines*, 131.
5. Smith, *An Autobiography*, 147–64.

I began to examine my work, my life, every day, and I could see nothing. Then I said, "Lord, help me to understand what Thou meanest. I want to hear Thee speak."

Brother Gould, then pastor of the Fleet Street Church, took his text. I was sitting with my eyes closed in silent prayer to God, and after he had been preaching about ten minutes, as I opened my eyes, just over his head I seemed to see a beautiful star, and as I looked at it, it seemed to form into the shape of a large white tulip; and I said, "Lord, is that what you want me to see? If so, what else?" And then I leaned back and closed my eyes. Just then I saw a large letter "G," and I said: "Lord, do you want me to read in Genesis, or in Galatians? Lord, what does this mean?"

Just then I saw the letter "O." I said, "Why, that means go." And I said "What else?" And a voice distinctly said to me "Go preach."

The voice was so audible that it frightened me for a moment, and I said, "Oh Lord, is that what you wanted me to come here for? Why did you not tell me when I was at home, or when I was on my knees praying?" But His paths are known in the mighty deep, and His ways are past finding out. On Monday morning, about four o'clock, I think, I was awakened by the presentation of a beautiful, white cross—white as the driven snow—similar to that described in the last chapter. It was as cold as marble. It was laid just on my forehead and on my breast. It seemed very heavy; to press me down. The weight and the coldness of it were what woke me; and as I woke I said: "Lord, I know what that is. It is a cross."

I arose and got on my knees, and while I was praying[,] these words came to me: "If any man will come after Me let him deny himself and take up his cross

and follow Me." And I said, "Lord, help me and I will . . ."

. . . [In] October, 1870, when I left my home at God's command, and began my evangelistic work. I did not know then that it meant all that it has been. I thought it was only to go to Salem, as the Lord had showed me. Shortly after this I was off to Salem. Got as far as Philadelphia, where I purposed leaving my little girl with her grandfather, while I went on to Salem. But strange to say, notwithstanding all the light, and clear, definite leading of the Lord, my heart seemed to fail me. I said to myself, "After all, to go on to Salem, a stranger, where I don't know a minister, or anybody. No, I will do some work here in Philadelphia."

So I got some tracts, went away down in the lower part of town, on St. Mary's street, and Sixth, and Lombard, and all in that region. I went into saloons and gave tracts; gave tracts to people on the corners; spoke a word here and there; some laughed and sneered; some took a tract. Then I went to the meetings, and sang and prayed and exhorted. I went about among the sick, and did all I could. And I said, "After all, the Lord may not want me to go to Salem."

After spending a week in Philadelphia I thought I would go home. Friday came, and I thought to myself, "Well, I will go home Saturday." But, Oh! there came such an awful horror and darkness over me. On Friday night, after I had come home front an excellent meeting, I could not sleep, all night. Oh how I was troubled. I did not know what to do, for I had spent all my money; father did not have much means, and when Mazie and I were at home I generally provided, not only for ourselves, but for all the family; so that my means went almost before I knew it; I had not much, anyhow. But it seemed to me I would die. So I told the Lord if He would spare me till morning, though I had not any money, I would go and see my sister, and if she could lend me a dollar so as to get on to Salem, I would go.

Saturday morning came. I borrowed a dollar, came home, and spent twenty-five cents of it for breakfast; then with what it cost me to ride down to get on the boat, in all about fifteen cents, I had left about sixty cents. My ticket on the boat was fifty cents; I had had some little hymns struck off; we colored people were very fond of ballads for singing.

A little while after I got on the boat, who should come in but Brother Holland, who used to be my pastor eight years before, in Lancaster, Pa. All this had come to pass in the years after I had known him; so that he did not know anything at all about it. He was very glad to see me, and asked me where I was going. I told him the Lord had sent me to Salem. Then I began to tell him my story. How the Lord had led me. How He had called me to His work. Dear old man, he listened to me patiently, and when I had got through he said:

"Well, Sister Smith, you know I don't believe in women preaching. But still, honey, I have got nothing to say about you. You go on. The Lord bless you."

I was dumbfounded; for I thought he was in the greatest sympathy with woman's work, though I had never heard him express himself with regard to it. But I was glad of the latter part of what he said.

It was quite a cool day, and the boat got in about two o'clock in the afternoon. There were no street cars then, as there are now. There was a big omnibus. They didn't let colored people ride inside an omnibus in those days. So I took my carpet bag and had to sit outside on the top of the omnibus.

They didn't let colored people off till all the white people were off, even if they had to go past where they wanted to stop; so I had to ride round on the omnibus at least three-quarters of an hour before I was taken to where I wanted to go.

The woman's name, where I had been told to go, was Mrs. Curtis. She was a widow, and owned her own house and grounds; she had quite a nice, comfortable little house. But she was a queer genius. Old Father Lewis, who had once been pastor of the A. M. E. Church at Salem, and at this time was pastor of the church at Jersey City Heights, N. J., had recommended me to Sister Curtis, because she was alone and had plenty of room, and he thought it would be so nice for me. It was more than a half mile from the locality in which the colored church was situated, and in which the majority of the colored people lived. But Sister Curtis seemed as though she was frightened at me. I told her who had sent me to her house, and how the Lord had called me to His work, and all my story of the Lord's doing. She listened, but was very nervous. Then she said she didn't know what in the world she would do, for she hadn't anything but some hard bread to give me to eat, and she hadn't any sugar; and I said, "Well, no matter for that. I can eat hard bread, and I can drink tea without sugar, if you can only accommodate me till Monday, at least."

Well, she said she could keep me all night, but she didn't like to leave any one in the house on Monday, because she generally went away to wash; and she generally had the cold pieces given her from the hotel where she went to wash dishes, and that was all she could give me to eat.

She knew how we colored people are about eating; we do like to eat; so I think she told me that thinking she would frighten me; but I agreed to everything. Then I asked her if she could tell me where Brother Cooper, who was then pastor, lived. She said, "Yes, it is about a mile and a half."

I asked her if she would show me which way to go. She did so, but did not give me anything to eat. I was very hungry, but I did not ask her for anything. So I started off about three o'clock, or a little after, and went to see Brother Cooper.

I was tired, and walked slowly, and it was about half-past four when I got up to the little village above. I inquired my way, and was told that Sister Johnson lived right close by Brother Cooper's, and if I would go to her house she could tell me, for it was just through her yard to Brother Cooper's house. So I went. I knocked at the door. The sister was in; several nice looking little children were playing around, and an elegant pot of cabbage was boiling over the fire. My! how nice it did smell; and I did wish and pray that the Lord would put it into her heart to ask me to have something to eat. I hinted all I knew how, but she did not take the hint. I knew by the sound of it that it was done and ought to come off!

I told her my story; told her about Brother Lewis; she was very glad to hear from him. I asked her if I could stay all night, because I felt so tired that I thought I could not walk back to Sister Curtis'. She said at once she could not possibly have me stay all night. Her mother had been dead about three months, and she had taken down the bedsteads, and she was so overburdened with her grief she had never put them up, and they were all lying on the floor.

I told her no matter for that; I could sleep on the floor just as well. No, she did not have room. She could not possibly do it.

Well, I stayed till it was pretty dark. It was after six o'clock. The more I talked the more she gave me to see that she was not going to ask me to have any cabbage, or to stay all night.

So I said to her, "Will you tell me where Brother Cooper, the minister, lives?"

"Oh, yes," she said, "I will send one of the children with you."

When I got to Brother Cooper's I knocked, and Brother Cooper came to the door; he was an awful timid man; so he stood at the door, holding it half open and leaning out a little ways, and asked me who I was. I told him that I was Amanda Smith; that the Lord sent me to Salem. Then I went on, standing at the door, telling him how the Lord had led me, and all about it. His wife, who was a little more thoughtful than he, heard me, and she called out to him, and said, "Cooper, why don't you ask the sister to come in." So then he said, "Come in, Sister."

I was awful glad, so I went in. Sister Cooper was getting supper. The table was set, and I thought, "Maybe, I will get something to eat now."

So I went on and finished my story, and they seemed to be greatly interested; and when the supper was quite ready, she said, "Will you have some supper, Sister Smith?" I thanked her, and told her I would.

While I was eating my supper who should come in but good Brother Holland, that had been on the boat. He said to Brother and Sister Cooper, "I am glad you have Sister Smith here. You needn't be afraid of her, she is all right; I have known her for years. I have not seen her since I was pastor at Lancaster."

Then they brightened up a little bit, and seemed to be a little more natural. My heart was glad. It was quarterly meeting, and Brother Holland was to preach in the morning and Brother Cooper in the afternoon. So Brother Holland said, as he was Presiding Elder, I might speak at night and tell my story.

"All right," I said.

After a little talk, Brother Holland left. Sister Cooper said she would be very glad to have me stay all night, but they had no room. They had not been long there, and had only fitted up one room for their own use. They thought they would make out with that for the winter. So then I was obliged to walk a mile and a half back to Sister Curtis'. I did hate to do it, but the Lord helped me.

So I stayed that night at Sister Curtis', and she gave me a little breakfast on Sunday morning, but it was mighty skimpey! But I found out that a good deal of praying fills you up pretty well when you cannot get anything else! On Sunday morning we went to Love Feast, and had a good time. Prior to this I had been asking the Lord to give me a message to give when I went to Salem. I said, "Lord, I don't want to go to Salem without a message. And now you are sending me to Salem, give me the message. What shall I say?"

Two or three times I had gone before the Lord with this prayer, and His word was, "It shall be made known to you when you come to the place what you shall say." And I said, "All right, Lord." So I didn't trouble Him any more till this Sunday morning. The Lord helped Brother Holland preach. When he got through preaching and the collection was taken, Brother Cooper made the announcement that I was there; he said, "There is a lady here, Mrs. Amanda Smith" (he had never seen me before or heard of me, and he was a rather jovial kind of a man, and in making this announcement he said, in a half sarcastic and half joking way), "Mrs.

Smith is from New York; she says the Lord sent her;" with a kind of toss of the head, which indicated that he did not much believe it. Oh, my heart fell down, and I said, "Oh! Lord, help. Give me the message."

The Lord saw that I had as much as I could stand up under, and He said, "Say, 'Have ye received the Holy Ghost since ye believed?'" (Acts 9:2). That was the message; the first message the Lord gave me. I trembled from head to foot.

A good sister took me home with her to dinner. The people all seemed very kind. I felt quite at home when I got with them. We came back in the afternoon and had a wonderful meeting.

At night after Brother Holland had preached a short sermon, he called me up to exhort. As I sat in the pulpit beside him, he saw I was frightened. He leaned over and said, "Now, my child, you needn't be afraid. Lean on the Lord. He will help you."

And He did help me. There was a large congregation. The gallery was full, and every part of the house was packed. I stood up trembling. The cold chills ran over me. My heart seemed to stand still. Oh, it was a night. But the Lord gave me great liberty in speaking. After I had talked a little while the cold chills stopped, my heart began to beat naturally and all fear was gone, and I seemed to lose sight of everybody and everything but my responsibility to God and my duty to the people. The Holy Ghost fell on the people and we had a wonderful time. Souls were convicted and some converted that night. But the meeting did not go on from that.

Thursday night was the regular prayer meeting night. Brother Cooper said I was there, and would preach Thursday night. He was going to give me a chance to preach, and he wanted all the people to come out.

There was no snow, but Oh! it was cold. The ground was frozen. The moon shone brightly, and the wind blew a perfect gale. One good thing, I did not have to go back to Sister Curtis'. Another good sister asked me to her house to stay. She made me very comfortable, but said I would have to be alone most of the day, as she was going to some of the neighbors to help with the butchering, as they do in the country. I was very glad of that, for it gave me a chance to pray. So I fasted and prayed and read my Bible nearly all day. Oh, I had a good time. And then I thought I would visit a neighbor nearby, another friend. So I did; and this was a good old mother in Israel. I told her a little of my experience, and then I told her the message the Lord had given me to speak about, and how it would lead to the subject of sanctification.

"My child," she at once said, "don't you say a word about sanctification here. Honey, if you do, they will persecute you to death. My poor husband used to preach that doctrine, and for years he knew about this blessing. But, Oh! honey, they persecuted him to death. You must not say a word about it."

Well, there I was again! So I went home, and the next day I prayed to God all day. I asked Him to give me some other message. If this message was going to do so much damage, I did not want it. But no, the Lord held me to it. Not a ray of light on anything else but that. I didn't know what to do, but I made up my mind it was all I ever would do, so I would obey God and take the consequences. I thought sure from what the dear old mother told me that the results would be fatal; I didn't know but I would be driven out. But not so. "Obedience is better than sacrifice, and to hearken than the fat of rams."

Thursday was a beautiful, bright day; but Oh! cold, bitterly cold. So I got down and prayed and said, "Lord, Thou hast sent me to Salem, and hast given me the message. Now for an evidence that Thou hast indeed sent me, grant to cause the wind to cease blowing at this fearful rate. Thou knowest Lord, that I want people to hear Thy message that Thou hast given me. They will not mind the cold, but the wind is so terrible. Now cause the wind to cease to blow, and make the people come out."

The wind blew all day; all the afternoon. I started to go across the field, about a half mile from where I was, to talk and pray with a friend. On my way back, about five o'clock, as I was crossing a ditch which ran through the field, bordered on either side by a row of hedge trees, and a little plank across it for a kind of a foot bridge, the wind wrapped me round and took me down into the ditch. I could not hold on, could not control myself. I expected to be thrown up against the trees, and I cried out to Him all alone, "Oh! Lord, Thou that didst command the wind to cease on the Sea of Galilee, cause this wind to cease and let me get home."

Just then there came a great calm, and I got up out of that ditch and ran along to the house. By the time we went to church it was as calm as a summer evening; it was cold, but not a bit windy—a beautiful, moonlight night.

The church was packed and crowded. I began my talk from the chapter given, with great trembling. I had gone on but a little ways when I felt the spirit of the Lord come upon me mightily. Oh! how He helped me. My soul was free. The Lord convicted sinners and backsliders and believers for holiness, and when I asked for persons to come to the altar, it was filled in a little while from the gallery and all parts of the house.

A revival broke out, and spread for twenty miles around. Oh! what a time it was. It went from the colored people to the white people. Sometimes we would go into the church at seven o'clock in the evening. I could not preach. The whole lower floor would be covered with seekers—old men, young men, old women, young women, boys and girls. Oh! glory to God! How He put His seal on this first work to encourage my heart and establish my faith, that He indeed had chosen, and ordained and sent me. I do not know as I have ever seen anything to equal that first work, the first seal that God gave to His work at Salem. Some of the young men that were converted are in the ministry. Some have died in the triumph of faith. Others are on the way. I went on two weeks, day and night. We used to stay in the church till one and two o'clock in the morning. People could not work. Some of the young men would hire a wagon and go out in the country ten miles and bring in a load, get them converted, and then take them back.

One night I was so weary they said they would get on without me, and I could have a rest. A Mr. Huff had asked me to go to his house. Two of his sons had been converted. He had been a member of the church, but had got cold and backslidden. His wife was pretty much in the same condition. They had three younger children, ten and thirteen years of age. So I went to their house to have a rest. Before we went to bed that night we had family prayer. They had got out of the way of that, Mrs. Huff told me. She had got stirred up, so was anxious about her husband. I read the Bible and explained the Word the best I could; then I sang; then I got down to pray. There was a young man by the name of Williams, Mr. Huff's nephew, about twenty-one years of age, with them at the house. We knelt down to pray. I told Sister Huff she ought to pray in her family. Poor thing, she had prayed so little for a long time, it was rather hard; but she did. After she prayed, I sang a verse, then prayed. Archie Huff, the son, had been converted two or three days before, wonderfully. I asked him to pray. So he prayed, as a young convert, simply and earnestly, though he was very hoarse; but the Lord helped him. When he got through praying I sang another hymn; and by that time old Mr. Huff had tumbled over on the floor and was praying out loud for the Lord to save him; so I began to pray; and while I was praying, the young nephew, Williams, fell out and shook the house. And there we were. And while these two brethren were praying, and Archie and I were praying, and the old woman was praying, (as it was out in the country we didn't whisper at all; we talked right out), these younger children, a little girl ten years old, and the boys, twins, about thirteen years old, got converted. The little girl was sitting up at the opposite side of the room (her mother had put her to bed), praying for the Lord to bless her. The two boys had got up and come down, and they were praying that the Lord would bless them. I said, "Oh, Lord, what will I do? I have no help but Thee only. Help, Lord!" I thought if I only had somebody to sing; but there was nobody—only Archie and I; and we had got so hoarse that we could not do much. But it was beautiful just to see God do it all!

The whole five of them were converted that night. Oh, what a time. And so we were into it till about twelve or one o'clock. Then I slipped off and lay down a little while.

The news got out through the neighborhood, so they sent for me to come to another house next day, about a mile and a half away. Old man Huff hitched up his team, and he and his nephew and Archie and I went over to the neighbor's. This man was a very moral kind of a man. He had been seeking the Lord, but he had got a little discouraged, so they thought if I would go and talk to him it would help him. I thought "I will have a quiet time over here."

I got there about four o'clock in the afternoon. We talked and had a pleasant time, and had supper; and I thought we would have prayers after awhile. Well, about eight o'clock one or two persons came in, neighbors; that made five or six of us.

"Dear me," I thought to myself, "I have not strength to talk any longer, so I will just give out a hymn, and we will sing and have prayers."

So I did, and we got down to pray. I asked somebody to pray. While we were praying, three or four more came in. When we got through that prayer someone else struck in, and two or three more came in; so we had twelve or thirteen persons, packed in like sardines in it box. And pretty soon this man that had been seeking, cried out for salvation. Oh, how he prayed! It was not long till he began to believe; and what always follows earnest faith is victory. When he shouted victory it struck terror to the others that were not converted, and that night there were five or six converted in that house. Oh! what a victory!

Next day we visited round through the neighborhood. How the shouts of praise and hallelujah to God seemed to be everywhere we went. So I went back to church, for I did not get any rest there, and we went on two or three weeks longer. From there I went to Millville, N. J., with similar results. I remember one night at Millville, after Brother Leonard Patterson

had preached, he said I was to take the services and go on indefinitely.

There had been some little misunderstanding between two or three of the members, so there was not a very good feeling existing all around; and while we had good meetings, we would come right up to a point and stick. So after I had gone on three or four nights, I proposed to have a day of fasting and prayer, which they all quite readily agreed to. I said: "Now, I don't want anybody to promise to fast that cannot; some people cannot stand it; but just you who think you can fast one day, and pray to God for the outpouring of His Spirit—I want you to stand up."

Among those who stood up was an old Brother Cooper; they called him "Father Cooper." He had enjoyed the blessing of sanctification for about forty years. Oh, what a grand man he was! When that old man prayed, something gave way. There were several old brethren that I did not expect would fast at all. So Father Cooper got up and I said: "Brother Cooper, you cannot stand it. I don't mean you."

"Oh," he said, "Honey, I don't mean to let the children outrun me."

Another old man got up and said: "No, indeed, the children can't get ahead of me; I'm going with them." So one or two of the sisters and I visited from house to house. We prayed and talked and sang. I was led to visit two white families. They were poor people. The Devil tried to scare me; told me they were Roman Catholics, and would put me out. I had quite a little struggle, but finally I got victory and went. I do not know whether they were Roman Catholics or not; but the Lord helped me to speak to them and pray. One woman was so glad; she had a sick child. I talked to her and comforted her.

That night when we came together the Lord helped me to speak to them, and

He sent His Spirit. When I asked them to come forward to the altar, those that were seeking purity, and those that were seeking pardon, I asked Father Cooper to lead in prayer. I shall never forget that prayer. I seem to see it all, and hear it yet.

There were two that had been leading sisters in the church, that did not speak to each other, and were neighbors, were standing in pews close to each other. They did not come forward to the altar when the others came, but I saw the Spirit of the Lord had hold of them; and while brother Cooper was praying, the Holy Ghost fell on the people, and these two sisters were struck by the power of God like lightning. One of them walked out of her seat and went over to the seat of the other and shook hands and wept, and one of them, a few minutes after, whirled over the back of the seat and down on the floor, and she walked on her back clear down the aisle up to one side and into the altar. I think if anybody had told her to do it she never could have done it.

It was a marvelous time. I have never seen anything like it before or since. There was one man that had been seeking the Lord for eight years. Everybody thought he was converted. He lived with his mother, who was a widow. Everybody, white and colored, liked and respected him. He was a good man, always went to church, and so the people said he was converted; but he did not know it. So when they told me this a day or two before the day of fasting and prayer, I had this man, with some others, specially on my mind. After this great victory, we worked till about eleven or twelve o'clock. I said, "Well, we will take up these who are seeking. We will just have them rise now."

We colored people did not use to get up off our knees quick like white folks; when we went down on our knees to get something, we generally got it before we got up. But we are a very imitative people, so I find we have begun to imitate white people, even in that. The Lord help us.

This poor young man got up and put his overcoat on, and he was sitting down and looking so sad, as though he was nearly heart-broken. I had talked and prayed and tried to help him all I could; and there never was a soul prayed more earnestly and sincerely than he did. But there he stuck. I stood and looked at him for a moment. O, how they sang. At last I went up to him and said: "Look here, Charlie D., why don't you let go and shout?"

"Oh!" he wept, "Lord save me!"

"Well," I said, "The Lord does save you; but you won't believe Him." And I said, "Let go and shout!"

And the Spirit of the Lord seemed to fall upon him, just like you would sprinkle hot coals on any one. He sprang to his feet, and the light went all over him like fire, and it seemed as though he would tear himself to pieces for a minute. "Oh," he said, "I have found it, I have found it, I have found it!"

This sent a thrill through the whole church, and again there was a shout; such a shout you never heard nor saw. It was about one o'clock before we got out that night. I shall never forget that meeting at Millville. Praise the Lord! He does all things well. Amen. Amen.

JULIA FOOTE
1823–1900

African Methodist Episcopal Zion Church

In 1894, Julia Foote, the New York–born daughter of former slaves, became the first woman ordained as a deacon in the African Methodist Episcopal Zion Church. Foote had a conversion experience at fifteen and subsequently sought and received the experience of sanctification. When her request for ordination was denied several years earlier, Foote's decision to conduct a Bible study in her home without her pastor's approval led to her being disfellowshipped from her local congregation. At one point in 1851, Foote temporarily ceased evangelistic work because of the loss of her voice and the need to care for her invalid mother. Eighteen years later, after experiencing a divine healing, she began to preach again. Her ministry gained her recognition throughout the black Holiness movement, yet her ordination occurred only six years before her death. Foote's fruitful preaching career involved conducting evangelistic campaigns throughout the Northeast, as far west as Ohio and up into Canada. On one occasion in 1878, an estimated five thousand people heard her preach at a Holiness meeting.

A Brand Plucked from the Burning

My Conversion

I was converted when fifteen years old. It was on a Sunday evening at a quarterly meeting. The minister preached from the text: "And they sung as it were a new song before the throne, and before the four beasts and the elders, and no man could learn that song but the hundred and forty and four thousand which were redeemed from earth." Rev. 14:3.

As the minister dwelt with great force and power on the first clause of the text, I beheld my lost condition as I never had done before. Something within me kept saying, "Such a sinner as you are can never sing that new song." No tongue can tell the agony I suffered. I fell to the floor, unconscious, and was carried home. Several remained with me all night, singing and praying. I did not recognize anyone, but seemed to be walking in the dark, followed by someone who kept saying,

"Such a sinner as you are can never sing that new song." Every converted man and woman can imagine what my feelings were. I thought God was driving me on to hell. In great terror I cried: "Lord, have mercy on me, a poor sinner!" The voice which had been crying in my ears ceased at once, and a ray of light flashed across my eyes, accompanied by a sound of far distant singing. The light grew brighter and brighter, and the singing more distinct, and soon I caught the words: "This is the new song—redeemed, redeemed!" I at once sprang from the bed where I had been lying for twenty hours, without meat or drink, and commenced singing: "Redeemed! redeemed! glory! glory!" Such joy and peace as filled my heart, when I felt that I was redeemed and could sing the new song. Thus was I wonderfully saved from eternal burning.

I hastened to take down the Bible, that I might read of the new song, and the first words that caught my eye were: "But now, thus saith the Lord that created thee, O Jacob, and he that formed thee, O Israel, fear not, for I have redeemed thee; I have called thee by thy name; thou art mine. When thou passest through the waters, I will be with thee, and through the rivers, they shall not overflow thee; when thou walkest through the fire, thou shalt not be burned, neither shall the flame kindle upon thee." Isa 13:1–2.

My soul cried, "Glory! glory!" and I was filled with rapture too deep for words. Was I not indeed a brand plucked from the burning? I went from house to house, telling my young friends what a dear Savior I had found, and that he had taught me the new song. Oh! how memory goes back to those childish days of innocence and joy.

Some of my friends laughed at me, and said: "We have seen you serious before, but it didn't last long." I said: "Yes, I have been serious before, but I could never sing the new song until now."

One week from the time of my conversion, Satan tempted me dreadfully, telling me I was deceived; people didn't get religion in that way, but went to the altar, and were prayed for by the minister. This seemed so very reasonable that I began to doubt if I had religion. But, in the first hour of this doubting, God sent our minister in to talk with me. I told him how I was feeling, and that I feared I was not converted. He replied: "My child, it is not the altar nor the minister that saves souls, but faith in the Lord Jesus Christ, who died for all men." Taking down the Bible, he read: "By grace are ye saved, through faith, and that not of yourselves; it is the gift of God" [Eph. 2:8]. He asked me then if I believed my sins had all been forgiven, and that the Saviour loved me. I replied that I believed it with all my heart. No tongue can express the joy that came to me at that moment. There is great peace in believing. Glory to the Lamb!

A Desire for Knowledge— Inward Foes

I studied the Bible at every spare moment, that I might be able to read it with a better understanding. I used to read at night by the light of the dying fire, after the rest of the family had gone to bed. One night I dropped the tongs, which made such a noise that my mother came to see what was the matter. When she found that I had been in the habit of reading at night, she was very much displeased, and took the Bible away from me, and would not allow me to have it at such times any more.

Soon after this, my minister made me a present of a new Bible and Testament. Had he given me a thousand dollars, I should not have cared for it as I did for this Bible. I cherished it tenderly, but did not read in it at night, for I dared not disobey my mother.

I now felt the need of an education more than ever. I was a poor reader and a poor writer; but the dear Holy Spirit helped me by quickening my mental faculties. O Lord, I will praise thee, for great is thy goodness! Oh, that everything that hath a being would praise the Lord! From this time, Satan never had power to make me doubt my conversion. Bless God! I knew in whom I believed.

For six months I had uninterrupted peace and joy in Jesus, my love. At the end of that time an accident befell me, which aroused a spirit within me such as I had not known that I possessed. One day, as I was sitting at work, my younger brother, who was playing with the other small children, accidentally hit me in the eye, causing the most intense suffering. The eye was so impaired that I lost the sight of it. I was very angry; and soon pride, impatience, and other signs of carnality, gave me a great deal of trouble. Satan said: "There! you see you never were converted." But he could not make me believe that, though I did not know the cause of these repinings within.

I went to God with my troubles, and felt relieved for a while; but they returned again and again. Again I went to the Lord, earnestly striving to find what was the matter. I knew what was right, and tried to do right, but when I would do good, evil was present with me. Like Gad, I was weak and feeble, having neither might, wisdom nor ability to overcome my enemies or maintain my ground without many a foil. Yet, never being entirely defeated, disabled or vanquished, I would gather fresh courage, and renew the fight. Oh, that I had then had someone to lead me into the light of full salvation!

But instead of getting light, my preacher, class-leader and parents, told me that all Christians had these inward troubles to contend with and were never free from them until death; that this was my work here, and I must keep fighting and that, when I died, God would give me a bright crown. What delusion! However, I believed my minister was too good and too wise not to know what was right; so I kept on struggling and fighting with this inbeing monster, hoping all the time I should soon die and be at rest—never tor a moment supposing I could be cleansed from all sin, and live.

I had heard of the doctrine of Holiness, but in such a way as to give me no light, nor to beget a power in me to strive after the experience. How frivolous and fruitless is that preaching which describes the mere history of the work and has not the power of the Holy Ghost. My observation has shown me that there are many, ah! too many shepherds now, who live under the dreadful woe pronounced by the Lord upon the shepherds of Israel (Ezek. 34.).

Various Hopes Blasted

The more my besetting sin troubled me, the more anxious I became for an education. I believed that, if I were educated, God could make me understand what I needed; for, in spite of what others said, it would come to me, now and then, that I needed something more than what I had, but what that something was I could not tell.

About this time Mrs. Phileos and Miss Crandall met with great indignity from a pro-slavery mob in Canterbury, Conn., because they dared to teach colored children to read. If they went out to walk, they were followed by a rabble of men and boys, who hooted at them, and threw rotten eggs and other missiles at them, endangering their lives and frightening them terribly.

One scholar, with whom I was acquainted, was so frightened that she went into spasms, which resulted in a derangement from which she never recovered. We were a despised and oppressed people; we had no refuge but God. He heard our cries, saw our tears, and wonderfully delivered us. Bless the Lord that he is "a man of war!" [Exod. 15:3]. "I am that I am" is his name [Exod. 3:14]. Mr. and Mrs. Phileos and their daughter opened a school in Albany for colored children of both sexes. This was joyful news to me. I had saved a little money from my earnings, and my father promised to help me; so I started with hopes, expecting in a short time to be able to understand the Bible, and read and write well. Again was I doomed to disappointment: for some inexplicable reason, the family left the place in a few weeks after beginning the school. My poor heart sank within me. I could scarcely speak for constant weeping. That was my last schooling. Being quite a young woman, I was obliged to work, and study the Bible as best I could. The dear Holy Spirit helped me wonderfully to understand the precious Word.

Through temptation I was brought into great distress of mind; the enemy of souls thrust sore at me; but I was saved from falling into his snares—saved in the hour of trial from my impetuous spirit, by the angel of the Lord standing in the gap, staying me in my course.

"Oh, bless the name of Jesus! he maketh the rebel a priest and king; He hath bought me and taught me the new song to sing."

I continued to live in an up-and-down way for more than a year, when there came to our church an old man and his wife, who, when speaking in meeting, told of the trouble they once had had in trying to overcome their temper, subdue their pride, etc. But they took all to Jesus, believing his blood could wash them clean and sanctify them wholly to himself; and, oh! the peace, the sweet peace, they had enjoyed ever since. Their words thrilled me through and through. I at once understood what I needed. Though I had read in my Bible many things they told me, I had never understood what I read. I needed a Philip to teach me.

I told my parents, my minister, and my leader that I wanted to be sanctified. They told me sanctification was for the aged and persons about to die, and not for one like me. All they said did me no good. I had wandered in the wilderness a long time, and now that I could see a ray of the light for which I had so long sought, I could not rest day nor night until I was free.

I wanted to go and visit these old people who had been sanctified, but my mother said: "No, you can't go; you are half crazy now, and these people don't know what they are talking about." To have my mother refuse my request so peremptorily made me very sorrowful for many days. Darkness came upon me, and my distress was greater than before, for, instead of following the true light, I was turned away from it.

Disobedience, But Happy Results

Finally, I did something I never had done before: I deliberately disobeyed my mother. I visited these old saints, weeping as though my heart would break. When I grew calm, I told them all my troubles, and asked what I must do to get rid of them. They told me that sanctification was for the young believer, as well as the old. These words were a portion in due season. After talking a long time, and they had prayed with me, I returned home, though not yet satisfied.

I remained in this condition more than a week, going many times to my secret place of prayer, which was behind the chimney in the garret of our house. None but those who have passed up this way know how wretched every moment of my life was. I thought I must die. But truly, God does make his little ones ministering angels—sending them forth on missions of love and mercy. So he sent that dear old mother in Israel to me one fine morning in May. At the sight of her my heart seemed to melt within me, so unexpected, and yet so much desired was her visit. Oh, bless the Lord for sanctified men and women!

There was no one at home except the younger children, so our coming together was uninterrupted. She read and explained many passages of Scripture to me, such as, John 17; I Thess. 4:3; 5:23; I Cor. 6:9–12; Heb. 2:11; and many others—carefully marking them in my Bible. All this had been as a sealed book to me until now. Glory to Jesus! the seals were broken and light began to shine upon the blessed Word of God as I had never seen it before.

The second day after that pilgrim's visit, while waiting on the Lord, my large desire was granted, through faith in my precious Saviour. The glory of God seemed almost to prostrate me to the floor. There was, indeed, a weight of glory resting upon me. I sang with all my heart,

"This is the way I long have sought,
And mourned because I found it not."

Glory to the Father! glory to the Son! and glory to the Holy Ghost! who hath plucked me as a brand from the burning, and sealed me unto eternal life. I no longer hoped for glory, but I had the full assurance of it. Praise the Lord for Paul-like faith! "I am crucified with Christ: nevertheless, I live; yet not I, but Christ liveth in me" [Gal. 2:20]. This, my constant prayer, was answered, that I might be strengthened with might by his Spirit in the inner man; that being rooted and grounded in love, I might be able to comprehend with all saints what is the length, and breadth, and heighth,[6] and depth, and to know the love of Christ which passeth knowledge, and be filled with all the fullness of God.

I had been afraid to tell my mother I was praying for sanctification, but when the "old man" [Rom. 6:6] was cast out of my heart, and perfect love took possession, I lost all fear. I went straight to my mother and told her I was sanctified. She was astonished, and called my father and

told him what I had said. He was amazed as well, but said not a word. I at once began to read to them out of my Bible, and to many others, thinking, in my simplicity, that they would believe and receive the same blessing at once. To the glory of God, some did believe and were saved, but many were too wise to be taught by a child—too good to be made better.

From this time, many, who had been my warmest friends, and seemed to think me a Christian, turned against me, saying I did not know what I was talking about—that there was no such thing as sanctification and holiness in this life—and that the devil had deluded me into self-righteousness. Many of them fought holiness with more zeal and vigor than they did sin. Amid all this, I had that sweet peace that passeth all understanding springing up within my soul like a perennial fountain-glory to the precious blood of Jesus!

"The King of heaven and earth Deigns
to dwell with mortals here."

A Religion as Old as the Bible

The pastor of our church visited me one day, to talk about my "new religion," as he called it. I took my Bible and read many of my choice passages to him, such as— "Come and hear, all ye that fear God, and I will declare what he hath done for my soul." (Psa. 66:16.) "Blessed is he whose transgression is forgiven, whose sin is covered." (Ps. 32:1.) While reading this verse, my whole being was so filled with the glory of God that I exclaimed: "Glory to Jesus! he has freed me from the guilt of sin, and sin hath no longer dominion over me [Rom. 6:14]; Christ makes me holy as well as happy."

I also read these words from Ezekiel 36: "Then will I sprinkle clean water upon

6. [Ed.] Foote's spelling of *height*.

you, and ye shall be clean; from all your filthiness and from all your idols will I cleanse you; a new heart also will I give you, and a new spirit will I put within you, and I will take away the stony heart out of your flesh, and I will give you a heart of flesh. And I will put my Spirit within you, and cause you to walk in my statutes, and ye shall keep my judgments, and do them."

I stopped reading, and asked the preacher to explain these last verses to me. He replied: "They are all well enough; but you must remember that you are too young to read and dictate to persons older than yourself, and many in the church are dissatisfied with the way you are talking and acting." As he answered me, the Lord spoke to my heart and glory filled my soul. I said: "My dear minister, I wish they would all go to Jesus, in prayer and faith, and he will teach them as he has taught me." As the minister left me, I involuntarily burst forth into praises:

> "My soul is full of glory inspiring my tongue,
> Could I meet with angels I would sing them a song."

Though my gifts were but small, I could not be shaken by what man might think or say.

I continued day by day, month after month, to walk in the light as He is in the light, having fellowship with the Trinity and those aged saints. The blood of Jesus Christ cleansed me from all sin, and enabled me to rejoice in persecution.

Bless the Lord, O my soul, for this wonderful salvation, that snatched me as a brand from the burning, even me, a poor, ignorant girl!

And will he not do for all what he did for me? Yes, yes; God is no respecter of persons. Jesus' blood will wash away all your sin and make you whiter than snow.

My Marriage

Soon after my conversion, a young man, who had accompanied me to places of amusement, and for whom I had formed quite an attachment, professed faith in Christ and united with the same church to which I belonged. A few months after, he made me an offer of marriage. I struggled not a little to banish the thought from my mind, chiefly because he was not sanctified. But my feelings were so strongly enlisted that I felt sure he would someday be my husband. I read to him and talked to him on the subject of a cleansed heart. He assented to all my arguments, saying he believed and would seek for it.

The few weeks that he remained with us I labored hard with him for his deliverance, but he left us to go to Boston, Mass. We corresponded regularly, he telling me of his religious enjoyment, but that he did not hear anything about sanctification. Great was my anxiety lest the devil should steal away the good seed out of his heart. The Lord, and he only, knows how many times I besought him to let the clear light of holiness shine into that man's heart. Through all this my mind was stayed upon God; I rested in the will of the Lord.

One night, about a month after his departure, I could not sleep, the tempter being unusually busy with me. Rising, I prostrated myself before the Lord. While thus upon my face, these words of God came to me: "For we have not an high priest which cannot be touched with the feeling of our infirmities; but was in all points tempted like as we are, yet without sin." (Heb. 4:15.) I at once rose up, thanking God for his precious words: I took my

Bible and read them over and over again; also the eighteenth verse of the second chapter of Hebrews. I was not conscious of having committed sin, and I cried out: "Leave me, Satan; I am the Lord's." At that the tempter left, and I surrendered myself and all my interests into the hands of God. Glory to his holy name! "For it pleased the Father that in him should all fullness dwell" [Col. 1:19], and of his fullness have I received, and grace for grace.

> "Praise God from whom all blessings
> flow
> Praise him all creatures here below."

The day following, this night of temptation was one of great peace—peace flowing as a river, even to overflowing its banks, and such glory of the Lord appeared as to almost deprive me of bodily powers I forgot all toil and care.

This was just a year after my heart was emptied of sin through faith I received the Saviour, and in the same have continued ever since and proved him able to keep from sin. Bless God! all my desires are satisfied in him. He is indeed my reconciled God, the Christ Jesus whose precious blood is all my righteousness.

> "Nought of good that I have done
> Nothing but the blood of Jesus."

Glory to the blood that hath bought me! glory to the blood that hath cleansed me! glory to the blood that keeps me clean!—me, a brand plucked from the fire.

George returned in about a year to claim me as his bride. He still gave evidence of being a Christian, but had not been cleansed from the carnal mind. I still continued to pray for his sanctification and desired that it should take place before our union but I was so much attached to him that I could not resist his pleadings; so, at the appointed time, we

were married, in the church, in the presence of a large number of people, many of whom followed us to my father's house to offer their congratulations.

We stayed at home but one day after the ceremony. This day I spent m preparing for our departure and in taking leave of my friends. Tenderly as I loved my parents, much as I loved the church, yet I found myself unwilling to leave them all in the divine appointment. The day following, accompanied by several friends, we started for Boston, in an old-fashioned stage-coach, there being no railroads at that time. As I rode along I admired the goodness of God, and my heart overflowed with gratitude to him, who had blessed me with power to choose his will and make me able to say with truth, "I gladly forsake all to follow thee."

Once, the thought of leaving my father's house, to go among strangers, would have been terrible, but now I rejoiced in being so favored as to be called to make this little sacrifice, and evince my love to him who saith: He that loveth father or mother more than me is not worthy of me" [Matt. 10:37].

Removal to Boston—
The Work of Full Salvation

On our arrival in Boston, after a long, wearisome journey, we went at once to the house of Mrs. Burrows, where my husband had made arrangements for me to board while he was away at work during the week. He worked in Chelsea, and could not come to look after my welfare but once a week. The boarders in this house were mostly gentlemen, nearly all of whom were out of Christ. Mrs. Burrows was a church-member, but knew nothing of the full joys of salvation.

I went to church the first Sabbath I was there, remained at class meeting, gave my letter of membership to the minister, and was received into the church. In giving my first testimony, I told of my thorough and happy conversion, and of my sanctification as a second, distinct work of the Holy Ghost.

After class meeting, a good many came to me, asking questions about sanctification; others stood off in groups, talking, while a few followed me to my boarding-house. They all seemed very much excited over what I had told them. I began to see that it was not the voice of man that had bidden me go out from the land of my nativity and from my kindred, but the voice of my dear Lord. I was completely prepared for all that followed, knowing that "All things work together for good to them that love God" [Rom. 8:28]. Change of people, places and circumstances, weighed nothing with me, for I had a safe abiding place with my Father. Some people had been to me in such an unchristianlike spirit that I had spoken to and about them in rather an incautious manner. I now more and more saw the great need of ordering all my words as in the immediate presence of God, that I might be able to maintain that purity of lips and life which the Gospel required. God is holy, and if I would enjoy constant communion with him I must guard every avenue of my soul, and watch every thought of my heart and word of my tongue, that I may be blameless before him in love. The Lord help me evermore to be upon my guard, and having done all, to stand. Amen and amen.

In a few months my husband rented a house just across the road from my boarding-house, and I went to housekeeping. "Mam" Riley a most excellent Christian, became as a mother to me in this strange land, far from my own dear mother. Bless the Lord! He supplied all my needs. "Mam" Riley had two grown daughters, one about my own age, married, who had two children. They were dear Christian women, and like sisters to me. The mother thought she once enjoyed the blessing of heart purity, but the girls had not heard of such a thing as being sanctified and permitted to live. The elder girl, who was a consumptive and in delicate health, soon became deeply interested in the subject. She began to hunger and thirst after righteousness, and did not rest until she was washed and made clean in the blood of Jesus. Her clear, definite testimony had a great effect upon the church, as her family was one of the first in point of wealth and standing in the community.

God wonderfully honored the faith of this young saint in her ceaseless labor for others. We attended meetings and visited from house to house, together, almost constantly, when she was able to go but Glory to God! the church became much aroused; some plunged into the ocean of perfect love, and came forth testifying to the power of the blood. Others disbelieved and ridiculed this "foolish doctrine" as they called it, saying it was just as impossible to live without committing sin as it was to live without eating, and brought disjointed passages of Scripture to bear them out.

New and Unpleasant Revelations

My husband had always treated the subject of heart purity with favor, but now he began to speak against it. He said I was getting more crazy every day, and getting others in the same way, and that if I did not stop he would send me back home or to the crazy-house. I questioned him closely respecting the state of his mind, feeling that he had been prejudiced. I did not attempt to contend with him on the danger and fallacy of his notions, but simply asked what his state of grace was, if God should require his soul of him then. He gave me no answer until I insisted upon one. Then he said: "Julia, I don't think I can ever believe myself as holy as you think you are."

I then urged him to believe in Christ's holiness, if he had no faith in the power of the blood of Christ to cleanse from all sin. He that hath his hope purifies himself as God is pure. We knelt in prayer together, my husband leading, and he seemed much affected while praying. To me it was a precious season, though there was an indescribable something between us—something dark and high. As I looked at it, these words of the poet carne to me:

> "God moves in a mysterious way,
> His wonders to perform."

From that time I never beheld my husband's face clear and distinct, as before, the dark shadow being ever present. This caused me not a little anxiety and many prayers. Soon after, he accepted an offer to go to sea for six months, leaving me to draw half of his wages. To this arrangement I reluctantly consented, fully realizing how lonely I should be among strangers. Had it not been for dear "Mam" Riley, I could hardly have endured it. Her precept and example taught me to lean more heavily on Christ for support. God gave me these precious words: "Be careful for nothing, but in everything by prayer and supplication, with thanksgiving, let your request be made known unto God [Phil 4:6]. Truly, God is the great Arbiter of all events and because he lives, I shall live also."

The day my husband went on shipboard was one of close trial and great inward temptation. It was difficult for me to mark the exact line between disapprobation and Christian forbearance and patient love. How I longed for wisdom to meet everything in a spirit of meekness and fear, that I. might not be surprised into evil or hindered from improving all things to the glory of God.

While under this apparent cloud I took the Bible to my closet asking Divine aid. As I opened the book, my eyes fell on these words: "For thy Maker is thine husband" (Isa 54:5). I then read the fifty-fourth chapter of Isaiah over and over again. It seemed to me that I had never seen it before. I went forth glorifying God . . .

My Call to Preach the Gospel

For months I had been moved upon to exhort and pray with the people, in my visits from house to house; and in meetings my whole soul seemed drawn out for the salvation of souls. The love of Christ in me was not limited. Some of my mistaken friends said I was too forward, but a desire to work for the Master, and to promote the glory of his kingdom in the salvation of souls, was food to my poor soul.

When called of God, on a particular occasion, to a definite work, I said, "No, Lord, not me." Day by day I was more impressed that God would have me work in his vineyard. I thought it could not be that I was called to preach—I, so weak and ignorant. Still, I knew all things were possible with God, even to confounding the wise by the foolish things of this earth. Yet in me there was a shrinking.

I took all my doubts and fears to the Lord in prayer, when, what seemed to be an angel, made his appearance. In his hand was a scroll, on which were these words: "Thee have I chosen to preach my Gospel without delay." The moment my eyes saw it, it appeared to be printed on my heart. The angel was gone in an instant, and I, in agony, cried out, "Lord, I cannot do it!" It was eleven o'clock in the morning, yet everything grew dark as night. The darkness was so great that I feared to stir.

At last "Mam" Riley entered. As she did so, the room grew lighter, and I arose from my knees. My heart was so heavy I scarce could speak. Dear "Mam" Riley saw my distress, and soon left me.

From that day my appetite failed me and sleep fled from my eyes. I seemed as one tormented. I prayed, but felt no better. I belonged to a band of sisters whom I loved dearly, and to them I partially opened my mind. One of them seemed to understand my case at once, and advised me to do as God had bid me, or I would never be happy here or hereafter. But it seemed too hard—I could not give up and obey.

One night as I lay weeping and beseeching the dear Lord to remove this burden from me, there appeared the same angel that came to me before, and on his breast were these words, "you are lost unless you obey God's righteous commands." I saw the writing, and that was enough. I covered my head and awoke my husband, who had returned a few days before. He asked me why I trembled so, but I had not power to answer him. I remained in that condition until morning, when I tried to arise and go about my usual duties, but was too ill. When my husband called a physician, who prescribed medicine, but it did me no good.

I had always been opposed to the preaching of women, and had spoken against it, though, I acknowledge, without foundation. This rose before me like a mountain, and when I thought of the difficulties they had to encounter, both from professors and non-professors I shrank back and cried, "Lord, I cannot go!"

The trouble my heavenly Father has had to keep me out of the fire that is never quenched, he alone knoweth. My husband and friends said I would die or go crazy if something favorable did not take place soon. I expected to die and be lost, knowing I had been enlightened and had tasted the heavenly gift. I read again and again the sixth chapter of Hebrews.

Heavenly Visitations Again

Nearly two months from the time I first saw the angel, I said that I would do anything or go anywhere for God, if it were made plain to me. He took me at my word, and sent the angel again with this message: "You have I chosen to go in my name and warn the people of their sins." I bowed my head and said, "I will go, Lord."

That moment I felt a joy and peace I had not known for months. But strange as it may appear, it is not the less true, that, ere one hour had passed, I began to reason thus: "I am elected to preach the Gospel without the requisite qualifications, and, besides, my parents and friends will forsake me and turn against me; and I regret that I made a promise." At that instant all the joy and peace I had felt left me, and I thought I was standing on the brink of hell, and heard the devil say:

"Let her go! let her go! I will catch her." Reader, can you imagine how I felt? If you were ever snatched from the mouth of hell, you can, in part, realize my feelings.

I continued in this state for some time, when, on a Sabbath evening—ah! that memorable Sabbath evening—while engaged in fervent prayer, the same supernatural presence came to me once more and took me by the hand. At that moment I became lost to everything in this world. The angel led me to a place where there was a large tree, the branches of which seemed to extend either way beyond sight. Beneath it sat, as I thought, God the Father, the Son, and the Holy Spirit, besides many others, whom I thought were angels. I was led before them: they looked me over from head to foot, but said nothing. Finally, the Father said to me: "Before these people make your choice, whether you will obey me or go from this place to eternal misery and pain." I answered not a word. He then took me by the hand to lead me, as I thought, to hell, when I cried out, "I will obey thee, Lord!" He then pointed my hand in different directions, and asked if I would go there. I replied, "Yes, Lord." He then led me, all the others following, till we came to a place where there was a great quantity of water, which looked like silver, where we made a halt. My hand was given to Christ, who led me into the water and stripped me of my clothing, which at once vanished from sight. Christ then appeared to wash me, the water feeling quite warm.

During this operation, all the others stood on the bank, looking on in profound silence. When the washing was ended, the sweetest music I had ever heard greeted my ears. We walked to the shore, where an angel stood with a clean, white robe, which the Father at once put on me. In an instant I appeared to be changed into an angel. The whole company looked at me with delight, and began to make a noise which I called shouting. We all marched back with music. When we reached the tree to which the angel first led me, it hung full of fruit, which I had not seen before. The Holy Ghost plucked some and gave me, and the rest helped themselves. We sat down and ate of the fruit, which had a taste like nothing I had ever tasted before. When we had finished, we all arose and gave another shout. Then God the Father said to me: "You are now prepared, and must go where I have commanded you." I replied, "If I go, they will not believe me." Christ then appeared to write something with a golden pen and golden ink, upon golden paper. Then he rolled it up, and said to me: "Put this in your bosom, and, wherever you go, show it, and they will know that I have sent you to proclaim salvation to all." He then put it into my bosom, and they all went with me to a bright, shining gate, singing and shouting. Here they embraced me, and I found myself once more on earth.

When I came to myself, I found that several friends had been with me all night, and my husband had called a physician, but he had not been able to do anything for me. He ordered those around me to keep very quiet, or to go home. He returned in the morning, when I told him, in part, my story. He seemed amazed, but made no answer, and left me.

Several friends were in, during the day. While talking to them, I would, without thinking, put my hand into my bosom, to show them my letter of authority. But I soon found, as my friends told me, it was in my heart, and was to be shown in my life, instead of in my hand. Among others, my minister, Jehial [Jehiel] C. Beman, came to see me. He looked very coldly upon me and said: "I guess you will find out your mistake before you are many months older." He was a scholar, and a fine speaker; and the sneering, indifferent way in which he addressed me, said most plainly: "You don't know anything." I replied: "My gifts are very small, I know, but I can no longer be shaken by what you or anyone else may think or say."

Public Effort—Excommunication

From this time the opposition to my lifework commenced, instigated by the minister, Mr. Beman. Many in the church were anxious to have me preach in the hall, where our meetings were held at that time, and were not a little astonished at the minister's cool treatment of me. At length two of the trustees got some of the elder sisters to call on the minister and ask him to let me preach. His answer was: "No; she can't preach her holiness stuff here, and I am astonished that you should. ask it of me." The sisters said he seemed to be in quite a rage, although he said he was not angry.

There being no meeting of the society on Monday evening, a brother in the church opened his house to me, that I might preach, which displeased Mr. Beman very much. He appointed a committee to wait upon the brother and sister who had opened their doors to me, to tell them they must not allow any more meetings of that kind, and that they must abide by the rules of the church, making them believe they would be excommunicated if they disobeyed him. I happened to be present at this interview, and the committee remonstrated with me for the course I had taken. I told them my business was with the Lord, and wherever I found a door opened I intended to go in and work for my Master.

There was another meeting appointed at the same place, which I, of course, attended; after which the meetings were stopped for that time, though I held many more there after these people had withdrawn from Mr. Beman's church.

I then held meetings in my own house; whereat the minister told the members that if they attended them he would deal with them, for they were breaking the rules of the church. When he found that I continued the meetings, and that the Lord was blessing my feeble efforts, he sent a committee of two to ask me if I considered myself a member of his church. I told them I did, and should continue to do so until I had done something worthy of dismemberment.

At this, Mr. Beman sent another committee with a note, asking me to meet him with the committee, which I did. He asked me a number of questions, nearly all of which I have forgotten. One, however, I do remember: he asked if I was willing to comply with the rules of the discipline. To this I answered: "Not if the discipline prohibits me from doing what God has bidden me to do; I fear God more than man." Similar questions were asked and answered in the same manner. The committee said what they wished to say, and then told me I could go home. When I reached the door, I turned and said: "I now shake off the dust of my feet as a witness against you [Mark 6:11; Luke 9:5]. See to it that this meeting does not rise in judgment against you."

The next evening, one of the committee came to me and told me that I was no longer a member of the church, because I had violated the rules of the discipline by preaching.

When this action became known, the people wondered how anyone could be excommunicated for trying to do good. I did not say much, and my friends simply said I had done nothing but hold meetings. Others, anxious to know the particulars, asked the minister what the trouble was. He told them he had given me the privilege of speaking or preaching as long as I chose, but that he could not give me the right to use the pulpit, and that I was not satisfied with any other place. Also, that I had appointed meeting on the evening of his meetings, which was a thing no member had a right to do. For these reasons he said he had turned me out of the church.

Now, if the people who repeated this to me told the truth—and I have no doubt but they did—Mr. Beman told an actual falsehood. I had never asked for his pulpit, but had told him and others, repeatedly, that I did not care where I stood—any corner of the hall would do. To which Mr. Beman had answered: "You cannot have any place in the hall." Then I said: "I'll preach in a private house." He answered me: "No, not in this place; I am stationed over all Boston." He was determined I should not preach in the city of Boston. To cover up his deceptive, unrighteous course toward me, he told the above falsehoods.

From his statements, many erroneous stories concerning me gained credence with a large number of people. At that time, I thought it my duty as well as privilege to address a letter to the Conference, which I took to them in person, stating all the facts. At the same time I told them it was not in the power of Mr. Beman, or anyone else, to truthfully bring anything against my moral or religious character—that my only offence was in trying to preach the Gospel of Christ—and that I cherished no ill feelings toward Mr. Beman or anyone else, but that I desired the Conference to give the case an impartial hearing, and then give me a written statement expressive of their opinion. I also said I considered myself a member of the Conference and should do so until they said I was not, and gave me their reasons, that I might let the world know what my offence had been.

My letter was slightingly noticed, and then thrown under the table. Why should they notice it? It was only the grievance of a woman, and there was no justice meted out to women in those days. Even ministers of Christ did not feel that women had any rights which they were bound to respect.

CHARLES PRICE JONES
(1865–1949)

Church of Christ (Holiness) USA

Charles Price Jones, founder of the Church of Christ (Holiness) USA, emerged as the most prominent leader of the early twentieth-century African American Holiness Movement. Converted at age twenty, he became the head of a successful Baptist congregation and a prominent member of the local Baptist convention, when he became dissatisfied with his religious state and sought a deeper experience of God, which led him to embrace the Holiness doctrine of sanctification. This move caused him to be disfellowshipped from the local Baptist convention and removed from his prominent pastorate. For a short time, Jones worked closely with his colleague Charles Harrison Mason, evangelizing throughout the Tennessee Valley and organizing congregations into a loose Holiness fellowship that would eventually become a denomination. A fissure developed between the two, however, after Mason accepted the Pentecostal doctrine of Holy Spirit baptism being accompanied with the evidence of speaking in tongues. On the contrary, Jones maintained that Holy Spirit baptism was an inner work of the heart that required no outward sign accept a life lived in holiness and obedience the Lord.

Jones, who was educated at Arkansas Baptist College and one of the most prolific writers within black Holiness, developed several manuscripts on Holiness doctrine and penned more than one hundred hymns. Several of these would become mainstays of the Holiness and Pentecostal movement. Among his most noted works are "Deeper, Deeper," "I'm Happy With Jesus Alone," and "All I Need."

Baptism of the Holy Spirit

This former treatise have I made, O Theophilus, of all that Jesus began both to do and teach, Until the day in which He was taken up, after that He through the Holy Ghost had given commandments unto the apostles whom He had chosen: To whom also he shewed Himself alive after his passion by many infallible proof," being seen of them forty days, and speaking of the things pertaining to the kingdom of God: And, being assembled together with them, commanded them that they should not depart from Jerusalem, but wait for the promise of the Father, which, saith he, ye have heard of me. For John truly baptized with water; but ye shall be baptized with the Holy Ghost not many days hence. When they therefore were come together, they asked of Him, saying, Lord, wilt Thou at this time restore again the kingdom to Israel? And He said unto them, it is not for you to know the times Of the seasons, which the Father hath put in His own power. But ye shall receive power, after that the Holy Ghost is come upon you: and ye shall he witnesses unto me first in Jerusalem, and in all Judea, and in Samaria, and unto the uttermost part of the earth. Acts 1:8.

The Gospel dispensation is called "the ministration of the Spirit" (II Cor. 3:7, 8). Jesus went away, having fully completed the atonement, having taken away sin by the sacrifice of Himself, that the Comforter might come, He in coming was to convince the world of sin, of righteousness and of judgment to come and to guide the believer into all truth.

This is Christ's epitome, our Savior's own summing up of the dispensation and work of the Holy Spirit. The Savior in this wonderful dispensational administration of the Spirit thoroughly and personally identifies Himself with the Holy Spirit, as the following passages show:

> "If ye love Me, ye will keep My commandments. And I will pray the Father, and He shall give you another Comforter, that He may be with you forever. Even the Spirit of truth. whom the world cannot receive; for it beholdeth Him not, neither knoweth Him: ye know Him, for He abideth with you, and shall be in you. I will not leave you desolate: I come unto you. Yet a little while, and the world beholdeth Me no more but ye behold me: because I live, ye shall live also. In that day ye shall know that I am in My Father, and ye in me, and I in you." John 14:15–20.

> "Now the Lord Is the Spirit: and where the Spirit of the Lord is, there is liberty. But we all, with unveiled face beholding as in a mirror the glory of the Lord, are transformed Into the same image from glory to glory, even as from the Lord the Spirit." II Cor. 3:17, 18.

Our Savior and the Spirit are one. The Holy Spirit is Christ at work in the world saving men in His divine, invisible, omnipresent and almighty aspect. In Romans eighth chapter the statement, "If any man have not the Spirit of Christ, he is none of His," is followed by the statement, "If Christ be in you the body is dead because of sin but the Spirit is life because of righteousness."

Jesus Began—Jesus Continues

This throws light on the statement made in the text, "Of all that Jesus began both to do and to teach." Indeed as our propitiation, as our sacrifice and officiating high-priest, He completed, finished, yes, perfected forever, His work; as teacher of men, administrator of the will of God, and Savior of the world He only began His work when He was personally here in the flesh. He is to carry it on in the person of tile Holy Ghost. The work of Jesus Christ, the son of Mary, endued with the Holy Ghost is given us in the four records made by Matthew, Mark, Luke, and John. The record of Christ Jesus the Holy Spirit (see Rom 8:8, 9; Acts 16:7; II Cor 3:17, 18, and Rev 1, 2 & 3) is given in the book of Acts; how enduing His church with His own power; filling it with and baptizing it in His own presence; and imparting to it His own love, zeal, wisdom, and holiness; He continued the work many years. In the same Holy Spirit He will continue this work till He comes again. (Phil 1:6; Heb 1:20).

The Church Is God at Work

As God was in Christ reconciling the world unto Himself He is in the church doing the same thing. This is clear from I Corinthians twelfth chapter where the baptism of the Holy Spirit as an abiding blessing is explained as it is nowhere else. To understand this chapter is to get much rest and blessing, and will save from terrible delusions and fanatical mistakes. Yet, only those who are taught of the Lord by the Spirit will ever understand God. This is clear from I Corinthians second chapter.

Jesus bade His disciples to wait for the promise of 'the Father. This promise it is made clear from the text, was the baptism, outpouring, coming upon, receiving gift or enduement of the Holy Ghost.

Figures of Speech

Any student of Acts can see that our Saviour's real aim was to get the church to be still till He could come back and fill her with Himself in the Holy Spirit; because He is both the power of God and the wisdom of God. I Cor 1:24. To convert a man it takes divine power, to sanctify a man takes divine power. To take care of the church it takes wisdom divine, to understand God, to appreciate Him takes a divine revelation in the soul. It took the Holy Spirit to make Christ of quick understanding in the fear of the Lord (Isa. 11:1–11) that He might recover His remnant.

The baptism of the Holy Ghost therefore expresses the divine presence in and upon the church empowering her for her work. Sanctifying her in God, making her wise unto salvation, and sealing her as the bride of' Christ, (I Jn 2:20–27; Eph 1:13; 4:30).

But remember that only three times do Christ and the apostles refer to the Holy Spirit's presence as a baptism—twice in the book of Acts; once in I Corinthians 12th chapter. His presence is also called the gift of the Holy Ghost. As a gift to us He is referred to most. In John 7:37–9; 14:16, Acts 2:38; 5:32 and a number of other passages He is referred to as a gift, as given unto us. And surely He is a gift to us. He was not in any such sense a gift to the prophets as He is to us. To them He was given occasionally because they were leaders of the people. Now as the birthright of all He is the gift of Christ to every believer's heart who will receive Him. But of the meaning of these other figures in Acts by which the gift of the Spirit is known we want to speak in other discourses. Now we want to speak of the term "the baptism of the Spirit" and what is implied in it.

Two Events

We find the term "baptism of the Spirit" mentioned in the record of two events: the day of Pentecost and the case of Cornelius. In both cases the blessing was called an outpouring. In the one case He was out-poured on people some of whom had received the Spirit and been illuminated before. Now they seem to have received a larger infilling and empowering. With others it was their first experience. Yet we never hear of what is now preached to us in some quarters that we are converted or justified, then receive sanctification or an anointing, then go on and "get the baptism of the Holy Ghost." Nowhere in Acts or the epistles is such a process described; tho we do see that the Ephesians, after having received the Spirit, were prayed for that they might be strengthened with might by the Spirit in the inner man; and they are yet exhorted to be "filled with the Spirit." But this is not put as if they had received an anointing at first and must now receive their baptism, their Pentecost. There are deeper depths, even all the fullness of God, but it all belongs in the ministry of the Spirit and is not called the baptism of the Spirit. It is best to be literally scriptural, or else the spiritual man is in danger of going mad - "The spiritual man is mad," said the prophet, foreshadowing without doubt our days of delusions and false propagandas. And yet are not many of these the efforts of honest men to get out of the scriptures all that is in them? The only safe path is to literally, strictly, jealously scriptural to the law and the testimony. If they speak not according to this word it is because there is NO LIGHT IN THEM.

What It Means

What does baptism mean? It means an overwhelming, submersion, an immersion, a burial. And what happened on the day of Pentecost? The room was filled with the presence of the Spirit He having come as with the sound of a mighty rushing wind. We have been in many a room so filled with His presence that it seemed to us we could almost see Him. At no other time is it recorded in the Bible that He came with such a sound. Tongues of fire sat on those who were present At no other time did this occur, that we know of. Yet we know when those who have seen the minister lost in the Spirit have seen, as they said, a flaming light upon him.

It pleased the Holy Spirit to manifest Himself also by giving certain miraculous gifts to the disciples on this as on other similar occasions. They began to speak with other tongues "as the Spirit gave them utterance." It is to be remarked that all were filled, it is not said that all spake with tongues. Yet all might have done so had it so pleased the Spirit; for all power is in Him. To manifest Himself with one gift is as easy as to manifest Himself with another. Blessed be He!

The Greek here is *Kai epleestheesan pantes pneumatos hagiou, kai eerxanto lalein heterais glossais kathos to Pneumia edidou apophtheggesthai autois.* "And they were all filled with the Holy Spirit, and they began to speak with other tongues, as the Spirit gave them utterance." "They BEGAN to speak with tongues" carries a different idea from "they all DID speak with tongues." We object not to the Spirit's so manifesting Himself at any time; we

only would not have Him misrepresented and so exalt a gift above the Lord Himself. For as the scriptures are being strained and misinterpreted in certain quarters a false doctrine is gone abroad giving place to the devil and greatly deluding earnest souls.

The great, the mighty fact of the day of Pentecost was that all were FILLED WITH THE SPIRIT and were overwhelmed in Him. They in God, God in them. He, the Spirit, made them conscious of that glorious consciousness that we are in God and God in us! We know it because "God is love, and he that dwells in love dwells in God and God in him." We know it because "God is light and in Him is no darkness at all."

Cornelius' Case

The only other time the gift of the Spirit is called a baptism is in tile book of Acts" in the case of Cornelius. Here too the blessing is called an outpouring. Here, too, is a crowd "all of one mind," tho they have not been clearly converted till the same sermon under which they are filled. The inference seems clear that where a large number are filled with the Spirit at once and He at the same time falls without the laying on of hands is called an outpouring or baptism. From the twelfth of first Corinthians we see that the gift of the Spirit to tile church as a whole is so-called— "baptized by (Greek "in") one Spirit into one body, whether we be Jews or Gentiles, whether we be bond or free."

In the case of Cornelius, too, tile gift of tongues was bestowed on certain ones but not all. Evidently some spoke with tongues while others prophesied and prayed and praised. There is no telling in how many ways they magnified God. We know that. Mary magnified God without speaking in a foreign language. Yet every man's tongue is new when he is converted and especially so when he is filled with tile Spirit, for "old things are passed away and all things are become new" (II Cor 5:14–17). The language by no means justifies the inference that all speak with tongues (I Cor 12:30–31). The language is, "For they heard them speaking with tongues and glorifying God." The glorifying of God was not necessarily glorifying except in the sense that God is glorified in all men in the Spirit. The justifiable inference of the language is that some spoke with tongues while others shouted "Glory to God!" in the tongue then and there in common use. Praise God for whatever [w]ay it pleases Him to manifest Himself. We would not make light of His gifts; we would only calmly and humbly examine the scriptures and get their literal sense, lest thru false interpretations we magnify error instead of the Lord and give place to Satan. Again it comes that those were noted as speaking ill tongues there understood, were men. Now it is deluded women and irresponsible children mostly. Evidently, the day of Pentecost has not returned yet. We pray its return in God's time.

A Certain Truth

One thing is certain, we are told to "be filled with the Spirit," we are to receive the Holy Ghost after we believe; and when He fills us we know it. He manifests Himself in bearing fruit (Gal 5:22, 3) and such gifts as it pleases Him to give us He giveth, above all boldness to witness that the Savior dwells within.

"Now if any man have not tile Spirit of Christ He is none of His. And if Christ be in you the body is dead because of sin, but the Spirit is life because of righteousness." Amen.

The scriptures nowhere say the gift of tongues or some sort of unknown jabber is evidence, that we are filled or baptized. Stand firm! Be true to the traditions left us by written scripture. It will save in these times.

chapter three

The Azusa Street Revival

Baptized with the Holy Ghost

Do you long to be full of Joy and free,
To be strong in God and his glory see,
Then obey His word and you shall be,
Baptized with the Holy Ghost.

Will you consecrate to Him now your all,
Let Him have his way while to Him you call,
As in faith you wait the power will fall,
Baptized with the Holy Ghost.

"This is that" which fell at Pentecost,
To prepare the church to redeem the lost,
We must then be led at any cost,
Baptized with the Holy Ghost.

'Tis the gift of God to the sanctified,
He will comfort, lead and will be our guide,
And will dwell In us, coming to abide,
Baptized with the Holy Ghost.

Will you gladly fall at the Saviour's feet,
Give your doubtings o'er, and be made complete,
There to dwell in peace, and communion sweet,
Baptized with the Holy Ghost.
You can sing God's praise now, and by and by,
Ye shall speak with tongues, and shalt prophesy,
In the power of God ye shall testify,
Baptized with the Holy Ghost.

Chorus:
"Ye shall be baptized," Jesus said,
Baptized with the Holy Ghost,
Tarry then until with the power endued.
Baptized with the Holy Ghost.
Yes I'll be baptized with His power,
Baptized with the Holy Ghost,
Tis the gift I see, Father's promise to me,
Baptized with the Holy Ghost.

—Author Unknown

The Apostolic Faith

Within several months of the beginning of the Azusa Street Revival, William Seymour had enlisted the assistance of Clara Lum and Florence Crawford to publish the *Apostolic Faith*, a newspaper that would herald its events to supporters around the world. A few months later, the circulation of the free periodical had reached fifty thousand. In its pages, Seymour and his colleagues not only reported on the phenomenal experiences unfolding within the revival—salvation, sanctification, Holy Spirit baptism, healing, deliverance, and exorcism; they expounded Pentecostal doctrine, exhorted the faithful, and solicited workers for the home and foreign missions field. But the periodical also highlighted reports of Pentecostal revivals breaking out across the national and global landscapes. Some of its contributors—Mason, Fisher, Barrett, and others—would go on to lead major segments of the movement. Circulation of the newspaper is credited by some as helping to spur the phenomenal rapid growth of the revival. Further, its abrupt decline, fueled by a rift in Seymour's relationship with Lum and Crawford is seen as at least partly responsible for the later decline in the meetings.

Pentecost Has Come[1]

Los Angeles Being Visited by a Revival of Bible Salvation as Recorded in the Book of Acts

The power of God now has this city agitated as never before. Pentecost has surely come and with it the Bible evidences are following. many being converted and sanctified and filled with the Holy Ghost, speaking in tongues as they did on the day of Pentecost. The scenes that are daily enacted in the building on Azusa street and at Missions and churches in other parts of the city are beyond description, and the real revival is only started, as God has been working with His children mostly, getting them through to Pentecost, and laying the foundation for a mighty wave of salvation among the unconverted.

The meetings are held in an old Methodist church that had been converted in part into a tenement house, leaving a large, unplastered, barn-like room on the ground floor. Here about a dozen congregated each day, holding meetings on Bonnie Brae in the evening. The writer attended few of these meetings and being so different from anything he had seen and not hearing all speaking in tongues, he branded the teaching as third-blessing heresy and thought that settled it. It is needless to say the writer was compelled to do a great deal of apologizing and humbling himself to get right with God.

In a short time God began to manifest His power and soon the building could not contain the people. Now the meetings continued all day and late into the night and the fire is kindling all over the city and surrounding towns. Proud, well-dressed preachers come in to investigate. Soon their high looks are replaced with wonder, then conviction comes, and very often you will find them in a short time wallowing on the dirty floor, asking God to forgive them and make them as little children. It would be impossible to state how many have been converted, sanctified, and filled with the Hob Ghost. They have been and are daily going out to all points of the compass to spread this wonderful gospel.

1. *Apostolic Faith* 1/1 (September 1906) 1.

Bro. Seymour's Call

Bro. W. J. Seymour has the following to say in regard to his call to this city: "It was the divine call that brought me from Houston, Texas, to Los Angeles. The Lord put it in the heart of one of the saints in Los Angeles to write to me that she felt the Lord would have me come over here and do a work, and I came, for I felt it was the leading of the Lord. The Lord sent the means, and I came to take charge of a mission on Santa Fe Street, and one night they locked the door against me, and afterwards got Bro. Roberts, the president of the Holiness Association, to come down and settle the doctrine of the Baptism with the Holy Ghost, that it was simply sanctification. He came down and a good many holiness preachers with him, and they stated that sanctification was the baptism with the Holy Ghost. But yet they did not have the evidence of the second chapter of Acts, for when the disciples were all filled with the Holy Ghost, they spoke in tongues as the Spirit gave utterance. After the president heard me speak of what the true baptism of the Holy Ghost was, he said he wanted it too, and told me when I had received it to let him know. So I received it and let him know. The beginning of the Pentecost started in a cottage prayer meeting at 214 Bonnie Brae."

The Old-Time Pentecost

This work began about five years ago last January when a company of people under the leadership of Chas. Parham, who were studying God's word, tarried for Pentecost in Topeka, Kan. After searching through the country everywhere, they had been unable to find any Christians that had the true Pentecostal power. So they laid aside all commentaries and notes and waited on the Lord, studying His word, and what they did not understand they got down before the bench and asked God to have wrought out in their hearts by the Holy Ghost. They had a prayer tower from which prayers were ascending night and day to God. After three months, a sister who had been teaching sanctification for the baptism with the Holy Ghost, one who had a sweet, loving experience and all the carnality taken out of her heart, felt the Lord lead her to have hands laid on her to receive the Pentecost. So when they prayed, the Holy Ghost came in great power and she continued speaking in an unknown tongue. This made all the Bible school hungry, and three nights afterward, twelve students received the Holy Ghost, and prophesied, and cloven tongues could be seen upon their heads. They then had an experience that measured up with the second chapter of Acts, and could understand the first chapter of Ephesians.

Now after five years something like 13,000 people have received this gospel. It is spreading everywhere, until churches who do not believe backslide and lose the experience they have. Those who are older in this movement are stronger, and greater signs and wonders are following them.

The meetings in Los Angeles started in a cottage meeting, and the Pentecost fell there three nights. The people had nothing to do but wait on the Lord and praise Him, and they commenced speaking in tongues, as they did at Pentecost, and the Spirit sang songs through them.

The meeting was then transferred to Azusa Street, and since then multitudes have been coming. The meetings begin about ten o'clock in the morning and can hardly stop before ten or twelve at night, and sometimes two or three in the morning, because so many are seeking, and some are slain under the power of God. People are seeking three times a day at the altar and row after row of seats have to be emptied and filled with seekers.

We cannot tell how many people have been saved, and sanctified, and bap- tised with the Holy Ghost, and healed of all manner of sicknesses. Many are speak- ing in new tongues, and some are on their way to the foreign fields, with the gift of the language. We are going on to get more of the power of God.

Mission in Los Angeles[2]

A visitor who has the gift of interpretation reports service in shorthand.

The power of God came down in a marked manner on Monday, April 29, at Azusa Mission beginning especially in the ministerial meeting held during the day and culminating in the evening service. While testimonies were being given by baptized witnesses to a returned missionary from China, upon whom the Pentecostal power is now resting, the message was given in Tongues by one brother and interpreted by another, "Open thy mouth wide and I will fill it, wait not for thy word, to be formed in your mind, but give out just what the Spirit puts within and let him control."

A sister who had been attending the meeting some time testified to having received liberty only recently, and said that on visiting a s sick woman during the day the Lord had convinced an unbelieving girl. Upon this the husband of this witness arose and spoke in tongues very forcibly, but the interpretation was not given until the brother in charge of the meeting had told how this sister had received liberty by going and for the first time seeking to help the unsaved. In a meeting after which the message in tongues was translated with even more power as: "oh how we praise the Lord for the way he works; when we go to do a work for him he will work another by his Spirit through us. He

wants to teach us that his ways are not our ways nor his thoughts our thoughts, but as the Heaven is High above the earth so are his ways higher than our ways and his thoughts than our thoughts."

A little later in the evening, as a young colored brother was testifying. he began to sing in another language: "O Jesus, thou wonderful saviour." After a few more words of praise to God in his own language he sang in another beautifully: "oh, and now the king comes in triumph," upon which the power was so great that many baptized Believers arose one after another and joined in a mighty chorus in the Spirit while the young brother went on with his testimony and then sang: "oh pour out Your hearts before him and bond yourselves in obedience" Whereat the leader of the meeting arose and Although he had not heard the interpretation of these messages, cried out: "Come to the altar! come to the altar!" And the young messenger continued in a tongue: "Oh seek the Lord while he may be found, call upon Him while He is near to you," and another brother spoke forcefully in another language, to the heart of the people: "Oh turn to Him while it is called today and seek Him while He may be found." The interpretation of these messages was not given out at that time but recorded in shorthand. The effect of the manifestation of the Spirit's power was, however, immediate and very marked, for the people came forward to the altar and fell all around under the power of the Holy Spirit, demons being cast out in the name of Jesus, saints being quickened, and four receiving the baptism with the Holy Ghost with the evidence of speaking in tongues.

To those who ask why we should speak in tongues and what use it is unless understood by those to whom the

2. [Ed.] *The Apostolic Faith* 1/7 (April 1907)
2. The depiction in this article is a compilation of characterizations of the worship occurring in the several Pentecostal missions that had sprung up around Los Angeles within several months of the beginning of the Azusa Street revival. The language of the testimonies in this depiction would become the standard language of Pentecostal testimonies for decades to come, and represents the liturgy of Pentecostalism.

message is given, this report is sufficient evidence that it is not by the understanding of mind or by great intellect that God would speak to the children of men, but in the mighty power and demonstration of the Holy Ghost.

The Pentecostal Assembly

At the Pentecostal Assembly, 327½ So. Spring St. in the Metropolitan Hall, an earnest band of Christians hold service every Tuesday and Friday afternoon and evening and all day Sunday of each week. These witness in the liberty of the Spirit, those who have received the baptism in the Holy Ghost often speaking in tongues, the interpretation edifying the church. On Tuesday evening, April 30, a drunken man was brought into the hall and before the meeting started the power of God had sobered him in readiness for the Gospel. More workers went out and each brought in another poor victim of intoxication, one brother capturing three, two of whom tried to restrain their mate but followed in. The Word of God was read by the brother in charge, from the passage in Luke 19 centering in the words: "The Son of Man came to seek and to save that which was lost" (v.10), the exposition being to the point and given by the Spirit. With songs of victory interspersed, the saints got to their knees and dealt with each case separately as they manifested an earnest desire to be saved; and. thus encouraged, these poor men themselves lifted up their voices to God, some of them really crying to Him from their hearts for pardon and Power. Before they received deliverance in some cases, the demon of drink had to be cast out, and all had to be encouraged like children to pray to their Father in heaven, but we believe a work was done

which will be seen through all eternity. The names and addresses of most of these men were taken by a brother in the Assembly, who will call upon them in the day and encourage them to look to God.

Azusa Mission, Thursday Evening, May 1

After some hearty singing and earnest prayer, a converted Jewish brother testified. Then a little boy mounted the altar and said plainly: "I thank the Lord for saving me and now I am seeking the baptism. I want you to pray for me that I may get it. Tonight I had the toothache and I prayed for the Lord to take it away, and He took it away."

A sister said: "Rejoice in the Lord. Rejoice always, and again I say rejoice. I am rejoicing in the Lord; I am rejoicing in his salvation, I am rejoicing in His life, I am rejoicing in His presence with me, I am rejoicing in His faithfulness, I am rejoicing in His unchangeableness, I am resting on His promises, and looking and expecting Him moment by moment. Hallelujah! Hallelujah! Praise our God forever."

A colored brother arose and sang the verses of a hymn, the people joining in the chorus: "The Blood, the Blood is all my plea; Hallelujah, it cleanseth me." He then said: "Hallelujah! I am so glad I can testify that the blood cleanseth me. Oh, the sweetness! My heart is full of love for Jesus. I am so glad I can take up the cross and. work with Him now, and follow him. Oh, I know I am leaning on the Almighty's arms."

An old gentleman who has recently received the baptism said: "Just take the blessings that God sends down to us. Oh I thank God that He has found an old man, a sinner like me. I was not worthy of anything, but He gave Himself to me. glory, o glory! Then he spoke in another language the interpretation being): "Glory to Thee my great Redeemer for Thy great love toward me. O how I praise Thee. (He continued in English:) Oh glory to God for the gift he has given me. Now if there is any sinner here tonight seek Him. Now we all may have it without money."

Another testified as follows: "I praise God tonight that I am under the blood; Jesus' Blood covers me and cleanses me from all sin."

Someone else said: "I know that the Blood of Jesus saves me and sanctifies and keeps me from day to day. He is my healer, I praise him and thank Him for the way he is increasing my faith and instructing me today. The Lord gave me a verse since I have been standing here: 'Wait on the Lord, be of good courage, and he shall strengthen thine heart.' I am just standing on His promises. With His stripes I am healed. I praise Him and thank Him with all my heart. He saves me and sanctifies me and baptizes me with the Holy Ghost."

A new song of much power was then sung through in tile Spirit by all.

> Jesus Christ is made to me
> All I need, all I need;
> He alone is all my plea.
> He is all I need.
>
> *Chorus:*
> Wisdom, Righteousness and power,
> Holiness forever more,
> My Redemption full and sure,
> He is all I need.[3]

A brother testified, "The is power in my soul tonight because God put it

3. [Ed.] That song might have been new to the writer, but it was penned by Holiness leader Charles Price Jones in 1900.

in there; it is the power of the Spirit that came down from the throne of God, from the Everlasting Father, before whom we must one day stand and give an account of the deeds done in the body. Oh how careful we as professing Christians ought to walk before this ungodly generation. The Lord showed me a few years ago that out of California would come a movement that would startle the world, and here is this prophecy fulfilled. Praise God for this personal Pentecost." He then said in another tongue: "Jesus died that you might be saved. Oh be saved tonight and seek Him with all the heart, and let Him have His way."

A young colored sister then said: "I want to praise God tonight. He is all in all to me. Glory to Jesus. Dear ones, you do not know how sweet it is to trust Jesus. Do not sit back laughing and scoffing—oh you are laughing at Jesus, not at us. (In tongues) He that sitteth in the heavens shall laugh, the Lord shall have them In derision. Oh why will ye not come unto him that ye might have life? Oh why do you resist my pleadings with you at this time? Oh why do you not come to Me and turn to Me with thy heart? Dear ones, accept this blessed salvation. I do praise my blessed Redeemer for saving me from sin, for giving me a clean heart. When I was a sinner, I would go to church and look around laughing, but oh I did not know I was laughing at Jesus, but, praise God, He is all in all to me now. He has taken all the laugh out of me, all criticism. He has given me a perfectly clean heart and filled me with love. Dear ones, oh it is precious to have a clean heart. He saved my soul and He has baptized me with the Holy Ghost. (In tongues) O why do you resist the strivings of the Spirit. Why not turn to Him in repentance? Dear ones, it is sweet to walk with Jesus. I take Him as my Healer. He heals all my diseases. O Glory to God. (In tongues:) "Why do you not look to Him and live at this 'time?'"

Bro. W. J. Seymour then started the congregation singing:

> Jesus, Jesus, how I trust thee,
> How I've prove thee o'er and o'er;
> Jesus, Jesus, precious Jesus,
> Oh, for grace to trust Thee more.

He then said: "Glory! Beloved, I want to say 'Goodnight' to you all for a short while. It has now been over a year since I left Texas and came up in this portion of the country to labor and work for the Lord. And I am going back there through that old state where the Lord called me from a year ago. I am going to pass through there and see those precious children who prayed with me for Pentecost, and while I am gone I want you all to pray that God may use me to His own honor and glory.

"I want to read some of God's precious Word in the first chapter of the book of Isaiah. (He read to verse 9 and then said:) I am so glad the Lord God has raised up a people right in Los Angeles, and Francisco, they seem like Sodom and Gamorrah, but out of these cities the Lord. God has raised up a people for His holy name. He has cleansed them from sin, He has sanctified them, and has baptized them with the Holy Ghost and sealed them unto the day of Redemption. Glory to His holy name! I can go and rejoice with the people in Texas, telling them of the wonderful things, that God has done In Los Angeles. They said I should be back in a month's time, and now this is the first chance I have had to get back.

(He then read to the end of verse 20). 'But if ye refuse and rebel ye shall be devoured with the sword: for the mouth of the Lord hath spoken it.' Every man,

every church, every home that rejects the full Gospel of the Lord and Savior Jesus Christ, shall be devoured. We are living in a time when the Holy Ghost is working—bless God—convincing men and women of righteousness and judgment, and every man and every woman that hardens their heart against the Word of God shall fall. If the men and women of this city will repent and turn from their sin and accept our Lord and Savior, Jesus Christ, 'ye shall eat the good of the land.' Glory to His holy name! God has fat things to feed all his hungry people. Oh, He will fill you tonight. Oh, the music will be singing in your soul and, oh, the love of Christ that passes all understanding will be dwelling in your heart. Just read what he says: 'If ye be willing and obedient ye shall eat the good of the land.' Jesus says: 'Abide In me, as the branch cannot bear fruit of itself except it abide in the vine, no more can ye except ye abide in Me: Oh, beloved, if we abide in the words of the Lord Jesus Christ and feed off Christ, I'll tell you, we shall live off the good of the land—bless His holy name. We will have the fat—bless God. We will have everything to cheer our heart, we shall have healing and health and salvation in our souls. Oh, glory to His holy name. Oh, do not refuse the Word of God; oh, accept it, accept all the doctrine of our Lord. and Savior, Jesus Christ, and oh, beloved, it will fill your hearts with good things.

"But just listen to what He says; 'If ye refuse and rebel, ye shall be devoured with the sword: for the mouth of the Lord hath spoken it.' Beloved, if you reject Christ, if you reject His precious Blood, if you reject the Holy Ghost, ye shall be devoured with the sword; but if you accept Jesus Christ He will prepare a table before you, and the Lord God Himself will spread it and He will feed you Himself.

When Jesus had gotten through feeding His disciples He told His disciples to feed His lambs and sheep. What are we going to feed them with? We are going to feed them with the precious Word of God; we are going to teach them to accept Jesus Christ as their Savior and as their Sanctifier to destroy the root of sin, and then we are going to teach them to accept the Holy Ghost. He shall baptize them with the Holy Ghost and fire, and when He comes in: He is going to speak through them and He says, 'In the last days I will pour out of My Spirit on all flesh.' Glory to His holy name. I want to say 'Goodnight' to you."

"God be with you till we meet again" was then sung as Brother Seymour shook hands with as many as possible. We then left for the train. Brother Anderson spoke a few words of encouragement to the saints on the necessity of our continuing faithful in the pastor's absence."

There is a Swedish Pentecostal Mission in Los Angeles at 8th and Wall streets. The power of God is falling there. The Swedish people have been among the foremost in accepting the doctrine of the baptism with the Holy Ghost and many are endued with power from on high.

Russians and Armenians m Los Angeles are seeking the baptism. The Armenians have a Pentecostal cottage meeting on Victor Street, between 4th and 5th. Some have been baptized with the Holy Ghost.

At the Pentecostal Mission on Central avenue and 53rd Street, in Los Angeles, meetings are going on in power. Conviction is on the sinners. Numbers are seeking Pentecost. Bro. Lyttle gave up half of his store for this mission and an unconverted man offered to do the work himself putting up a partition. God is working there.

WILLIAM JOSEPH SEYMOUR (1871–1922)

Apostolic Faith Mission

William Joseph Seymour has been called the father of the modern Pentecostal movement by some, for his leadership of the 1906 Azusa Street Revival in Los Angeles, that catapulted the fledging movement into national prominence. The Louisiana–born son of former slaves was baptized as a Catholic and probably raised in the Baptist Church. On moving to the North to escape rigid racial segregation, he aligned himself first with the Methodist Church and then with the Evening Light Saints, a Holiness group that would become the Church of God (Anderson, Indiana). The largely self-educated pastor was introduced to the doctrine and experience of Pentecostal Spirit baptism and speaking in tongues by his ministry colleague Lucy Farrow, who also introduced him to Charles Parham (formulator of the formal doctrine of speaking in tongues as initial evidence of Holy Spirit baptism), with whom he studied for a short while before moving to Los Angeles.

Most scholars now agree that Seymour was the leader at the Azusa Street Revival, and until his death he served as the pastor of the mission church out of which it sprang. But as the revival waned, Seymour's influence among other Pentecostal leaders suffered the same fate, and throughout much most of the twentieth century his contributions to the Pentecostal movement were largely ignored by white scholars, and unknown by common African American Pentecostal believers. Within the last quarter of the twentieth century, Seymour's importance was rediscovered, largely spurred by work such as that undertaken by J. Douglas Nelson and James S. Tinney to reinsert him into American Pentecostal historiography.

Doctrines and Disciplines of the Azusa Street Mission of Los Angeles, California

Apostolic Address

To the Members of the Apostolic Faith Church

Dearly beloved brethren:

We esteem it our privilege and duty to most earnestly to recommend to your this volume which contains the Doctrines and Disciplines of our Church, both of which we believe are agreeable to the Word of God, the only sufficient rule of faith and practice. Yet the Church, using the liberty given to it by its Lord, and taught by the experience of a long series of years and by observations made on ancient and modern Churches, has from time to time modified its Discipline so as better to secure the end for which it was cofounded.

We believe that God's design in raising up the Apostolic Faith Church in America was to evangelize over these lands. As a proof hereof we have seen since 1906 that time of an extraordinary work of God extending throughout all of the United States and Territories and throughout the whole world.

In 1906, the colored people of Los Angeles felt they were led by the Spirit that they decided to have Elder W. J. Seymour of Houston, Texas to come to Los Angeles, Cal, and give them some Bible teaching. He came Feb. 22nd, and started Feb 24th, 1906. From his teaching one of the greatest revivals was held in the city of Los Angeles. People of all nations came and got their cup full. Some came from Africa, some came from India, China, Japan, and England.

Very soon division arose through some of our brethren, and the Holy Spirit was grieved. We want all of our white brethren and white sisters to feel free in our churches and missions, in spite of all the trouble we have had with some of our white brethren in causing diversion, and spreading wild fire and fanaticism. Some of our colored brethren caught the disease of this Spirit of division also. We find according to God's word to be one in the Holy Spirit, not in the flesh; but in the Holy Spirit, for we are one body (I Cor 12:12–14.) If some of our white brethren have prejudices and discrimination (Gal 2:11–20), we can't do it, because God calls us to follow the Bible (Matt 17:8; Matt 23) We must love all men as Christ commands (Heb 12:14). Now because we don't take them for directors it is not for discrimination, but for peace. To keep down race war in the Churches and friction, so they can have greater liberty and freedom in the Holy Spirit. We are sorry for this, but it is the best now and in later years for the work. We hope everyone that reads these lines may realize it is for the best; not for the worse. Some of our white brethren and sisters have never left us in all the division; they have stuck with us. We love our white brethren and sisters and welcome them. Jesus Christ takes in all people in his salvation. Christ is all and for all. He is neither black nor white man, nor Chinaman, nor Hind[u], no Japanese, but God. God is a Spirit, because without his spirit we cannot be saved. St. John 3:3–5; Rom 8:9.

We don't believe in the doctrine of artificial dancing that lots of people are calling the Holy Ghost dancing. David danced before the Lord. He danced with all his might. The Ark of the Lord was a type of the Presence of Christ. David, laying aside his royal majesty, and girdled himself with a linen ephod; this represent[ed] that he had come into the immediate presence of God as a sinner the [h]umble himself; it represented that he was naked before the Lord in his heart. He felt he could not be too humble, because God had been merciful to them in returning his Presence on the Ark which mean[s] his Glory. So David danced before the Lord, not before the people, for a show or form, but before the Lord; the people saw him and his wife, but it was God's Presence. So everything we do must be to the Glory of God.

We believe in rejoicing in the Spirit. We believe in shouting and leaping as the New Testament endorses.

Sound Doctrine

We must have sound doctrine in our work. We don't believe that the soul sleeps in the grave until the resurrection morning. The next, we don't believe in being baptized in the name of Jesus only. We believe in baptizing in the name of the Father, and the Son, and the Holy Ghost, as Jesus taught his disciples (Matt 28:19–20). We do not believe in keeping Saturday as the Christian Sabbath, we do not believe in dipping a person three times in order that he may be properly baptized. We believe in burying the candidate once in the name of the Father, and the Son and the Holy Ghost, Amen. We don't believe in the fleshly doctrine of the male and female kissing and calling it the Holy Kiss. It hurts the cause of Christ, and cause[s] our good to be evil spoken of. We believe in the Holy Brethren greeting the Brethren and the Holy Sisters greeting the Holy Sisters with a kiss.

—William Joseph Seymour, from *Doctrines and Disciplines of the Azusa Street Mission in Los Angeles*, 11–12.

LUCY FARROW
(1851–1911)

Apostolic Faith Mission

Lucy Farrow played a pivotal role in the unfolding of the Azusa Street Revival. Several months before it started, Farrow had served as the pastor of the Houston congregation where Seymour first came into contact with the doctrine and experience of Pentecostal Spirit baptism. Farrow also introduced Seymour to Charles Fox Parham, formulator of the doctrine of initial evidence. Once Seymour moved to Los Angeles, Farrow joined him to help lead the Bible study at Bonnie Brae Street and then the Azusa Street Revival. She left the revival to carry the message of the Pentecostal experience across the United States, stopping in Virginia to plant at least one, and possibly two, congregations. She then moved on to Liberia where she continued to conduct revivals and was reported to have been one of the few Azusa Street missionaries who successfully employed the gift of xenolalia,[4] to be able to deliver a number of messages in the Kru dialect. Farrow's untimely death came before the end of the heyday of the revival. But during her short five years with the Azusa Street Mission, she appeared to be revered as one of its most spiritual leaders, and was sought out by many who attended for her powerful ministry.

The Work in Virginia
907 Glasken St, Portsmouth, VA[4]

We had a glorious meeting last night. It was the sixth night and we have six speaking in tongues. It is wonderful to see how the Lord is working with His believing children, but there is much to be done here. There is a band of saints that do not read the Bible like saints. They say the Bible is for unbelievers so they do not read it at all. O for someone to help. Won't you come and help if you can, and as soon as you can?

God is making a short work in the earth today. He is soon corning to earth again. He said we should not get over the cities until the Son of Man should come, so we have not much time to lose. Remember me to all of the saints. Tell them to pray for me much. I can't write to all, so you remember me to all as one. Ask them to pray for the work in Virginia. It is much needed. I don't know how long the Lord is going to keep me here. There is so much to still to be done. I did not come through Danville, but I am going there soon as I can get off from this place. I came through New Orleans and changed cars there, and laid hands on two sick, and sowed seed on the way from Houston here.

—Lucy Farrow

A later report is that twenty have received the baptism of the Holy Ghost in Portsmouth.

4. The ability to supernaturally speak in a known tongue without having learned it.

OPHELIA WILEY

Apostolic Faith Mission

Among the women who played important roles in the Revival, Ophelia Wiley is perhaps one of the least known. Wiley was actively involved in the revival from its early days, and the evangelist and songstress was a trusted member of the missionary team that accompanied Florence Crawford, taking the Pentecostal message throughout the Pacific Northwest, finding enthusiastic reception, and on at least one occasion garnering the attention of the secular press. The inclusion of this short, unremarkable piece in the *Apostolic Faith* newspaper, among several similar articles submitted by workers and visitors to the mission, shows the openness of the periodical's editors to receiving and publishing contributions from all sorts of Pentecostal believers from around the globe.

Sermon from a Dress

The Lord make's His truth so plain that a wayfaring man, though a fool, shall not err therein. You have all seen a dirty dress washed. But you never saw a person take a dirty dress and iron it. And you never saw them take a dress and wash and iron it all at once. And you never saw a person put on a dress and iron it.

The dirty dress represents a person in sin. Your righteousness is filthy rages. "Though your sins be as scarlet, they shall be as white as snow." When you get the dress washed, that represents a justified experience. When the dress is washed and on the line, you rejoice because the washing is through.

But the clothes need [something[5]] else before they are ready to wear. What do they need? Why, they need to be ironed. You would be ashamed to take the clothes off the line and wear them without ironing. Jesus would be ashamed to pres-

ent you before the Father if you were not sanctified, but when you are sanctified He is not ashamed to call you brethren. Christ gave Himself for His church that He might wash it and present it without spot of wrinkle. So we must let Him iron out all the wrinkles.

What next? You take an ironed garment and there is something lacking yet. What is it? Why you need to put it on and wear it. But that is no work. The work was done when you washed and ironed it. So the Holy Ghost is a free gift. It is the promise of the Father to the soul that is sanctified. You do not have to repent to get the Holy Ghost, but you must be washed clean and be whiter than snow. Now you have nothing to mourn over, but something to rejoice over. You can know you are baptized. The Holy Ghost will cut your tongue loose and let you praise Him in an unknown language. God will not iron a dirty piece. He will take out the spots and then the wrinkles, and after these two works, He will baptize you with His free gift—the Holy Ghost.

5. [Ed.] The text here has "nothing."

JENNIE EVANS SEYMOUR
(?–1936)

Apostolic Faith Mission

Jennie Evans Moore had been a member of Joseph Smale's New Testament Church, a thriving Holiness congregation, before joining the Bible study meeting across the street from her home on Bonnie Brae Street. She was one of the first members of the group to experience the Pentecostal Holy Spirit baptism, and with that baptism, reportedly receiving the gift of playing the piano, an instrument she had never studied. Moore moved with the group to Azusa Street where she took an active part in the ministry. But Easter Sunday found her at her home congregation where she broke out into a message in tongues at some point during the worship service, igniting the interest of several in the congregation who would later in the week find their way to the revival.

Within a couple of years, she and Seymour were married, sparking a schism between the couple and Florence Crawford, which would lead to disruption in the publication of the *Apostolic Faith*, and the dwindling of the Azusa Street Mission congregation. In the following years, Jennie joined her husband in leading the mission, and after Joseph's death took over as pastor of the even smaller congregation, serving as it head until her death a decade later.

Music from Heaven[6]

It has been often related how the Pentecost fell in Los Angeles over a year ago in a cottage prayer meeting. Sister Jennie Moore who was in that meeting and received her 'Pentecost' gives her testimony as follows:

> For years before this wonderful experience came to us, we as a family, were seeking to know the fullness of God, and He was filling us with His presence until we could hardly contain the power. I had never seen a vision in my life, but one day as we prayed there passed before me three white cards, each with two names thereon, and but for fear I could have given them, as I saw every letter distinctly. On April 9, 1906, I was praising the Lord from the depths of my heart at home, and when the evening came and we attended the meeting the power of God fell and I was baptized in the Holy Ghost and fire, with the evidence of speaking in tongues. During the day I had told the Father that although I wanted to sing under the power I was willing to do whatever He willed and at the meeting when the power came on me I was reminded of the three cards which had passed me in the vision months ago. As I thought thereon and looked to God, it seemed as if a vessel broke within me and water surged up through my being, which when it reached my mouth came out in a torrent of speech in the languages which God had given me. I remembered the names on the cards: French, Spanish, Latin, Greek, Hebrew, Hindustani, and as the message came with power, so quick that but few words would have been recognized. Interpretation of each message followed in English, the name of the language would come to me. I sang under the power of the Spirit in many languages, the interpretation both words and music which I had never before heard, and in one home where the meeting was being held, the Spirit led me to the

6. *Apostolic Faith* 1/8 (May 1907) 3.

piano, where I played and sang under inspiration, although I had not learned to play. In these ways God is continuing to use me to His glory ever since that wonderful day, and I praise Him for the privilege of being a witness for Him under the Holy Ghost's power.

—J. M., 312 Azusa St. Los Angeles

JULIA HUTCHINS (1872–?)

Apostolic Faith Mission

Pastor Julia Hutchins was the leader of the Nazarene congregation that issued the invitation that first brought Seymour to Los Angeles. Hutchins hoped he would work with her as assistant pastor. But Seymour's first encounter with the group did not go well. His teaching that the baptism of the Holy Spirit was accompanied by the initial evidence of tongues did not resonate with Hutchins's understanding that she and the sanctified members of her Holiness congregation were already baptized with the Holy Ghost. After severing the pastoral relationship, however, she was instrumental in orchestrating a hearing for Seymour among other Holiness leaders who also rejected his contention and forbade him to proffer his teaching in their congregations. Sometime between that period and when the Azusa Street Revival moved into full swing, Hutchins had a change of heart and joined Seymour and other Pentecostal believers as a regular at the revival. Once she received her own Pentecostal Spirit baptism, Hutchins was ready to make good on the call she had earlier received from the Lord to go to Africa as a missionary, leading her own team to Liberia. Once there, she kept in touch with the Los Angeles saints, filing correspondences that spoke of her successes in using her newly acquired gift of tongues to carry on her ministry.

Sister Hutchins' Testimony[7]

I was justified on the 4th of July, 1901, and at that time I felt that the Lord wanted me in Africa, but I was not then at all willing to go. But on the 28th of July, 1903, the Lord sanctified me. Before He sanctified me, He asked me if I would go to Africa. I promised Him I would. From that time on, I have felt the call to Africa, and have been willing to go at any moment, but not knowing just when the Lord would have me leave.

On the sixth of last month, while out in my back yard one afternoon, I heard a voice speaking to me these words: "On the 15th day of September, take your husband and baby and start out for Africa." And I looked around and about me to see if there was not someone speaking to me, but I did not see anyone, and I soon recognized that it was the voice of God. I looked up into the heavens and said:

"Lord, I will obey." Since then I have had many tests and temptations from the devil. He has at times told me that I would not even live to see the 15th of September, but I never once doubted God. I knew that He was able to bring everything to pass that He told me to do.

After hearing the voice telling me to leave Los Angeles on the 15th, I went to one of my neighbors and testified to her that the Lord had told me to leave for Africa on the 15th of September. She looked at me with a smile. I asked her what she was smiling about. She said: "Because you have not got street car fare to go to Azusa Street Mission tonight, and talking about going to Africa." But I told her I was trusting in a God that could bring all things to pass that He wanted us to do. He has really supplied all may needs in every way, for the work where He has called me.

I want to testify also about my husband. He was a backslider, and how the devil did test me, saying: "You are going

7. [Ed.] *Apostolic Faith* 1:2 (October 1906) 1.

out to cast the devil out of others and going to take a devil with you." My husband was not saved, but I held onto God and said: "Lord, I will obey."

I continued to testify and to make preparation to leave on the 15th. The Lord reclaimed my husband and sanctified him wholly and put the glory and shout in him. So now it is my time to laugh. The devil has oppressed and mocked me; but praise the Lord, now I can mock him. Glory to God!

It is now ten minutes to four o'clock on the afternoon on the 15th day of September.

I am all ready and down to the Mission with my ticket and everything prepared, waiting to have hands laid on and the prayers of the saints, and expect to leave at eight o'clock from the Santa Fe Station en route for Africa. We expect to go to Mt. Coffee, Monrovia, Liberia.

Feeling the need for a real companion in the Gospel that was out and out for God, I prayed to God that He might give me one to go with me. I had my eyes upon one that I wanted to go, but in prayer and humbly before God, I found that was not the one the Lord wanted to go. So I said: "Anyone, Lord, that you would have to go will be pleasing to me." And, to my surprise, He gave me my niece—a girl that I had raised from a child. Now she is nineteen years of age, is saved, sanctified and baptized with the Holy Ghost, and is going with me out into the work of the Lord. So instead of giving me one Companion, He gave me two – my niece and my husband.

Our first stop will be Chattanooga Tenn., Harge Row. I want the prayers of the saints that I may stay humble.
—Mrs. J. W. Hutchins.
Address Mt. Coffee, Monrovia, Liberia, Africa.

CHARLES HARRISON MASON
(?–1961)

Church of God in Christ

For more than forty-five years, C. H. Mason served at the helm of the Church of God in Christ—the largest African American Pentecostal body in the United States. As a young man he gained some prominence throughout the black Tennessee Valley community before he fell into disfavor for accepting and preaching the Holiness doctrine of sanctification. For nearly a decade, he worked with his colleague Charles Price Jones to found the Church of God in Christ as a Holiness denomination. After visiting the Azusa Street Revival and having the Pentecostal Holy Spirit baptism experience, Mason disagreed with Jones over the necessity of tongues as an initial evidence of Holy Spirit baptism. After the split, Mason reconstituted the Church of God in Christ as a Pentecostal denomination.

In 1907, the two decided to investigate the validity of the phenomenon being reported from the West Coast, Mason made the two-thousand-mile trip, and after having the Pentecostal Holy Spirit baptism experience was convinced that what he had found at Azusa Street was an authentic move of God. Mason disagreed with Jones over the necessity of tongues as an initial evidence of Holy Spirit baptism and a schism ensued between the two. After the split, Mason reconstituted the Church of God in Christ as a Pentecostal denomination.

Tennessee Evangelist Witnesses[8]

Dear ones, It Is sweet for me to think of you all and your kindness to me while I was with you. My soul is filled with the glory of the Lord. He is giving great victory wherever He sends us in His name, many being baptized with the Holy Ghost and speaking In tongues. Praise the Lord. The fight has been great. I was put out, because I believed that God did baptize me with the Holy Ghost among you all. Well, He did It and It just suits me. Glory In the Lord. Jesus is coming. Take the Bible way, It Is right. The Lord is leading me out of all that men have fixed up for their glory. Be strong In Him. (Isa. 41:10, 20) The Lord is casting out devils, healing the sick, and Singing the sweetest songs. He has sung hundreds of songs. I do not have time to go back over one to practice it, for the next will be new. Praise His name. I sit under His shadow with great delight. His banner over me is love.

—C. H. Mason,
Lexington, Miss.

8. *Apostolic Faith* 1/6 (Feb–Mar, 1907).

EMMA COTTON
(?–1952)

Church of God in Christ

Thirty years after the Azusa Street Revival began, eyewitness Emma Cotton set out to recapture the spiritual fervor of the meeting and report on it to a new generation of believers as well as to remind the older saints of the heritage that they shared. Cotton and her husband, Henry, pastored an independent congregation that would become one of the leading Church of God in Christ congregations in California during the mid-twentieth century. She would also become a close friend and confidant of famed evangelist Aimee Semple McPherson, and was one of few women that McPherson allowed to speak from her coveted pulpit at Angelus Temple. Cotton attended the revival as a young woman and did not seem to have played a major role in it. Yet her depiction of the event uniquely pays attention to the role that women played in its unfolding and success.

The Inside Story of the Outpouring of the Holy Spirit, Azusa Street, April 1906[9]

Brother W. J. Seymour, the one whom God used to bring the message that stirred the world, was born in Louisiana. He was saved and sanctified under the Evening Light Saints, a Holiness group. Later, he came to Houston, Texas, where he met Sister Farrar,[10] who had a small Holiness mission. She was led to go to Kansas to attend Bible School and Brother Seymour, who was now one of the congregation is asked to act pastor during her absence.

While away Sister Farrar received the light of Acts 2:4. She began at once to seek for more of God, and the Spirit came upon her so strong that she was unable to remain at Bible School. She then returned to Houston to tell the story of her wonderful new experience.

It was not this time that a Sister Terry went to Houston, Texas. Before she left for Houston she heard of a group of Nazarene colored saints in Los Angeles who had organized a little Holiness church on Santa Fe Avenue. Sister Terry went to these meetings where she met the pastor, Julia Hutchins . . . Sister Terry finally arrived Houston that summer to visit her folks, she visited the Houston mission there, where she met Brother Seymour.

Sister Terry later returned to Los Angeles where she immediately went out on Santa Fe to the little Nazarene group, and told Sister Hutchins about the very godly man she had met in Houston. Right away interest was stirred and the group invited the Holiness preacher, Brother Seymour, to their little church.

Just before Brother Seymour received this invitation to the Coast Sister Farrar had returned from Kansas to the little mission with her new experience. After she made it known to the preacher that she had received the baptism with the Holy Ghost he was amazed because he had thought the Holy Ghost was received when one was sanctified

He then began to seek the Lord through prayer and the Word of God. It was then the Lord, in His faithfulness to Brother Seymour, as he is faithful to

9. [Ed.] *Message of the Apostolic Faith* 1/1 (April 1939) 1–3.

10. [Ed.] She is referring to Lucy Farrow.

everyone who is honest. Began to show him that he was mistaken about being baptized with the Holy Spirit; that he was only sanctified.

Brother Seymour began asking the Lord to empty him of his false ideas, and when he was emptied of every false thought and idea that he had, the Lord then made plain to him Acts 2:4 as a personal experience.

By this time, the fare from Los Angeles had reached him and when he arrived here, he found the saints waiting for him with eagerness to the man of God . . .

Everybody was happy to see him, but on Sunday morning, when Brother Seymour preached on Acts 2:4 as a personal experience, oh! what a surprise to those old saints who had claimed the baptism of the Holy Ghost for years. There they were told by the preacher they did not have the Holy Ghost; they were only sanctified.

When the meeting was dismissed, Brother Lee, a precious colored saint who was a member of the Peniel mission invited Brother Seymour to his home to dinner. When they returned to the mission to the afternoon service, the lock was on the door, because the saints thought he had a false doctrine, and they would not permit him in the mission any more. So then, Brother, Lee, out of courtesy for the stranger, (not that he believed that he was right) had to take him back to his home. He could not leave the stranger in the street.

Brother Seymour had no money to get out of town and the saints did not believe in him and he did not know anybody, so he stayed in the room and prayed. Brother and Sister Lee did not feel so good toward him, but they just could not invite him to leave. They had the unwelcomed guest on their hands.

After a few nights in the home Brother Seymour asked them if they would pray when Brother Lee would come in from his work, so they did. In a few nights, the Spirit of God began to bike hold of the hearts of Brother and Sister Lee for prayer, and they felt differently toward the stranger. Then in a few day more, the saints from the little mission began to come around to see if the stranger was still in town or had gone.

They found such a wonderful spirit of prayer in that home that they began to humble themselves before the Lord. It was them the Lord began to talk to them and everyone that came into that home would get down and pray. The news began to spread among the people about that praying man. They would not receive his doctrine, but they would pray with him.

Then came a neighbor into the home, a Baptist sister: Sister Asbury of 214 North, Bonnie Brae, and invited the stranger, Brother Seymour, to hold, the prayer meeting in her home.—So they began the prayer meeting in Brother and Sister Asbury home, and they tarried day and night. In the meantime, the Spirit of the Lord had taken hold of Brother Lee's heart in such a way that he now was in constant prayer. He was a janitor in the bank at Seventh and Spring for years and he said he used to go down into the basement of' the bank and hide away and spend hours and hours in prayer.

One day the Lord gave him a vision. He plainly saw two men come to him; apparently Peter and John. He said he was not asleep; he was praying. They stood and looked at him; then they lilted their hands to heaven and they began to shake under the power of God and began to speak in other tongues. And he said he jumped up and he was just shaking under the power of God and did not know what was the matter with him. When he went home that night he said to Brother Seymour, "I know how people act when they get the Holy Ghost." Brother Seymour had explained the manifestation of the Spirit to the group.

This sounded so foolish to them. And Brother Seymour could not explain it enough for them to understand: they just had to get it. After he had this vision a deeper hunger was stirred in his heart. Brother Seymour could not impress the people; but after Brother Lee had the vision they began to believe it was [a] real, experience. The Lord created such a hunger in Brother Lee that he began to seek more earnestly for that experience.

One evening he came in from his work, and he said to Brother Seymour, "If you will lay your hands on me. I will receive my baptism." And Brother Seymour said, "No, the Lord wants me to lay hands suddenly on no man." Later in the evening, Brother Seymour said to Brother Lee, "Brother, I lay my hands on you, in Jesus name," and when he laid his hands on him Brother Lee fell under the power like dead, and Sister Lee was so frightened that she screamed and said, "What did you do to my husband?"

In a few minutes, Brother Lee rose up and sat in a chair. Brother Seymour said afterwards that he prayed and asked the Lord to let him get right up as they all seemed so frightened that the Lord could not finish the work at that time. Brother Lee had a heavenly touch then and he sought the Lord day and night.

Brother Seymour told about Sister Farrar, whom he had met in Texas who had given him the light on Acts 2:1, so after Brother Lee had this experience with the Lord, they were anxious to see the woman who had had this wonderful experience in the Holy Ghost and they got together the money and sent for her.

When Brother Lee came home one evening and found Sister Farrar there, he fell on his knees: at her feet, and he said, "Sister, if you will lay your hands on me, I believe I will get my baptism right now." And she said, "I cannot do it, unless the Lord says so." Later while at dinner Sister Farrar rose from her seat and she walked over to Brother Lee and said, "The Lord tells me to lay my hands on you for the Holy Ghost." And when she laid her hands on him, he fell out of his chair like dead; and began to speak in other tongues. It was so strange to Sister Lee and her brother that the Lord did not do much through Brother Lee; he just spoke in tongues a few minutes and got up.

They went on over to the prayer meeting at Sister Asbury's home. When Brother Lee walked into the house, six people were already on their knees praying. As he walked in the, door he lifted his hands and began to speak in tongues and the power fell on them and all six of them began to speak in tongues. Then came the great noise that was spread abroad.

They shouted three days and nights. The people came from everywhere, By the next morning, there was no way of getting nearer the house. As the people came in they fell under the Power; and the whole city was stirred. They shouted there until the foundation of the house gave away, but no one was hurt. During those three days, there were many people who received their baptism, who had just come to see what it was. The sick were healed, and sinners were saved just as they came in.

Then they went out to find another meeting place, and they found Old Azusa. It was an old discarded building on Azusa Street that had been used for a Methodist church but had been vacant for years: It seemed to have been waiting for the Lord and there began that great world-wide revival, where the people came from all over the world by the hundreds and thousands. That meeting lasted for three years without a break.

While I write this my soul is lifted up, because I saw house in its first glory and when I remember those days; I feel like going down into the dust of humility, if only to bring back that old-time Power. I am willing to give my life.

I feel that this is the time now for the refreshing of the saints. The old-time Azusa work stood for and still stands for the earnestly contending for the faith once delivered to the saints. This message of the Lord is a great getting together, that we all might be renewed in the old-time Spirit and Power; that we might do a greater work for Jesus in this last hour.

The noise of the great outpouring of the Spirit drew me, and I had been nothing but a walking drug store all my life, with weak lungs and cancer. As they looked on me, they said, "Child, God will heal you." In those days of that great outpouring when they said God would heal you, you were healed.

For thirty-three years, I have never gone back to the doctors, thank God, nor any of that old medicine! The Lord saved me, baptized me with the Holy Ghost and healed me, and sent me on my way rejoicing. This is what I saw and heard. I have much more to say about the wonderful working of the power or God among the people next time, if it is the Lord's will.

chapter four

African American Trinitarian Denominations

MARY MAGDALENA LEWIS TATE
(1871–1930)

Church of the Living God Pillar and Ground of the Truth

Some time after 1890, around the age of nineteen, Tate had a conversion experience and subsequently felt a call to preach. For years, she traveled throughout the Ohio Valley preaching Holiness doctrine and establishing "holiness bands" she called "do-right bands," but making no attempt to organize them into a body. Magdalena Lewis Tate, founder and first presiding bishop of the Church of the Living God Pillar and Ground of the Truth had been part of William Christian's Holiness group of a similar name, but she reportedly had no knowledge of the Azusa Street Revival that was unfolding in Los Angeles. In 1906, the same year the revival broke out, Tate had a supernatural experience of healing accompanied by Pentecostal Holy Spirit baptism in which she spoke in tongues without prompting from anyone or acknowledged awareness of the occurrence elsewhere. She subsequently began preaching Pentecostal doctrine throughout Tennessee and organizing the group she had formed into a denomination.

At her consecration, Tate became the first woman to serve as presiding bishop of a nationally recognized denomination. That body saw itself as divinely ordained of God to restore the church to its New Testament purity, and Tate imposed a rigid standard of personal piety on its members, which included sanctions on specific foods, social activities, and involvement with those, even within the Pentecostal community, who did not share her vision. Tate's importance, however, stems from the fact that at least seven denominations can trace their roots back to the original body that she founded.

A Special Message from Mother to Her Children[1]

P.O. Box 658
Nashville, Tennessee
June 6, 1928

Dear Saints:

This is to say there has been a mistake grievously made and sent on the written notice called "a vision." My P.O. address was written up wrong so I am herein saying, be careful to send my mail to me at P.O. Box 658 as some just will at times write me at P.O. Drawer 870. So don't write me there any more please do not, as P.O. Box 870 has never been my box at all, so don't write me there. Please to send me a donation at once to this number as above explained. I am sick and in need. Now, I am truly your Chief Overseer, the only and true founder of the House of God, which is the Church of the Living God, the Pillar and Ground of the Truth. I am definitely expressly known to be the one through whom the Lord in these last days did choose to set up this above herein named church, beginning in Greenville, Alabama, then in many other places in Alabama and from there to Paducah, Kentucky, also to Waycross, Georgia. The Lord preached through me twenty-four nights in succession when building up the work in Waycross, Ga., without the aid of anyone but Jesus to help me and set up the church in number of twenty-four members before any ones

1. [Ed.] This version of the letter appeared in a collection titled *Mary Lena Lewis Tate: Collected Letters and Manuscripts*, compiled and edited by Meharry H. Lewis.

arrived to assist me in the meeting. While rejoicing over the twenty-fourth person having already received the blessed Holy Ghost, I lifted up my eyes and did wait the arrival of one who was my helper at that time. So the meeting in Waycross continued on until about a hundred or more were filled with this wonderful blessing in Waycross, Ga., after which my son arrived. So the Spirit bade me continue the meeting and souls continued to be saved until the number of the band was two hundred and sixty. So, I am yet praising God for yet being that honored vessel of gold in the great house of God as He kindled a fire in my soul in the South as He spoke of in Ezekiel, chapter 20 and verses 47–48. So as it is known of many that my words are true, so be it continuously known unto all that you may tell your children of it and let your children tell their children and their children another generation.

Now, I truly know God did set His house in order through me His humble servant in these last days and through me founded and delivered to His people the right and true name of His church as it was already written in First Timothy, chapter 3 and verse 15, but he chose me, Mary Magdalena to call your attention to it whereby bringing it out in oneness that all of His followers might be one, that the world might believe also, and know that the Father sent Jesus Christ (see Jn 17:1–12, and 17:19–23).

Now, loving children, upon some things I have held my peace as long as is needful and I believe all who fear God will follow me in what I shall herein with few words strive to make plain by the Word of God after showing a few Scriptures as a platform as I have always taken heed in building (see I Cor 3:10). They who love His law have great peace and nothing shall offend them (see Ps 119:165). So all

of you I am sure desire to be a companion of all of them that fear God and them that keep His precepts (see Ps 119:63, 74–165; and Ps 20:7–11, 18). David declared that God's Word is true from the beginning (Ps 119:160).

Now dears, really what I am saying is a true centerpiece of my discourse as follows: Let us all ever remember the Sabbath Day and keep it Holy. Now, as for myself, I shall never anymore in life do any carnal labor on the day which the world calls Sunday, as the Lord has given it to us to be the seventh day of the week, if we count that Monday is the first day of the week according to Friday being the first day that Jesus laid in the heart of the earth and according to the Word, He was in the earth three days and nights so it would be that Monday morning, He arose and early when it began to dawn upon the first day of the week and it was in the end of the Sabbath (see St. Matthew, chapter 23 and verse 1; St. Mark, chapter 16 and verse 1; St. Luke, chapter 24 and verse 1; St. John, chapter 20 and verse 1). Now, comparing the record of these four Gospel writers, we find that the first day of the week means the first day of the seven days given and six of them are working days and the seventh one is a rest day. The Sabbath, the day we call Sunday, so as Monday was the first day and as it began to advance or dawn which means come into existence, it was the end of the Sabbath, so by counting six working days of the [week], then the seventh day of the week is the Sabbath Day. So count from Monday to Saturday, it is six days, and the next day, which we call by name Sunday, is the seventh day which, according to the sweet Word of God beyond a shadow of doubting, is truly the Sabbath day. Praise our God for this wonderful light. There have been much doubting and disputing over the real certainty of really what day is truly the Sabbath, as most everybody without a doubt has some zeal of God concerning his commandment found in Exodus; chapter 20, verse 8 (and continued in 11), "Remember, the sabbath day, to keep it holy." (See also Gen 2:2) We are taught that on the seventh day God ended His work which He had made and He rested on the seventh day from all His work which He had made. (Also see Hebrews, Chapter 4 and verse 4; Lev 33:3). Truly every child of God, when once considering such plain sweet honey comb words of God as already outlined herein, certainly does truly have some zeal of God in the matter that God meant what He had said in the subject. And I see it like this, if all cannot understand why He wants His people to recognize six days as work days and rest the seventh day, they should be willing to obey anyway because it is the word of God Almighty and His words shall stand forever (Isa 40:8; Matt 24:35; Mk 13:31; Lk 21:33). Now it is plain to be seen that remembrance of the Sabbath Day on the keeping of it is much needed now because most people are very fast in these last days and don't take up much time with hearing the Word of God neither obeying, Therefore, the true friends of God and Christ should, as the Apostles and saints in time past, keep a heart and eye single to the fact that the Sabbath Day (Sunday) is a time when most people of all towns, cities or countries are mostly at leisure and it is a very convenient time to gather people together to hear the Word of God, wherewith you can go to them or get them to come to you the true friends to Jesus Christ and [thereby, get them to come] to His dear father. Once the true light of God's command concerning the Sabbath (or anything else) shines plainly unto them, they will all say along with me and David and all the saints of Light, "The law of thy mouth is better unto me than thousands of gold and silver," (see Ps 119:72). Now let us realize that there could not be any Sabbath Day unless there was six days of labor (see Ex 31:14–16, Deut 5:13–14; Ex 35:2). These Scriptures have already shown and hereby is plain proof enough to show to all that after six days, the next day would be the seventh, which is the Sabbath.

Now we are sensible of the fact that there will be many people who will not work at all and are not ministers; neither have they any excuse for not working. But, it is good for them to know what is the Sabbath Day as the Sabbath has always been a convenient time to hear the Word of God. Probably such persons could, on the Sabbath Day, arrange to get in company with those who do recognize the Sabbath according to the Word of God, and it could be a means of those who had not believed to really believe, for how can they believe in whom they have not heard and how can they hear without a preacher, and how shall they preach except they be sent (see Rom 10:14–15).

Now all of us who are in Christ Jesus, who walk not after the flesh, but after the Spirit, the righteousness of the law must be fulfilled in us (see Rom 8:1–52). It's plainly shown that being mindful of the Sabbath Day keeping is some of the righteousness in the law to be fulfilled in us, the true people of God who are in Christ Jesus by the baptism of the Holy Spirit and not of water as some no doubt have thought (see Rom 12:13; Gal 3:27). The saints and Apostles in times past always made convenient to have the people to meet them or else they met the people on the Sabbath Day and disputed with the people and taught the Word of God (see

Acts 13:14 and 27; 16:13; 17:2; 18:4; 28:14; also, Ezk 20:12; Isa 58:13; Jer 17:21).

Dearly beloved, let us all remember the Sabbath Day and keep it Holy ever after. Since this true light on the real Sabbath shined unto all, let the work that we do on the Sabbath ever be on the highest standard like God, our heavenly Father and His dear Son, Jesus Christ, as we do know it is right to do good on the Sabbath. All preparation of oil. such as cooking and all arrangements should be made perfectly on Saturday, that nothing of the sort be done on Sunday at all because it is the seventh day, which makes it truly the Sabbath. All who desire may fast that day and all who desire may eat, but the food should be prepared on the day of preparation (see Matt 27; Mk 15:42; Lk 23:54). Many other Scriptures could be referred to in reference to the seventh day Sabbath, as I shall continue from time to time, teach it and preach it all the days of my life and also continue to insert such teaching in all my scriptural tracts and write up all along as God will. And I am sure these things will ever be wholesome, digestive, spiritual fruits and meats which shall be relished among all of my true ministers and followers in Jesus Christ as some have been patiently waiting upon me to bring out these things as they knew is was my right and business to do so that they not be busy bodies in my matters. It was so sweet for you all to wait on me. May God ever bless you and I don't believe a one on my true children will prove a fool in meddling with me, for the Spirit says in Proverbs, it is an honor for a man to cease from strife, but every fool will be meddling (Proverbs, chapter 20 and verse 3). I say, as David did in Psalms, chapter 119 and verse 71, it is good for me that I have been afflicted one day, as I was feeling sad and lonely and feeling as the Spirit says in

Second Corinthians, chapter 4 and verses 8–10. So while meditating with the Lord, in the Spirit, He commanded me to take my pencil in hand and begin writing what He had shown me for several years concerning the seventh day as Sabbath and the six working days for labor and carnal work. And as I took my pencil in my hand and began to write, the Lord did wonderfully and supernaturally brighten up my room and strengthened up my eyes and I have been feeling better in my eyes than I have since I have been afflicted in them. Praise God for ever more, bless His holy Name! I haven't eaten or drunk anything for three days and have been writing on this *vision* which God has showered upon me. Now pray for me that I may ever be instrumental in bringing out the mysteries for this church on time as it may please God. "If ye be willing and obedient, ye shall eat the good of the land: But if ye refuse and rebel, ye shall be devoured with the sword: for the mouth of the Lord hath spoken it," (Isa 1:19–20).

Now, all of the saints should keep the Sabbath as already herein explained, but if there be any serious hindrance to block the way to prevent any of them from keeping the Sabbath as soon as this message reaches them, they should stay willing to keep it and not rebel in any way whatsoever until the hindrance be moved, then get in line in the matter to stay forever. I want to also herein . . . [allay] concern by saying, when the voice spoke to brother Paul as we read in Acts, chapter 12 and verse 16, and said to him, "And now why tarriest thou? Arise, and be baptized and wash away thy sins, calling on the name of the Lord," it had no reference at all to the water baptism, because Paul rose up and was baptized (see Acts 9:18). So this baptism which Paul came in contact with by calling on the name of the Lord, was the baptism of the Holy Ghost, the real washing of regeneration and renewing of the Holy Ghost! (See Tit 3:5). The baptism of water cannot wash away sin, neither bury anyone with Christ as it will take the Spirit to do such work. Water cannot do such work. We are buried with Christ by baptism of the Spirit because Jesus Christ is in heaven on the right hand of the Father. We cannot get with Him in baptism[,] only by the Spirit for by one Spirit are be baptized into one body (see I Cor 12:13; Rom 6:4). Now, if the word baptism was not referred to in several instances, biblically, we could be allowed to think that the water baptism could do all these great things, but since there is the baptism of the Spirit, then let us see it that the baptism of the Spirit is the greatest of all and is the one baptism to be experienced by faith as spoken of in Ephesians, chapter 4 and verse 5. Therefore, it is plain to be seen that this baptism alone is the one referred to that is doing such great work, such as burying us with Christ and washing away our sins and planting us together in the likeness of His death and baptized in Jesus, etc. (see Gal 3:27).

Next thought on this, no one can be ready to meet Jesus unless they become *God's son.* "He came unto His own, and His own received Him not. But, as many as received Him, to them gave He power to become the sons of God, *even* to them that believe on his name," (Jn 1:11–12). "He that hath overcometh shall inherit all things; and I will be his God, and he shall be my son," (Rev 21:7). It is plainly to be seen according to these Scriptures referred to that all people who become the sons of God must overcome all evil and low-down dirty things and really live above committing them. And all who are yet being overcome by evil shall have to fast and watch and pray much that they be delivered from the bondage of corruption into the glorious liberty of the children of God, for we know that the whole creation groaneth and travailleth in pain together until now, and not only they but ourselves groan within ourselves waiting for the adoption, to wit, the redemption or our bodies (see Rom 8:19–23; II Cor 5:1–4). The reason we groan is that we want countenance in feeling the Spirit of God moving about in our soul. Therefore we do groan daily waiting for the adoption, which is of the Spirit in witness to the daily and continued spiritual redemption. The redemption is the forgiveness of sins (see Col 1:14). So as we who are true do know our sins have been forgiven. We want the Spirit to continue to *witness* and see it continuing, as the word *wit* means to "look and see" as did Miriam, the sister of Moses, who stood afar off to witness what would be done to Moses, after he could be hid no longer than three months for his mother had made bulrushes and put Moses into it and laid it in the flags by the river. So Miriam doubtless knew that somebody would find her little brother there, but she wanted to witness, which means she wanted to know of a certainty, what would be done to Moses, her baby brother (see Ex 2:4).

So the earnest expectation of the creature waiteth for the manifestation of the sons of God, so the manifestation of the sons of God is that overcoming power and overcoming statute and standard which is for all who strive to get to it. All creatures who are yet weak and subject to mistakes which is vanity will be delivered from such corruption if they would keep obedient to God's Word through those who are over them in the Lord and those who are stronger than themselves, because it was through and by the fall of Adam that we all were by our Creator made subject to vanity not by willingness, but by God's own reason. That is why He has planned a way for all to be delivered into the glorious liberty of the children of God. When people are made entirely free from sin and have grown to the place whereby they can remember their body and keep it under subjection to the Word of God, it is truly glorious liberty. So in this all who desire to come to this liberty do groan and travail in pain (see Rom 8:19–24). We see plainly that all can be saved by hope and are saved by hope if saved at all, which means that you are traveling to the honored height or place as above herein explained by keeping yourselves from idols as taught in the First Epistle of John, chapter 5 and verse 21, confessing your faults, and walking in the light. If you confess your sins (that is, your faults), God is faithful and just to forgive your sins. He will also cleanse you from all unrighteousness. When cleansed from all unrighteousness, you are in that glorious liberty and not under bondage (see Lk 1:74–75). Any person who, after being blessed, if they live after the flesh will die—will die out of the Spirit, spiritually and temporally. But, if they, through the Spirit, do mortify the deeds of the body, they shall live (Rom 8:13–14).

Now, let us ever in all things obey the Word of God that we by obeying may follow the Spirit, that the adoption witness the redemption of our body every day for the weak people are not the only ones who groan within themselves, but we who have the first fruits are also groaning within ourselves. We are not groaning that we be unclothed, but we groan earnestly that we be clothed upon with our house from on high. The clothing is *the power* from that house not made with hands, *the power* that comes upon us

and comforts us, glory to the Name of the Lord (see Rom 8:23).

Now dears, as this message is directly to the people of my churches, I am, so to speak, compelled to make it as *Duke's mixtures,*[2] on account of my financially embarrassed condition. This will say, all of you have been notified of the General Assembly time and place and representing funds. So please obey. We may send another notice, but if not, don't fail to come in to the Assembly on time, also write me after reading these contents.

I am thine and thou are mine, so all pastors send me a special offering after reading this message as I have asked you. Now a hint to the wise is sufficient. Just pray that the time will come when I won't have to call on you as often and patiently wait for it to really come to pass. I showed you on those notices how to help me and not conflict with assemblies and other official days. So I am worthy to be considered at any time as I am complying with instructions in Philippians, chapter 4 and verse 5. Now, I have suffered much having my teeth adjusted, but have not taken one drop of medicine yet, praise God! I feel if ever there was a time I needed the care of my children in Jesus, it is now. I need cereals of different kinds to eat in soft food and fruits. I am pitiful. I am just from the dentist today for the first dentist left about 4 or 5 roots in my jaws and I have been too weak to have them taken out until today. So he took out three today and let me rest until Thursday, the 7th, praise God! So he requested that I bring him fifty dollars ($50.00) Thursday. Now you all know I need help. I am suffering much. I do thank those who have sent me some little aid. You know your own selves when you

2. [Ed.] A widely used pomade that could be used for all grades of hair, hence an "all in one" message serving a number of purposes.

send me in anything and I am having my little secretary to keep tab on all. I have many things to say to you all, but if God will, I shall live and shall see you all face to face in the Assembly, perhaps.

Bye, bye, from your own Dear Mother, M. L. Tate, P.O. Box 653, Nashville, Tennessee. My home address is 1811–1819 Heiman Street, Nashville, Tennessee.

Elder Mason Tells of Receiving the Holy Ghost[3]

The first day in the meeting I sat to myself, from those that went with me. I saw and heard some things that did not look scriptural to me, but at this I did not stumble. I began to thank God in my heart for all things for when I heard some speak in tongues I knew it was right, though I did not understand it. Nevertheless it was sweet to me. I also thank God for Elder Seymour who came and preached a wonderful sermon. His words were sweet and powerful and it seems that I hear them now while writing. When he closed his sermon, he said, "All of those that want to be sanctified or baptized with the Holy Ghost, go to the upper room, and all those that want to be healed go to the prayer room, and those that want to be Justified, come to the altar." I said that is the place for me, for it may be that I am not converted, and if not, God knows it and can convert me.

Satan says to me, 'If you get converted, will you tell me?' I said yes, for I knew if I were not convinced and God did convert me, it would tell for itself. I stood on my feet while waiting at the altar fearing someone would bother me, but I said in my mind, that if I ever get to that alter and get my back turned on the people, I will see them about getting me away. Just as I attempted to bow down someone called me and said, 'The pastor wants you three brethren in his room.' I obeyed and went up. He received us and seemed to be so glad to see us there. He said, 'Brethren, the Lord will do great things for us and bless us.' He cautioned us not to be running around all the city seeking worldly

pleasure, but seek pleasure of the Lord. The word just suited me.

At that time a sister came into the room at the time we were bowing to pray, one that I had a thought about that night not have been right, I had not seen her a number of years. I arose, took her into a room and confessed it to her. And we prayed. I arose and returned to the pastor's room and began to pray again, and the enemy got into a minister, a brother to tempt me. He opened his Bible and said, 'Look.' I said to him, go away, I do not want to be bothered. And he temped me the third time. but I refused to hear him. I told him that he did not know what he wanted, I knew what I needed. I did not intend to be interfered by anyone, so he gave me up and ceased to annoy me further, though he was a man that I loved as myself.

Eld. J. A. Jeter, of Little Rock, Ark., and D. J. Young of Pine Bluff, Ark., we three went together, boarded together and prayed for the same blessing. The enemy had put into the ear of Bro. Jeter to find fault of the work but God kept me out of it.

That night the Lord spoke to me, that Jesus saw all of this world's wrong but did not attempt to set it right until God overshadowed Him with the Holy Ghost. And He said that "I was no better than my Lord," and if I wanted him to baptize me, I would have to let the people's rights and wrongs all alone, and look to Him and not to the people, and He would baptize me. And I said yes to God, for it was Him who I wanted to baptize me and not the people.

"Glory!" The second night of prayer I saw a vision. I saw myself standing alone and had a dry roll of paper. I had to chew it. When I had gotten it all in my mouth, trying to swallow it, looking up towards

3. Originally published in *The History and Life Work of Elder C. H. Mason, Chief Apostle, and His Co-Workers* (1924).

the heavens, there appeared a man at my side. I turned my eyes at once, then I awoke and the interpretation came. God had me swallowing the whole book, and that if I did not turn my eyes to anyone but God and Him only, He would baptize me. I said yes to Him, and at once, in the morning when I arose I could hear a voice in me saying, 'I see.'

I had joy but was not satisfied. A sister began to tell me about the faults that were among the saints, but stopped as she did not want to hinder me by telling me of them. I sat and looked at her and said, 'you all may stand on your heads, God has told me what to do. God is going to baptize me.' So I came to the mission and found the brother that I had left, fighting. He had turned the other way, a Sister began speaking in tongues and said:

"'The voice of the Lord says in my heart that here is something in that for Jesus.' And he said if there is anything for Jesus I want it. So he went and bowed down at her feet for all to pray for him. I was going to take my seat by him, I was left standing on my feet. Then the enemy came to show me what I had missed by being out of the meeting, I would not reason with him. but said, 'Go from me.' He was trying to get me to condemn myself, when I would reason with him, he tried to show me that it was only deceit in Bro. Jeter for he knew that I knew his way toward women, but I would not reason with the devil.

"I got me a place at the altar and began to thank God. After that, I said, 'Lord if I could only baptize myself I would do so.' For I wanted the baptism so bad that I did not know what to do. I said, 'Lord you will have to do the work for me.' So I just turned it all over in to His hands to do the work for me, a brother came and prayed for me. I did not feel any better or any worse. One sister came and said, 'Satan will try to make you feel sad, but that is not the way to receive him—you must be glad and praise the Lord.' I told her that I was letting the Lord search my heart, for I did not want to receive new wine in old bottles, But I said, 'My heart does not condemn me.' Then I quoted the scripture to her which readeth thus: 'Beloved, if our hearts condemn us not, then have confidence towards God, and whatsoever we ask, we receive of him.' I John 3:21–22. Then I realized in my heart that I had confidence in God and did not have to get it, for my heart was free from condemnation.

"Then I began to seek for the baptism of the Holy Ghost according to Acts 2:44, which readeth thus: 'Then they that gladly received His word were baptized,' Then I saw that I had a right to be glad and not sad. As the enemy was trying to make me believe the way 'to receive the Holy Ghost was to be sad, but the light of the word put him out. There came a reason in my mind Which said, "Were you sad when you were going to marry!" I said "NO, I was glad." It said that this meant wedlock to Christ. Then I saw more in being glad than in being sad.

"The enemy said to me, 'There may be something wrong with you.' Then a voice spoke to me and said. 'If there is anything wrong with you, Christ will find it and take it away and will marry you, at any rate, and will not break the vow." More light came and my heart rejoiced! Some said let us sing. I arose and the first song that came to me was, "He Brought Me Out of the Miry Clay; He Sat My Feet on the Rock to Stay." The Spirit came upon the saints and upon me! After which I soon sat down and soon my hands went up and I resolved in my heart not to take them down until the Lord baptized me.

"The enemy tried to show me again how much pain it would cause me to endure not knowing how long it would be before the Lord would baptize me. The enemy said that I might not be able to hold out. The Spirit rebuked him and said that the Lord was able to make me stand and if not I would be a liar. And the Spirit gave me to know that I was looking to God and not to myself for all things. The sound of a mighty wind was in me and my soul cried, "Jesus, only, none like you." My soul cried and soon I began to die. It seemed that I heard the groaning of Christ on the Cross dying for me. All of the work in me until I died out of the old man. The sound stopped for a little while. My soul cried, Oh. God, finish your work in me. Then the sound broke out in me again. Then I felt something raising me out of my seat without any effort of my own. I said, 'It may be imagination.' Then looked down to see if it was really so. I saw that I was rising. Then I gave up, for the Lord to have His way with in me. So there came a wave of glory into me, and all of my being was filled with the glory of the Lord. So when He had gotten me straight on my feet there came a light which enveloped my entire being above the brightness of the sun. When I opened my mouth to say glory, a flame touched my tongue which ran down in me. My language changed and no word could I speak in my own tongue. Oh, I was filled with the glory of the Lord. My soul was then satisfied. I rejoiced in Jesus my Savior, whom I love so dearly. And from that day until now there has been an overflowing joy of the glory of the Lord in my heart.

"After five weeks I left Los Angeles, California, for Memphis, Tennessee, my home. The fire had fallen before my arrival. Bro. Glenn Cook, of Los Angeles, Cal., was there telling the story and the Lord was sending the rain. I was full of the power and when I reached home, the Spirit had taken full control of me and everything was new to me and to all the saints. The way that he went after things was all new. The way he did change was the same. At the same time, I soon found that he could and was teaching me all things and showing the things of the Lord. He taught how and what to sing and all his songs were new. The third day after he began with me in Memphis I asked him to give me the interpretation of what was spoken in tongues, for I did not understand the operation of the Spirit. I wanted the church to understand what the Spirit was saying through me, so that they might have been edified. My prayers were in vain. The Lord stood me up on the day and began to speak in tongues and interpret the same. He soon gave me the gift of interpretation, that is, He would interpret sounds, groans and any kind of spiritual utterance."

The Fire Baptized Holiness Church of God of the Americas

Basis of Union—Who We Are

Section 5

We believe that the Pentecostal baptism of the Holy Ghost and Fire is obtainable by definite act of appropriating faith on the part of the wholly sanctified believer, and that the initial evidence of the reception of this experience is speaking with other tongues as the spirit gives utterance (Acts 1:5; 2:1–4; 9:14–17; 10:44–46; 19:6).

The Bible teaches that the coming of the Holy Spirit into the hearts of men was prophesied. Joel declared, "And it shall come to pass afterward, that I will pour out my Spirit upon all flesh; and your sons and your daughters shall prophesy, your old men shall dream dreams, your young men shall see visions: and also upon the servants and upon the handmaids in those days will I pour out my Spirit" (Joel 2:28, 29).

John the Baptist also declared, "I indeed baptize you with water unto repentance: but he that cometh after me is mightier than I whose shoes I am not worthy to bear: He shall baptize you with the Holy Ghost, and with fire (Matt 3:11). John the Baptist here speaks of the Holy Ghost as an experience received which is separate from water baptism unto repentance.

Jesus also speaks of the sending of the Holy Spirit, "In my Father's house are many mansions, if it were not so, I would have told you. I go to prepare a place for you . . . And I will pray to the father, and he shall give you another Comforter, that he may abide with you forever. Even the Spirit of truth; whom the world cannot

receive, because it seeth him not; for he dwelleth with you and shall be in you" (Jn 14:2, 16, 17).

Jesus tells His disciples that He is going back to heaven to prepare a place for them and that He will pray to the Father to send another Comforter. He also makes it known that the Comforter has dwelt with them, but then shall be in them. There is a difference in the Holy Ghost being in you and being with you.

In John 15:26,27, Jesus indicates that the Holy Spirit would talk when He came ". . . He shall testify of me."

In the following Scriptures, John 15:26, 27; 16:7–16: Jesus declares that the Holy Ghost would talk when He came. This is a point to remember, as this becomes a "bone of contention" in discussions of the Baptism of the Holy Ghost.

In Acts 1:4, 5, 8, 9; Lk 24:49–53 we see the prophecies of the Holy Ghost on the verge of coming to pass. They will, of course, come to pass. They will be enacted as we go farther into our discussion.

John the Baptist spoke to the people who came to him for water baptism, and who had repented, telling them that there was a baptism to follow, which was greater than any he could administer unto them.

Jesus also was talking to His followers who had left the things of the world and were now considered "not of the world." Their sins had been forgiven and they were walking in the light. He told them that the "world cannot receive" this experience; therefore it is settled that it is for the people who already have an experience with God. In the above Scriptures we see Jesus blessing His disciples as He ascended to heaven, they received great joy, and in this attitude they returned to Jerusalem from Bethany where they went to the upper room, tarrying for seven days, praising and blessing God before the

Holy Ghost came. It cannot be denied that these people were saved and sanctified, because the prayer for joy and oneness, which is to be a part of sanctification, as recorded in John 17:11 and 17:13, was in evidence in their lives. In the above Scriptures we see them with "great joy" and they are seen in oneness in Acts 2:1, "And when the day of Pentecost was fully come, they were all with one accord in one place." Thus it is concluded that they had received the experiences of "past sins forgiven" and sanctification, prior to the day of Pentecost when they received the Baptism of the Holy Ghost.

Acts 2:1–8 is the account of that great and glorious day. These Scriptures also see the fulfillment of the prophecy of Joel.

It would be useless for anyone to deny the experience of the Baptism of the Holy Ghost as an actual occurrence, or any part of it, because the above Scriptures are too clear to be denied; however, attempts have been made to discredit the experience and to keep man from believing in a reception of the experience. The thought has also been advanced that only the Twelve Apostles were recipients of the Baptism of the Holy Ghost on the day of Pentecost, in answer let us look at Acts 1:15; "And in those days Peter stood up in the midst of the disciples, and said, (the number of names together were about an hundred and twenty)" and Acts 2:4; "And they were all filled with the Holy Ghost, and began to speak with other tongues, as the Spirit gave them utterance."

Acts 2:39; 9:17; 1 Corinthians 14:18, further shows that this experience was received on the day of Pentecost and can be had today.

Paul was not even saved or forgiven on the day of Pentecost, but rather a great persecutor of the church. He has now met the Lord and received the Holy Ghost, as they did on the day of Pentecost (I Cor 14:18).

There are others, both Jew and Gentile, who even at a later date received the Baptism of the Holy Ghost. Read Acts 10:22, 24–28; 10:34, 35; 10:44–47; 19:1–7. The above Scriptures show different people at different times receiving the Baptism of the Holy Ghost: First, on the day of Pentecost; next, Saul of Tarsus; Cornelius with kindred and friends and then disciples at Ephesus. It is interesting to note that on each of these occasions the people spoke with tongues, thus fulfilling the prophesy of Jesus, "He will testify of me, and ye shall bear witness."

Many today claim to believe in the Baptism of the Holy Ghost, but will not accept the teaching of speaking with tongues, even though it is clearly taught in the Scriptures.

We are often told that Paul's letter to the Corinthian church was a condemnation of speaking with tongues, and we are cited to the 14th Chapter of 1 Corinthians for proof, but no Scripture in this chapter supports this argument. Paul's purpose is to instruct the church how to "excel to the edifying of the church."

We must note that the Apostle is talking about the gift of tongues and tongues as the initial evidence of the reception of the Baptism of the Holy Ghost. 1 Corinthians 14:1–4, is an explanation of the difference in benefits gained by prophesying or speaking with tongues. Both are edifying, but one edifies the individual speaker, the other edifies the church.

Paul wants the church to understand that tongues does not take the place of preaching and the purpose of our gathering in church is to edification. Therefore he says, "Seek that ye may excel to the edifying of the church."

Section 6

We believe in divine healing as in the atonement (Ex 15:26; Ps 103:3; Isa 53:4–5; Matt 8:14–17; Acts 8:7; Js 5:14–15).

God is able to heal men without the aid of natural means and without medical technology. Adam's sin brought sickness and ill health into the human race but God has made provisions for our healing.

The word atonement describes the restoration of the harmonious relationship between God and man. Man was separated by sin but God in His mercy provided a covering for man. He also satisfied the love and holiness of God in the atonement.

Exodus 15:26 ". . . And said, If thou wilt diligently harken to the voice of the Lord thy God, and wilt do that which is right in his sight, and wilt give ear to his commandments and keep all His statures, I will put none of these disease upon thee, which I have brought upon the Egyptians: For I am the Lord that healeth thee."

Here, at the bitter waters of Marah, God assures His people that He would not cause the disease of the Egyptians to over take them. He declares Himself to be their healer. Many of the moral laws that He gave them later were designed to keep them from sickness. For example, following God's laws against prostitution and homosexuality would keep them free of venereal diseases.

Psalm 103:3, 4 ". . . Who forgiveth all thine iniquities; who healeth all thy disease; who redeemeth thy life from destruction; who crowneth thee with loving-kindness and tender mercies."

David praises God for all His benefits toward Him including his healing. He recognizes that God forgives all of our sins and heals all of our diseases. There is no sin or illness that we cannot take to God.

Isaiah 53:4–5 "Surely he hath borne our griefs, and carried our sorrows; yet we did esteem him stricken, smitten of God, and afflicted. But he was wounded for our transgressions, He was bruised for our iniquities; the chastisement of our peace was upon him: and with His stripes we are healed."

God pulls back the curtain of time for Isaiah and allows Isaiah to see Christ dying for our sins—actually bearing the punishment we deserved. In seeing this, it is also revealed to him the results of the suffering of the Suffering Servant. Our sin is taken away and we are healed.

Matthew 8:14–17 "And when Jesus was come into Peter's house, he saw his wife's mother laid, and sick of a fever. And he touched her hand, and the fever left her: and she arose, and ministered unto them.

When the even was come, they brought unto him many that were possessed with devils: and he cast out the spirits with his word, and healed all that were sick: That it might be fulfilled which was spoken by Esaias the prophet, saying, Himself took our infirmities, and bore our sickness."

In these verses we see Jesus at work healing the sick. A single touch makes Peter's mother-in-law whole. Her healing is so complete that she is able to serve guests. At His word the demonic forces, which invaded the bodies of others bringing sickness and torment, were cast out. Matthew sees Jesus moving in fulfillment of prophecy, as he heals the sick.

Acts 8:6, 7 "And the people with one accord gave heed unto those things which Phillip spoke, hearing and seeing the miracles which he did. For unclean spirits, crying with loud voices, came out of many that were possessed with them:

and many taken with palsies and that were lame, were healed."

While Jesus was with His disciples, He sent them out by two's to minister in the surrounding villages. They returned rejoicing that even devils were subject to them. They were warned that their joy should come from having their names written in the Lamb's book.

Phillip, who was not one of the twelve, is witness to the same experience as he ministers the Word in Samaria. He experienced that power at work in his life that was promised with the coming of the Holy Spirit (Acts 1:8). Phillip healed the sick and cast out demons through the power of the Holy Ghost just as Jesus and the Apostles did. The power to heal the sick comes with the Holy Ghost. Now, there is a specific gift of healing as spoken of by Paul in 1 Corinthians 12:9, 10, however, the Bible also teaches that God hears and answers the prayers of His children—period.

James 5:14, 15 "Is any sick among you? Let him call for the elders of the church; and let them pray over him, anointing him with oil in the name of the Lord: And the prayer of faith shall save the sick, and the Lord shall raise him up; and if he have committed any sins, they shall be forgiven him."

James refers to someone who is physically ill. In Scripture, oil was both medicine (Lk 10:30–37) and a symbol of the Spirit of God (as used in anointing kings, 1 Samuel 16:1–13). Thus oil can represent both the medical (physical) and spiritual spheres of life.

Christians should not separate the physical and the spiritual—Jesus Christ is Lord over both the body and the spirit.

Members of the body of Christ are not alone. They should be able to count on others for support and prayer, especially when they are sick and suffering. The leaders (lay and clergy) should stay alert to pray for the needs of all its members.

"And the prayer of faith", does not refer to the faith of the sick person, but to the faith of the church. God heals, faith doesn't, and all prayers are subject to the will of God. But our prayers are part of God's healing process. God waits to hear us pray on behalf of members of the body.

James also alludes to the fact that our healing is in the atonement. Through the prayer of faith, not only is the infirmity removed but, if there is any sin, that is also removed at the same time. This affirms that we have both, forgiveness of sin and healing in the atonement.

Section 7

We believe in the imminent personal premillennial second coming of our Lord, Jesus Christ (1 Thessalonians 4:14–18; Titus 2:13; II Peter 3:1–14; Matthew 24:20–44), and we love and await for His appearing (II Timothy 4:8).

1 Thessalonians 4:15–18 "For this we say unto you by the Word of the Lord, that we which are alive and remain unto the coming of the Lord shall not prevent them which are asleep. For the Lord himself shall descend from heaven with a shout, with the voice of the archangel and with the trump of God: and the dead in Christ shall rise first: Then we which are alive and remain shall be caught up together with them in the clouds, to meet the Lord in the air: and so shall we ever be with the Lord. Wherefore comfort ye one another with these words."

Because Jesus Christ came back to life, so will all who believe. All Christians, including those living when He returns will live with Jesus forever. Therefore, we need not despair when loved ones die or world events take tragic turn. God will turn our tragedies to triumphs, our poverty to riches, our pain to glory, and our defeat to victory. All believers in the very presence of God will be safe and secure. As Paul comforted the Thessalonians with the promise of the resurrection, so we should comfort and reassure one another with this great hope.

Titus 2:13 ". . . Looking for that blessed hope, and the glorious appearing of the great God and our Savior Jesus Christ."

We live the Christian life in hope and with great expectation. We must live in such a manner that we do not dread His coming. We must live morally and ethically pure in this present world.

II Peter 3:1–14 In this passage Peter warns the saints against scoffers—those who say, "We've heard that all our lives." He reminds us that God has His own time set. He does not need time. Time was created for mankind. God is eternal and will not be threatened by the words of mortal men.

The coming of the Lord will be sure and sudden. Presently, He is patiently waiting for more men to be saved. The Spirit of the Living God pleads with men to heed the call of God. When His patience has run out with evil men He will come, He will judge, and He will punish.

Matthew 24:20–44 In these verses Jesus Himself speaks of the character of His coming. He spoke of the Great Tribulation, the false cries of His coming, and how to determine His true coming. It will be swift and sudden. There will be no time for afterthought, last minute repentance, or bargaining. The choice that we have already made will determine our eternal destiny. Jesus' purpose in telling about His return is not to stimulate predictions, calculations, or debates, but to warn us to be ready.

Our Walk & Our Work

Sanctification

Sanctification is the second definite instantaneous work of faith in the fully justified (or born again) believer. It is a definite experience like being born again. Inborn sin is destroyed in the soul, and the heart completely cleansed from sin. (Heb 10:4–9) In sanctification, the born-again believer is cleansed by the Holy Spirit with the blood of Christ. We see in I Thessalonians 5:23 that it is Paul's desire that God sanctify the believers thoroughly. The writer of Hebrews argues that the blood of Jesus sanctifies within.

Paul says that the saints' whole spirit, soul, and body be preserved unto the coming of the Lord (I Thessalonians 5:23). An adequate understanding of the doctrines of sanctification is necessary for living our faith in this present world. Our bodies must be cleansed so that they become temples of the Holy Spirit.

There are those who contend that sanctification is a progressive work. To them we say, If Paul says for the preservation of the saints' spirits, souls, and bodies, they could not be preserved blameless in the process. That would negate our "blameless" standing. If we are preserved blameless, we must be blameless before preservation. We do not speak in terms of sinless perfection for this is a quality that can only be associated with God Himself. We must attain Christian perfection.

The Baptism of the Holy Spirit

The Baptism of the Holy Ghost is a definite experience like conversion and sanctification and the initial evidence of the reception of this experience is speaking with other tongues as the Spirit gives utterance (Acts 2:4).

The Bible shows conclusively that a person must be sanctified in order to receive the baptism of the Holy Ghost. Peter said, speaking before the Jerusalem Council, of the Gentile Pentecost at Caesera, "And God which knoweth the hearts, bear them witness, giving them the Holy Ghost, even as He did us and them, purifying their hearts by faith" (Acts 15:8, 9). The word purifying in the original text is the aorist tense, which denotes definite completed action. Rendered literally it is, ". . . having purified their hearts by faith."

A person receiving the baptism of the Holy Ghost will initially speak with new tongues. This does not mean that the person will continuously speak in tongues throughout his life nor does it mean he has the gift of tongues. In cases where persons claim the gift of tongues, there must be interpretation or silence in the public (1 Corinthians 14:26–28).

IDA BELL ROBINSON
(1891–1946)

Mt. Sinai Holy Church of America

In 1924, Ida Robinson left a promising ministry within the United Holy Church of America to answer what she perceived was God's call "come out on Mt. Sinai and loose the women" by establishing Mt. Sinai Holy Church of America as an organization that would provide women with the opportunity use their gifts and talents to move into every level of ministerial leadership.

Robinson was born in Hazelhurst, Georgia, lived most of her young life in Pensacola, Florida, and migrated to Philadelphia with her husband to look for better employment. Once there, she joined a local Church of God congregation and assisted the pastor in leading that flock until she was asked to take over the pastorate of a local United Holy Church of America congregation. For the first seventy-five years of its existence, from 1924 to early 2001, the denomination remained under the leadership of female presiding bishops. Robinson lead the Mt. Sinai organization for twenty-three years until her death at age fifty-five.

The Economic Persecution[4]

Text: I John 4:20; Acts 2:4

In the early days of Christianity, under the old order of things, everyone who openly called on the name of the Lord Jesus was persecuted indescribably. Many of them died calling on the name of the Lord to the very end.

During the dark days of early civilization[,] the gospel having spread itself into Persia, the pagan priests who worshipped the sun were greatly alarmed, and dreaded the loss of that influence they had hereto maintained over the people's minds and properties. Hence, they thought it expedient to complain to the emperor that the Christians were enemies to the state, and held a treasonable correspondence with the Romans, the great enemies of Persia.

Well, the Persian emperor Sapores, being naturally an enemy of Jesus and Christianity, easily believed the lie told on the Christians by the wicked officers, and gave orders to persecute them throughout his empire. Due to this mandate, many persons eminent in the church and state fell martyrs at the hands of the ferocious pagans whose scheme to humiliate the Christians went over in a big way, but God always finds a way to deliver His saints out of the hands of their enemies. It was through Constantine the great, [that] God worked during a consecration period of the saints. God heard the [fervent] and effectual prayers of the church and gave it favor in the eyes of Constantine the Great. For days after, the Christians prayed for the Emperor's conversion.

One day at high noon, God showed the great Constantine a sign in heaven[;] a flaming cross appeared in the element with the legend, (by this we conquer), which resulted in his confession of Jesus Christ. Meantime, a great persecution of the saints had begun as a result of the false

---

4. Ida Robinson, "The Economic Persecution," originally published in *The Latter Day Messenger* (May 23, 1935) 2. Reprinted in Collier-Thomas, *Daughters of Thunder*, 203–5.

report made by the Persian officers to Sapores, the Persian Emperor[.] Constantine the Great, now saved and a witness of Jesus Christ, and a powerful friend of the church[,] sent a letter to Sapores protesting the treatment of the Christians, [by the] wicked subordinates. In his letter he told just how God had prospered him and blessed all of his undertakings because of this friendship with Jesus and fellowship with His saints. At the reception of this letter the persecution was ordered ceased and the gospel was spread throughout the domain of Persia.

At present the same conditions [prevail] in substance. Our people in certain southern states are killed, their bodies dismembered and thrown to vultures. This, of course, is a common occurrence, and, unfortunately, [occurs] where "Christianity" is more prevalent than any other part of our Union. For in this section of the country laws are made to uphold "Christianity" in their states and to prevent any teachings in their institutions of learning that [tend] to distort, minimize or otherwise change the principle of the doctrine of Christianity as taught in the Bible.

We hereby decree as it is written in their laws condemning modernism or any other doctrine hostile to the teachings of Jesus "that if anyone is found guilty of teaching doctrine contrary to Christianity in any [state] supported schools . . . [that person] shall be punished to the extent of the law . . . ," mentioning the extent to which the law provides. But these same people, in these same sections will toss their own laws to the four winds and trample under feet the laws of Christianity and utterly ignore the words of the sacred "Book" they pretend to love so dearly, and esteem so highly which says: "If a man says he loves God and hateth his brother, he is a liar: for he that loveth not

his brother whom he has seen, how can he love God whom he has not seen" (I John 4:20).

Someone has questioned the brotherhood of all mankind. Well! let us appeal to the wisdom and justice of the sacred "book" as regards Christianity. There is but "One Lord one faith and one baptism" so that, if God is the Father of all, the relationship that [exists] between Gentile and Jew, as well as Ethiopians, is [inseparable] and unquestionably established[.] So let us saints, pray that the Constantine of our day (if there be one) sends a letter to the modern pagans in the [polluted] southland in the form of "Anti-lynch" legislation that is now pending in Congress. We can overcome and we will overcome, and we will overcome, right here in this present world, the persecutions we [are] made to suffer, by our unjust brethren. It is written that "Ethiopians shall stretch their hands in righteousness to God" and by the help of God and the agencies He has so gloriously provided, we shall overcome.

It is easy to understand why the God[s] of this world are working so feverishly to overthrow the kingdom and one doctrine that will not interfere with their disgraceful acts. At present many of the so-called preachers who are parading under ministerial banners with the loyal forces of righteousness are in reality enemies of Jesus Christ. For example, a recent survey was made by a very dependable organization with a wide reputation for its accuracy in sounding out public opinion[.] [This organization] just completed its work in quizzing ministers. They ask, "Do you believe in the existence of hell and the devil?" To this question 54 percent of the ministers that were asked answered No. In other words 54 ministers out of every 100 don't believe in the devil or hell . . .

Many of them are engaged at this very time in battling against the policies of our Lord Jesus through channels of so-called liberalism, modernism and various other kinds of isms and cisms which tend to minimize God's Word. But we who are children of the light, cannot be swerved by any of this present-day ministerial gossip.

We believe that Jesus died and rose again. We believe that if we acknowledge His death according to the Bible we have access to the father through this acknowledgement. We believe if we confess our sins He will forgive us of the same and by, through and with His blood, cleanse us from all unrighteousness, which is sanctification of course. We believe that if we pray to the Father He will send us another comforter which is the Holy Ghost according to Acts 2:4.

> Shakespeare—
> Life is but a walking shadow[.]
> Shadows are as changeable and [fidgety] as a little child.
> A shadow being made by the sun, follows its movements and is in

constant variation until at last it quietly vanishes and disappears.

In this the life of man is frequently compared to a shadow. The always-philosophical Job says "Our days on earth are as a shadow." Possibly he was also thinking of time. Long before man had sense enough to make a clock or watch he used his shadow to measure the time of day. The Mohammedan stands up against the sun and by the length of his shadow in the sand determines that the hour of prayer is come. Weary workmen did not watch the clock but their shadow.

Now I appeal to you who have clocks, watches, charts, maps, and various other scientific [materials] acquainting you with the knowledge of this world. But oh ye children of light can't you look out and see the shadow of our Lord Jesus and how His arrival is inevitable? We may look out and see wars developing in all parts of our land. Unrest and confusion are found everywhere. This truly indicates the shadow of our Lord and we know it is time to pray.

HERBERT DAUGHTRY
(1931–)

House of the Lord and Church on the Mount

Pastor and activist Reverend Herbert Daughtry was born in Savannah, Georgia, the son a minister, and rose from a troubled young life—one that included struggles with gambling, crime, and drug use; a dishonorable discharge from the army; and a stint in prison—to become national presiding minister of the House of the Lord Churches, chairman emeritus of the National Black United Front, and president of the African People's Christian Organization. Though he was raised in the church that his father founded, Daughtry's religious conversion came while he was in prison in the 1950s. After being released, he returned to the church, becoming a fourth-generation minister and activist.

In the 1960s, Daughtry became involved in the push for school integration jobs for Brooklyn's black community. But his global focus led him to involvement in Jesse Jackson's 1984 presidential campaign as well as international efforts to secure the release of South African liberation leader Nelson Mandela.

His several works include *No Monopoly on Suffering: Blacks and Jews in Crown Heights (and Elsewhere)*; *A Seed Planted in Stone—The Life and Times of Tupac Shakur*; and *Jesus Christ: African in Origin, Revolutionary and Redeeming in Action*.

Jesus: The Surprising Contemporary

"There is a fountain filled with blood, drawn from Emmanuel's veins; and sinners plunged beneath the flood, lose all their guilty stains."

"Forasmuch as ye know that ye were not redeemed with corruptible things, as silver and gold, from your vain conversation received by tradition from your fathers; But with the precious blood of Christ as of a lamb without blemish and without spot: Who verily was foreordained before the foundation of the world, but was manifest in these last times for you." 1 Ptr 1:18–20

The title "Jesus, The Surprising Contemporary" is not original with me. I first heard it from a Dutch theologian in Thailand. He wanted to convey the idea that Jesus was startlingly relevant, that He confronts humanity in every age with His timeless message and person.

I thought at that time what a striking characterization—Jesus, the Surprising Contemporary. It seemed to gather up in a dramatic and concise fashion my thinking about Jesus. He is a contemporary and He is relevant.

Whether we like it or not, if we engage in serious thinking, eventually we will meet Him and He forces us to do something with Him. He seems always to be there.

Who was this Jesus called the Christ? Some called Him a friend of sinners and prostitutes; demon-possessed, an impostor, a blasphemer. Others called Him the Son of God, the Lamb of God, the Son of Man, a Prophet, a Rabbi or teacher, the Messiah or Christ.

What did He call Himself? That always depended on to whom He was speaking. And when we read the Bible, we must always read it with an understanding that Jesus is always under surveillance.

The establishment, the police, the spies are always present.

Sometimes they try to trap Him with questions. Other times they try to tangle up His words so that He is made to say what is not intended. They feel threatened by Him. He is gathering masses of people around Him. All kinds of people; the poor, Zealots or revolutionaries, the dispossessed—they are not sure what His aim is. Maybe He will start an insurrection, maybe a revolution. He must be stopped! So, keep in mind that when Jesus speaks, or teaches, He knows enemies are around. He knows that eventually He will be killed, but He must take care that it does not happen before He has had time to build His movement.

So, what He calls Himself, and what He allows others to call Him, depends upon who is doing the calling and who is around at the time. I will discuss the names of Jesus and titles at another time—suffice it now to say that He accepted the title Messiah which is Hebrew; the Greek form is Christ. The name means the Anointed One.

It is believed that God would send a special representative to earth to save or liberate mankind from its sinfulness in all of its manifestations, and demonstrate to man the will of God. The Nation of Israel had been chosen by God to be the channel through which the Messiah would come, and all the people eagerly prayed and waited towards this end.

Now there are some problems posed by the so-called followers of Jesus which make it difficult for people to see His relevance. Sometimes the followers lock Him up in Heaven. They make Jesus some kind of "up-there-spirit," totally removed from the tension and turmoil of everyday ordinary earth living.

It was probably as a reaction to this concept of Jesus that people began to talk about the search for the historical Jesus. They wanted to find the real flesh-and-blood Jesus. They wanted to be done with spirits and myths. They wanted the real historical Jesus.

One group locked Him up in heaven, and the other group locked Him in . . . history. In neither instance, it would seem, did Jesus, the Surprising Contemporary appear. In each case He was either up there, or back there, but not here, now.

Then, probably reacting to both of these, some theologians began talking about the Jesus who is out there, ahead of us, beckoning us to come ahead. They talked about the future breaking in. In this view, the followers of Jesus are pilgrims; they have no stationary place; they must be continually pulling up stake and moving on. For it is not the will of Jesus that His followers should become comfortable, or captured in any culture, condition, or state of being. They were to follow their Lord out into the future. This Dutch theologian also said, "I had to get rid of my Western baggage that I might follow Christ through culture." He meant that he had to cast aside worn out value systems, outdated norms, old frames of reference, to follow Jesus who was leading him into new life styles and cultural expressions.

Now, I believe that [the concept of] Jesus as the Surprising Contemporary comprehends the best of those three approaches. It searches for and embraces the historical Jesus back there; it gathers to itself the spiritual Jesus located up there: and it merges the Jesus ahead of us, out there, Thus, Jesus becomes contemporaneous with us—right here.

Now, what do I mean that Jesus is contemporary? The Pentecostal movement in America is an example of Jesus' relevance, or his contemporaneousness. Also, the Pentecostal movement is an example of abortive development. Pentecostal, from a Greek word meaning "fiftieth," refers to a festive day which came fifty days after Passover in the calendar of the Israelites. It was the gathering of the first fruits, so there was great celebration. It was on this day that the Disciples of Jesus were filled with the Holy Ghost, speaking in tongues. So, Pentecostalism has come to refer to those who believe in being filled with the Spirit of God, and evidencing that fact by speaking in tongues.

Now, the Pentecostal movement really got going in America around 1906, through the efforts of a black, one-eyed preacher named Seymour. The place was an old Methodist Church, long since closed, in the city of Los Angeles, California. God demonstrated His presence miraculously, in healings of all kinds, in radically changed lives. But, perhaps the greatest miracle was that color and class lines were broken down. Everybody was the same. There was a democratization of the gifts.

People came from all over the world, and they carried the message back with them. Significantly, the Charismatic movement that has since swept the earth, was started in such humble surroundings.

Now, if this could have continued, if men and women would have permitted God to continue His work through them, we might have seen a change in American society. But, in a few years, the Pentecostal movement followed the racial and color patterns of the larger society. White men formed denominations and fellowships and groups with other white men and enjoyed the benefits of a racist institution. Instead of challenging, they conformed, and so the Spirit of Jesus was captured by culture.

What is interesting particularly for black Pentecostals and Evangelicals is that they too, in another kind of way, became supporters of the status quo. They saw their roles as preaching against sin, and they defined sin in terms of short dresses, lipstick, movie shows, smoking, drinking, and pornography. Moreover, living holy came to mean not only refraining from the above, but also withdrawing from all protest and programs designed to confront the unjust institutions of America and waiting for Jesus to return from up there in heaven.

Instead of following Christ into new and perhaps radical expressions, our Pentecostal brothers turned away from it all, got holy, and frowned on others who were trying to change social conditions. Their worship became a kind of escapism. You went to church not to be informed, educated, enlightened, or challenged, but you went to have a "good-time"—"in the Lord," of course; to "get high on God," as one preacher put it.

The only difference between white Pentecostalism and black Pentecostalism was the color. Both were conservative, both supported the system either consciously—as was the case with most whites, or silently—as was the case with most blacks. For, to be silent in the face of injustice is to help to sustain that injustice. As a result, many turned away from Jesus. But it wasn't really Jesus that they were rejecting. They were rejecting a white Jesus who was woven into an American racist, exploitative system, not the Jesus of Scripture, the surprising contemporary.

Jesus is relevant. He is here. He is real. We must seek Him as He is, and let Him express Himself, not according to our cultural patterns, but in whatever way He desires. It is then that we discover that He is in truth a startling contemporary. He meets us at the cross roads. He meets us in the market place, in the political arena, in the school room, in the barber shop, butcher shop, beauty shop. He meets us in the hospitals and institutions. He is the startling contemporary. He is inescapable. And when we meet Him we will not be the same, ever again.

When we seriously study the life of Jesus, . . . we shall be driven to the conclusion that Jesus was not [the] cheerful conformer to the systems of men, as his followers through their own fears, ignorance, and self-interest have often made Him to be.

In every age, some would have Jesus adjusting to the contemporary cultures, value systems, mores, and styles of life. They would have Him accepting the prevailing political, religious, and social structures. But Jesus was not a this world conformer, waiting on another world. He was a confronter. He confronted men and women and societies with their sins, individually and collectively. Nobody was spared. The highest as well as the lowest came under His judgment. But all were given the opportunity to start anew. He showed them that they could become the children of God.

He was a disturber of the peace. He disturbed the serene order of the status quo; which order was built upon the gratification of the few and the degradation of the masses.

He was a shatterer. He shattered the religious and social and political systems which were corrupt to the core.

In a word, He was a trouble maker. He just could not leave things alone. He had to always be meddling and poking around.

He came with a new order. And to inaugurate a new order it is always necessary to overturn or remove the old order.

Now that is true individually and it is also true collectively. "You can't put new wine into old bottles," He once said, "nor can you put old wine into new bottles." New wine must be put in new bottles. You need a complete newness, newness through and through.

He came with a new ethic, a new morality, a new way of looking at old problems and questions. He came with a new value system, not grounded in tribal preservation or ancient laws, but in the eternal rightness of things.

Now His disciples had learned their lesson well. For it was said of them that they were turning the world upside down. What a description. These are they that have turned the world upside down. What did that description mean?

It meant that they rejected the world's idea of justice and rightness. It meant that they refused to accept the society's concept of what was important and what was meaningful and what was authentic. It meant that the followers of Jesus, copying the example of their Lord, went everywhere with a disdain for political, social, religious systems; they cared nothing for old moralities, old authorities, old traditions, etc. For these things had not brought peace and justice to the world, to say nothing of producing an abundant life for all earth's inhabitants. And, therefore, the disciples felt that these things needed to be swept aside to make way for the new order which would start in the minds and spirits of humanity, and would issue forth into a new community comprised of all the people of the world, given rise to new social structures.

Jesus had said, "My Kingdom is not of this world." What He meant was that His Kingdom gathers its ethics, its rationale, its philosophy, its life styles, its values, its strategy, not from the systems of men, for these are bankrupt for they are built upon the wisdom and self-interest of men. But rather, His Kingdom is sustained and perpetuated by the infusion of the Eternal Spirit of the Almighty Himself, which captures the spirits of men and catapults them out into the world with messages of salvation for all; and, therefore, His Kingdom is incorruptible. Its treasures are in heaven, beyond the corruption of earth. You can't buy or bribe your way in; you've got to be born anew. You've got to undergo a radical reordering of your attitudes, values associations, and desires.

His Kingdom is irresistible, the gates of Hell cannot stop it. And it is eternal, for it flows from God Himself. And it is always in opposition to the Kingdom of this world, for the systems of men are demonic. They are conceived in pride, nurtured in arrogance, and raised on selfishness, yielding a harvest of injustice, violence, inhuman behavior, and misery. And one day His Kingdom, though small and insignificant now, shall grow and grow, and gather momentum with the passing years and shall destroy the systems of men, and a new nation will begin.

One of the most memorable experience that I have ever had occurred in Bangkok, Thailand. We had concluded a three-year study on the theme "Salvation Today" sponsored by the Commission on World Mission and Evangelism. There were about fifteen of us present from various countries including Japan, India, Korea, Geneva, Germany, and Africa. We gathered to discuss the theme "Giving Account for the Reason for the Hope With Us." This was sponsored by the Faith and Order Commission of the World Council of Churches. I spent about five days of intensive day-and-night discussion with the group . . .

To repeat, it was an exhilarating, unforgettable experience. Our discussion covered many areas. We pondered the meaning of history and time as it is perceived from different cultures. We touched on the church worldwide, its strengths and weaknesses and so on.

After several days, we discovered that our conversation invariably became 'Christological', that is, Christ-centered. So, I think it is appropriate to our sermon topic for me to relate some of the thinking from at least four different countries. We would hope to see how Christ is a contemporary in different parts of the world. Also, and what I think is equally appropriate, we shall see conclusively that Christianity is not a white man's religion, decaying all over the world.

There is a big lie in the land, and it's been around for some time now. It is that Christianity is the white man's religion, confined only to Europe and America.

Now, I have touched on this before, so there is no need for an in depth reply. But, I have to say a few things in this connection.

Christianity comes from Christ, and means to be in Christ or to follow Him. The followers of Jesus were first called Christians in Antioch between the year 30–40 A.D. (see Acts 11:26) It was started in the same part of the world that Judaism and Islam were begun—that is Asia or Asia Minor and Africa—all three of them trace their beginnings back to a man called Abraham. I have made the point that there is much evidence to support the claim that he was black.

In the first centuries the most influential theological schools were in North Africa. Christianity was not introduced into all of Africa by the white man. Some parts of Africa had already come under Christian influence long before the slave trade. The oldest church in Christendom isn't white, but black. It is the Coptic Church (Copt is another word for Egypt).

Now, just let me say a word about the so-called death or decay of Christianity. I thank God I have had occasion to travel. I have see things with my own eyes, and heard with my own ears. Therefore, what I say to you grows out of what I have seen and heard.

If I were able, I would put everybody on planes, boats, and buses and say, "Go visit other countries, talk to people of other cultures, religions, and ideologies." For I think if people did travel, so much of the prejudice, hatred, and ignorance which exists among people would disappear. I have often thought that 95% of the untruths about other people—and people build their lives around these untruths—would be erased with travel.

In Africa, perhaps the most massive movement in the history of man is among what is called independent churches or indigenous churches. South Africa [is 14 percent] Pentecostal alone. It has been estimated that one-fifth of the population in Brazil is Pentecostal. There are revivals in Korea, Indonesia, and so on, and I will be quoting shortly from people of these and other countries. I personally have talked with Christian people from Burma, Vietnam, and Mozambique.

The proof is incontrovertible that Christianity has an African-Asian origin and [the] evidence grows in many parts of the world, especially in what has come to be called the Third World Countries.

Now, if after studying the life and works of Jesus you want to reject Him, well, that's one thing. But to reject Jesus because of what someone with an axe to grind, or an organization to promote, says about Him, makes you immature and/or docile.

Now, there is no doubt that whites have used Christianity for their own purposes. In the name of Jesus they have done some abominable things. But then, so have blacks. In the name of Jesus, blacks sell numbers, dead prophets' bones, blessed cabbages, and anything else poor gullible souls will buy.

If you want to be critical of how folks have used Jesus for their own personal ends, I can be as harsh and cutting as anybody. In fact, I can be sharper. I know first-hand more about the church and the followers of Jesus than most people. But we must always be careful that we don't repudiate the real in our rejection of the false. There is counterfeit money—but I don't see anybody rejecting the genuine. No one goes out and shoots the cow because somebody dilutes the milk for his own profit.

I have been privileged to converse with people from practically every religion and background, and I have come to the conclusion that few people reject Jesus because they have studied His life and works. Rather, I find that the rejections come from false information and impressions conveyed by the so-called followers of Jesus or His enemies who feel they must tear Him down to build themselves up.

What we need to do is get to the source. If you sincerely want to learn about Jesus, go to the Bible yourself. Say in your heart, "God, I want the truth about Jesus. Teach me." I urge this method upon you for that is the way that I became a Christian and I have been a follower of Jesus for over twenty years.

I heard somebody say the other day, "Come on out of Christianity, it's the white man's religion." The truth is most of us have never been in Christianity in the first place. We have been the victims of the white man's use of Christianity. Few blacks, comparatively speaking, have been in Christianity, for to be in Christianity is, as I have pointed out, to be in Christ.

Now the next time you hear someone saying that Christianity is the white man's religion, he is either ignorant of the facts, or knows the facts, but is lying to you for his personal gain. Or he means that white people have used Christianity for their own purposes. If that is what he is saying, then you have no argument with him. For to say that is to speak the truth, and it does not detract from the life and works of Jesus.

. . . The God of our faith has always shown Himself to be for the down-and-outers, the misfits, and never-do-wells. Therefore, if He is to be consistent with Himself, He must come to us as He came in the person of Jesus, over 1900 years ago, despised, deprived, and persecuted. He must come to us as He identified Himself with the nation of Israel, a people enslaved, with the oppressors boot on their necks. God was not ashamed to say to this nation of slaves, "you are my people, I will bring you out of bondage; I will come in the person of Moses; I will liberate you and you shall worship me on this mountain; you shall celebrate my liberation." So, we look for Jesus again but where shall we locate Him[?]

If you look to whiteness you will not find Him there. Now, I mean whiteness as a symbol, just as blackness has always meant nothingness in this society—whiteness has always meant everythingness. Whiteness is more than a color, it is a value system; it is a certain mentality; it's a life style; it's a frame of reference; it's an attitude; it's availability of advantages; it's membership in the clubs; it's automatic inclusion in the American systems, it's a way of life; it is Nixon in the White House,

Rockefeller in Albany, and Lindsay downtown; it is the control of the educational system; it is control of the medical institutions, the banking system; it is the creator and sustainer of the ghettoes in America and in other parts of the world; it is arrogance; it is Jesus, God, the Saints and anybody else of any worth. For if a person isn't white in color, and he achieves anything—he is made white in his values, his lifestyles, his frame of reference the chances are very slim that he can be an achiever in this society without becoming white.

And there was a time when it was acceptable to try to be white. Negroes did everything they could to be white. They straightened their hair or wore wigs; bought skin-whiteners; boasted about their white friends and white wives and husbands. Look at poor Sammy Davis, a man of tremendous ability, allowed himself to be reduced to being Sinatra's little sambo and Nixon's little nigger.

Nowadays, one tries to be white on the sneak. He is black by day when he is with black people, then gets into whiteness later on. For he knows that if he is going to get the material prosperity he desires, he has to do some imitations. But, that's not so bad as long as he knows where his real identity is.

Moses is an example here. He was raised in the Pharaoh's house, he went to Pharaoh's school, he learned all of Pharaoh's tricks; but he always remembered who he was. He didn't lose his identity in the Pharaoh's house. For the day came when he was chosen by God to lead the people to freedom.

Let us remember that you are not what you are until you say that's what you are, and world conditions are meaningless until you internalize them. You can live anywhere, work anywhere, and so long as your mind is positive and right, you will be the one influencing and not being influenced.

So now, if you're looking for Jesus, it isn't likely you're going to find him in the White House, no matter how many times the President says, "God bless you." It isn't likely you're going to find him amongst the bankers and insurance companies. You're not going to find Him in the offices of huge corporations. You're not going to find Him in Congress no matter how many congressional prayer meetings are held. For the existing mind set in those places is anti-God, anti-righteous, and anti-justice. The God of our faith is on record as opposing those who practice injustice.

It's very interesting that white theologians a few years ago began to inform the world that God was dead. Paul Van Buren, a Professor of Theology at the Episcopal Theological Seminary wrote, "God had died of neglect, a quiet displacement has taken place." William Hamilton, another theologian at Colgate Rochester Divinity School wrote, "I am here referring to a belief in the non-existence of God. When we speak of the 'death of God,' we speak not only of the death of idols, we speak as well of the death in us of any power to affirm any of the traditional images of God. I mean that the world is not God and that it does not point to God." In another place he said, "We are not talking about the absence of the experience of God but about the experience of the absence of God."

Now, what is the meaning there? To me the death of God is a contradiction—for if He is God, He cannot die. If he died, He could not have been God. He was an impostor. It seems to me that the problem with these theologians is that they had located God in the wrong places. They had thought that God was synonymous with the white culture; that God and the flag were one; that white politics, white economics, white values were one with God. In a word, they thought, as many others thought and still think, that God and whiteness are one and the same thing.

But then they discovered that the name of God was being harnessed to every conceivable kind of oppression, dehumanization, and those who talked about God didn't really believe in Him, at least not the God of justice and truth. And so, it became obvious that God had become a game. And then with technological development, whites didn't need to invoke the name of God anymore. Why, they were God themselves.

So, it became obvious to them that God must have died. But the truth of the matter is, He never lived in their style, political system, churches or cathedrals. God was never there. At least, not the God of our faith.

Now, it is significant that even our black forefathers, during slavery, without any formal education, knew that God of the Bible and the God of the slave master wasn't the same one. So what uninformed blacks in the most deplorable condition knew, and scholars and theologians and preachers were ignorant of, is that God was not in the big house on the hill; that God was not in the slave traffic; but God was in the slave hut, there amongst the bleeding black bodies of the slaves.

And when they talked about God, they weren't playing games with words. Talking about God, or God talk, as the white theologians called it, and they say that's useless too, wasn't an exercise in proper grammar or exquisite English, but talking about God was a matter of life and death.

Jesus as the Surprising Contemporary is found amongst the outcasts of the earth. And also among the rich and powerful who have seen the illusion of these things, or who are using their resources in the furtherance of God's kingdom.

End of Compartmentalization

There is another dimension which we need to add to make the picture complete. Evangelical Christians and others have sought to divide social action and spiritual action. However, in the scripture which depicts Jesus in the temple we discover the beginning of the solution to the compartmentalization problem.[5]

There in these verses, we see Jesus move from a furious assault upon the money changers, to healing the sick and lame. There is no dichotomy in Jesus' behavior. He confronts exploitation and at the same time, in the same place, comforts the victims. He is a condemner and a consoler. Thus, in spite of what religionists say, even the most well intentioned, regarding the need to separate the social from the spiritual, radical social action and personal religion—Jesus gave us the example.

Christians must be prophetic as well as pastoral. There is an Old Testament example in the Book of Isaiah. The prophet is seen going to advise King Hezekiah regarding the threats of Assyria.[6] Then we see the prophet again in the sick room of King Hezekiah assuring him that God had heard his prayers.[7] In the next chapter Isaiah is back in the royal court again, this time he warns the King about the Babylonians.[8] Isaiah, like Jesus, moves from one kind of action—political involvement at the highest level, to minister to the sick; from the royal court to the room of the ill.

Yet, why it should have been thought otherwise must be attributed to European world view or stratagem. A compartmentalization of social and spiritual is absent in African world view and it is unsound Biblically. The God of our faith is presented as the Creator who is intensely concerned about the total person. Even the strands of our hair are numbered.[9] The sparrow cannot fall to the ground without His notice.[10]

5. Matt 21:12–14.

6. Isaiah 37:21–38.

7. Isaiah 38.

8. Isaiah 39.

9. St. Luke 12:7.

10. St Matthew 10:29–31.

chapter five

African American
Oneness Pentecostalism

The Waterway

Hattie Pryor

Long ago the maids drew water in the evening time they say
One day Isaac sent his servant to stop Rebekka on her way
My master sent me here to tell you
See these Jewels rich and rare
Would'st you not his lovely bride be in the country over there?

Chorus:
It shall be light in the evening time
The path to glory you will surely find
Through the water way it is the light today
Buried in his precious name!
Young and old repent of all your sins and the Holy Ghost will enter in
The evening light has come
Tis a fact that God and Christ are one!

So God's servants come to tell you Of a Bridegroom in the sky,
Looking for a holy people To be His bride soon, by and by;
He sends to us refreshing water In this wondrous latter day;
They who really will be raptured Must go thru the water way.

Are you on your way to ruin, Cumbered with a load of care?
See the quick work God is doing So that His glory you may share.
At last the faith He once delivered To the saints, is ours today;
To get in the Church triumphant You must go the water way.

Have you look'd and often wondered why the power is slack today,
Will you stay in that back number and go on in the man-made way,
O' saints who never have been buried in the blessed name Of God,
Let the truth now sanctify you, Tis the way Apostles trod.

GARFIELD THOMAS HAYWOOD
(1880–1931)

Pentecostal Assemblies of the World

Almost every African American Oneness Pentecostal denomination can trace its lineage back to one organization, the Pentecostal Assemblies of the World (PAW), and gives homage to one leader, Garfield Thomas (G. T.) Haywood. The prolific writer published nearly a hundred pamphlets and books, as well as several hundred essays defending the doctrines of baptism in Jesus's name, and the non-Trinitarian conception of the Godhead.

Haywood was one of the most respected early black leaders in the broader Pentecostal movement and was a close colleague of many of the framers of the (predominantly white) Assemblies of God (AG), and a frequent speaker at their meetings. His decision, however, to align himself with the "new issue" as Oneness understandings came to be known, would place him in direct confrontation with AG and other white Trinitarian leaders.

The Victim
of the Flaming Sword

Trinitarianism

Wherefore the Lord said, Forasmuch as this people draw near me with their mouths and their lips do honor me, but have remove their heart far from me AND THEIR FEAR TOWARD ME IS TAUGHT BY PRECEPTS OF MEN: therefore, behold I will proceed to do a marvellous work among this people, even a marvellous work and wonder: for the wisdom of their wise men shall perish and the understanding of their prudent men shall be hid. (Isa 29:13–14)

Today these Scriptures are again meeting their fulfillment even as it was at the close of the Jewish dispensation. Tradition has so filled the religious world that little regard is given to the WORD of GOD; for many honor God with their lips, but their heart is far from him. They are willing at any time to uphold their traditions, at the expense of the WORD of GOD; and when one begins to speak against the "Trinitarian Doctrine," (God in three persons) great fear seems to come upon the people that such teaching is dishonoring God, and any even prophesying judgment to come upon those who think it a light against such tradition. They think it a light thing to ignore water baptism, in the Name of JESUS; the One Person God, and the Holy Ghost New Birth; which are clearly set forth in the Scriptures. They don't mind saying that water is nonessential. They don't mind saying that Jesus is the Second Person in the "Trinity" when Jesus, Himself, declares, "I AM THE FIRST and I AM THE LAST." Truly their fear towards Him is taught by the precepts of men.

Touching the Doctrine of the Trinity, the Apostles knew of no such thing; they knew nothing about three Spirits; they had no knowledge of three separate Persons in the Godhead; they had not been informed that the Holy Ghost, the Spirit of God, and the Spirit of Christ were the Spirits of three separate Persons. They knew of but One GOD, One Spirit One LORD. They knew that God was a Spirit (Jn 4:24); and that the Lord was that Spirit (II Cor 3:17) and that Jesus Christ was that Lord.

The word "Trinity" is not found in the Bible from Genesis to Revelation. The term "three Persons in the Godhead" has no place there. The phrase, "God the Father, God the Son and God the Holy Ghost," is unscriptural. Tradition has coined these terms, and thrust them forth into the religious world and hath obscured the glorious vision of the Mighty God, the Everlasting Father, in the Person of Jesus Christ.

In the second chapter of Colossians, the Apostle Paul directs his words to "them of Laodicea," and so many as have not seen his face in the flesh.

According to the Church Age, the Laodicean period is the present age, in which we are now living. This being true, his admonitions in this chapter should have great bearing upon the minds and hearts of God's people at this time, for it is to them that he makes known his heart's desire that they might be comforted, knit together in love, and unto all riches of full assurance of understanding to the acknowledgment of the mystery of God, and of the Father, and of Christ, and further warns them against philosophy, vain deceit, tradition of men and the rudiment[s] of the world. From this it appears that God gave unto him a foreknowledge of errors that were to come upon the world touching the Person of the Godhead; therefore, in mentioning of Christ, he declares that in Him dwelleth the fullness of the Godhead bodily, and further adds, "And ye are complete in him, which is the head over all principality and power."

God, foreseeing the fear that would come upon the people in proclaiming Jesus to be our God, prophesied beforehand, saying, "O Zion, that bringeth good tidings get thee up into the high mountains; O Jerusalem, that bringeth good tidings, lift up your voice with strength, lift it up

and BE NOT AFRAID; say unto the cities of Judah, BEHOLD YOUR GOD! Behold, the Lord God will come with strong hand, and His arms shall rule for HIM; behold his reward is with HIM, and his work before Him. He shall feed his flock like a good SHEPHERD." That this Shepherd is Jesus Christ, no one can deny (Jn 10:14). Yet, in the Face of these words, many are afraid to proclaim that Jesus Christ is our God (Isa 40:9–11).

We hereby quote a clipping of an article entitled, "Holy Trinity Feast." The writer says, "The Feast of the Holy Trinity was observed in many Catholic and some Protestant churches throughout the city, yesterday, with special services, in which particular attention was paid to the doctrine of the Trinity. This Feast Day is considered the foundation of all Feast Days, and the day of celebrating a mystery which is not to be understood through human reason." He further states that there is no doubt the mystery cannot be understood. But who shall we believe, man of God? The WORD OF GOD declares that the Spirit will search all things, yea the deep things of God. He will teach us all things, and in this is included the mystery of God, and of the Father, and of Christ.

So long as man will endeavor to solve this mystery, apart from Christ Jesus, it will always be to him a mystery; but Christ is the true solution of all perplexing problems, for in Him are hid all the treasures of wisdom and knowledge. In Him dwelleth all the fullness of the Godhead in bodily form. When the Disciples declared to see the Father, apart from Christ, He pointed them unto his own body, standing in their midst and when he further made mention of the Comforter, the Holy Ghost, He again said, "You know Him; for

He dwelleth with you and shall be in you" (Jn 14:9, 16, 17).

In our Spirit, we have always known but one God; but in our theology we have recognized three. If the Father, Son and Holy Ghost are three separate Persons, Spirits and Personalities, we have on our hands three separate, distinct Gods. But if Father, Son and Holy Spirit bear God's relationship to mankind, then it can be clearly seen that there is but one God; and that God is manifested in the Person of the Lord Jesus Christ; for God hath declared, "Thus saith the Lord, the King of Israel, and his Redeemer, the Lord of Hosts; I am the first and I am the last; and beside me there is no God" (Is 44:6). Jesus, the King of Israel, the Redeemer declared, " I am Alpha and Omega, the first and the last . . . Fear not; I am the first and the last; I am He that liveth and was dead, and behold, I am alive forevermore. Amen" (Rev 1:11, 17, 18).

God help us to gird up our minds, be sober, and hope to the end for the grace that is to be brought unto us in the Revelation of Jesus Christ! Truly the time for this fulfillment is almost at hand. The glory of God is filling our vision; our eye has become single, and our body is being filled with light. We see no man save "JESUS ONLY." And we now, with open face, beholding as in a glass the glory of the Lord, are changed into the same image from glory to glory, even as by the Spirit of the Lord. For God, Who commanded his light to shine in our hearts to give the light of the knowledge of the glory of God in the face of Jesus Christ (II Cor 3:18; 4:6).

The Finest of the Wheat

The Glory of the Son of Man

The manifestation of the sons of God is evidently near at hand. The whole creation groaneth and travaileth in pain together until now for that grand and glorious event. It must come! It shall come! It will come and will not tarry.

For a number of years we have been touching upon this subject and many hearts have been made to rejoice when they beheld what the future held in store for them that love him. And like the Psalmist of old we are made to cry, "Glorious things are spoken of thee, O City of God!" The Bride of the Lamb, the Spirit-filled saints are the city of God. And to her shall be given power to rule over the nations.

To teach that these despised followers of the Lowly Nazarene, who are rejected, scoffed and ridiculed, will become rulers of the nations may seem a thing incredible to many, but with God all things are possible. Joseph was hated by his brethren. He was cast into a pit. He was taken out and sold into Egypt. In Egypt he was thrown into jail, but when the time had come he arose from the prison ascended to the throne. Daniel declares, "The kingdom and dominion, and the greatness of the kingdom under the whole heaven, shall be given to the people of the saints of the Most High." (Daniel 7:27) And in verse 22 he says, "And judgment was given to the saints of the Most High; and the TIME CAME when the saints POSSESSED the kingdom.

The Son of Man

The vision which Daniel saw of one like the Son of Man coming to the Ancient of Days and receiving a kingdom, has always been a conundrum to many. To most people, the "Son of Man" referred to is Jesus Christ personally, but this view can clearly be proven erroneous by comparing the vision (Verses 13, 14) with the interpretation given by "the one who stood by" (Verses 18, 22–27). He here declares in plain words that the one like the "Son of Man" is the saints of the Most High."

The saints of the Most High are one in Christ and are one body. "For as the body is one, and had many members, and all the members of that one body being many are one body; so also is Christ." (1 Cor 12:12) All who are baptized by that "one Spirit" and living a clean, holy life (1 Cor 12:13) are members of that one body. The Spirit that thrills and vibrates the bodies of the baptized saints of today, is the same that made up the one body in the "one body" in the days of old. And this is that body that Daniel saw in his vision of the "Son of Man." The Ancient of Days is Christ in His ancient and eternal Glory. (Compare Dan 7:9 with Rev 1:13–15). The Son of Man is the body of Spirit-filled saints. Jesus Christ is "our" Lord and we are "His Christ" and the Kingdoms of this world are to become the Kingdoms of OUR LORD and HIS Christ, or anointed ones.

The Great Question

But when and how shall these things be, is the thing that awaits solution. As to when shall it be, the Prophet states that he "beheld until thrones were cast down." In this we obtain a faint idea as to "when shall these things be." During the past world conflict there were evidently more "thrones cast down" that ever was known. Since that time "uneasy lies the head that wears the crown." Wars and rumors of wars have been precedent in the past few years in confirmation of the fact that "the time is at hand."

The Great War has left European nations in a desolate, restless, and suffering condition. Famine is rife, everywhere, and thousands are dying for lack of medical attention. In America, it was said, that many thousands are dying because there are not physicians to administer to them. What an opportunity is this for the people of God who know the power of the God who heals. What a mighty awakening it would be if only a company of Spirit-filled people was to march through this afflicted world and heal them in the name of Jesus. If ever there was a time for God to manifest his sons to the world it is now.

The conditions are growing from bad to worse. Medical science is proving a failure. The Christian world is beginning to realize that there is a possibility of the health of the people being restored by the prayer of faith. In certain nominal churches, the Episcopal churches of the middle Northwest, especially, have begun "weekly healing missions." Then comes Sadhu Sundar Singh, the apostle of India, reaching healing by the prayer of faith. He says, "I have come to help Christianize America." With faith revived to the old apostolic standard, and a world crying for God, how easily would it be for God to raise up his people in authority over this generation by the manifestation of His power through his people.

Is this not the event spoken of by the great apostle Paul, for which he declares that, "the whole creation groaneth and travaileth in pain together until now?" Has not the whole world been in pain and sorrow like the pains of travail during and since the world war? The very Scripture (Rom 8:18) which precedes

the above quotation has even been used by the secular press to console the torn and bleeding soldiers at the front and the wounded hearts at the fireside. It was used in connection with a painting which portrayed a wounded soldier being directed by an angel to the rays of light above him say, "For I reckon that the sufferings of this present time (referring to the wars) are not worthy to be compared with the glory which shall be revealed in us." How significant is this incident! What can the "glory" be but the manifestation of the sons of God! While the world is groaning without, we who have the first fruits of the Spirit "groan within ourselves waiting for the adoption: to wit, the REDEMPTION of our bodies."

The Day of Redemption is surely near. All creation bears witness to this glorious event. Note what St. Luke says of this day. (Lk 2:25–28). Can we find time for strife, envy, prejudice, bigotry and world honour at such a time as this? Now is the time for God to be glorified in His saints. WATCH and PRAY. Greater things than we have ever witnessed are near at hand. The power that now lies apparently dormant may revive and burst forth at any moment. The Church is rapidly coming to "the unity of the faith, and the knowledge of the SON of God, unto a perfect man, unto the measure of the stature of the fullness of Christ. (Eph 4:13). The works that Christ did, in the days of His flesh, must be done by the Church (Jn 14:12), and even greater. The people spoken of by the prophet Joel are about to appear (Jl 2:1–11). St. Paul speaks of it as the time when God "shall come to be glorified in his saints" (2 Thess 1:7–10). Surely the hour is come that the Son of man is glorified, and God id glorified in Him. If God be glorified in Him, God shall also glory him in himself, and shall straightway glorify him" (Jn 13:32–32.). When Judas was manifested[,] God became manifested in Christ. When the anti-Christ is manifested, God will be glorified in Christ, the church, which is His body. Be ready. We are all members of His body and the glory which He has shall be given us, that He might be glorified (Jn 17:22).

ROBERT CLARENCE LAWSON
(1883–1961)

Church of Our Lord Jesus Christ of the Apostolic Faith

One of the first nonracial schisms in Oneness Pentecostalism was, in part, over another volatile issue that would continue to resurface over the life of the movement. Robert Clarence Lawson placed himself at the center of that schism, challenging the practices of the Pentecostal Assemblies of the World regarding the leadership of women.

Lawson met Haywood in 1914 and became a member of Haywood's Christ Temple congregation after the latter prayed with him and he received healing from tuberculosis, a disease at that time considered terminal. Shortly after that, Lawson was converted, baptized in Jesus's name, and had received the Pentecostal Spirit baptism.

Lawson would become one of the most prominent black Pentecostal leaders in the country, a champion of progressive social causes among oneness thinkers, and a spiritual father of many who were to make a mark on the movement. Lawson's preaching gift prompted Haywood to tap him to plant churches in St. Louis and San Antonio before he assumed a pastorate in Columbus, Ohio. He served in a number of administrative positions within PAW before leaving to found the Church of Our Lord Jesus Christ (COOLJC) in 1919. As a prolific writer and hymnist, his work and writing were targeted to correct what he saw as the social injustices of his African American community, as in defending oneness doctrine.

The Anthropology of Jesus

This is the first division of our main subject matter. The word anthropology means the science of physical facts concerning man and his development and history. After the fall of man through the transgression of Adam, God came seeking the lost. Adam, who was afraid and hid himself in the thickets of the garden, heard God's voice upon the wind of the day. After eliciting out of Adam the confession of his guilt, the great Jehovah promised him a Savior: ". . . the seed of the woman that would bruise the head of the serpent." (Gen 3:15).

In order to fulfill this promise, the Lord set about the development of the seed. He chose Abraham of the branch of Shem—the father of the Semites. Abraham had inherited those fundamental qualities that make for the highest spiritual attainments and developments; namely faith and a spirit of obedience. Moreover, his quest for true knowledge of God brought him into contact with the Infinite, who said unto him, "Abraham, get thee out of thy country and from thy kindred, and from thy father's house, unto a land that I will show thee." Believing the voice that spake with him to be God, the God of Gods[1] above all, Abraham obeyed, not knowing where he was going. Thus, he became the father of faith and the reservoir of psychic forces; the inheritor of Adam's lost inheritance; and the possessor of the covenants and promises of God.

Through the obedience of Abraham, by his wanderings and journeys, God developed those psychic forces and ideals of faith, multiplied his promises, and

1. [Ed.] Lawson originally had "God's."

brought him to the stage of spiritual development that he became a worthy progenitor of the seed that would afterward bruise the serpent's head. Under the emotion of the ideal of a universal kingdom in which all nations of the earth would be blessed through the promised one, Abraham waxed strong in faith, not considering Sarah's body as dead, nor yet his own body. He staggered not at the promises of God, but was strong in faith, giving glory to God. Therefore God, being pleased, gave him a seed, saying, "In Isaac all nations would be blessed" Consequently, God multiplied the seed of Abraham, Isaac, and Jacob. He also multiplied the transmission of Abraham's spiritual ideals and promises along with the emotional and psychic inheritance to the twelve sons and their children-which compose the family (or nation) of Abraham—out of which Christ came. In passing it is good to note the continuous development of the physical virgin stalk out of which Abraham and Christ came: also the intensifying of those psychic qualities—along with the renewing of the promises and covenants of God to each succeeding generation.

Abraham married his half sister, Sarai. (Gen 11:29). Nahor, his brother, married Milcah, his brother Haran's daughter. After Abraham entered into the land of Canaan and so—journeying there, the time drew near to his death. Abraham therefore sent his servant Eliezer back to the land of Mesopotamia—unto the city of Nahor—the land of his forefathers and his people, to get a wife for his son Isaac. Rebecca was his brother Nahor's daughter, Isaac's first cousin. (Gen 27:30).

When Jacob fled from the face of his brother Esau, upon the entreaty of his mother, he also returned to the land of Ur of Chaldee to take a wife of his father's house; unlike Esau did of the Canaanites. Upon returning to the land of his fathers, unto the house of Laban his father's brother's son, Jacob took a wife—yea two. Rachel and Leah, his second cousins, bore for him the twelve patriarchs who form the national anthropological background of the physical foundation of Jesus Christ.

The second layer on this foundation is the development of the tribe of Judah—out of which Jesus came. The above strictly deals with the Semitic contribution to the anthropological development of Jesus Christ. The Hamitic contribution to the anthropological development of Jesus Christ comes in at the incipiency of the tribe of Judah—out of which Christ came; for it is written in Genesis 49, "The scepter should not depart from Judah until Shiloh come." The beginning of the tribe of Judah is recorded in Genesis, chapter 38. It reads on this wise:

> And it came to pass at that time, that Judah went down from his brethren, and turned into a certain Adullamite whose name was Hirah: And Judah saw there a daughter of a certain Canaanite Negro-woman—whose name was Shuah, whom he married, and she conceived, and bare him a son; and called his name Er. And she conceived again, and bare a son; and she called his name Onan. And she yet again conceived, and bare a son; and she called his name Shelah. In the process of time Judah took a wife for his firstborn, Er whose name was Tamar. But Er, Judah s first son was wicked in the sight of God; so the Lord caused him to die. Judah consequently said unto Onan, marry the wife of your brother and raise up an heir for your brother. But Onan knew that the heir would not be his own, therefore, before he approached his brother s wife, he did the

unspeakable thing, wasting the seed of his brother.

What Onan did was wicked in the sight of God, therefore, he caused him to die. The abominable act was not only wicked—it was great wickedness. Why[? B]ecause he refused and resisted the will and purpose of God in the mingling of the blood of the Hamitic, or Negro, race with Shem and that of Japheth in the anthropological development of Jesus Christ. It was necessary in the plan of God to develop the most perfect man of the human race, to mingle and inter-mingle the blood of the three branches to produce the best and most perfect man. Of course all of this is out of gear with the philosophical and pseudo-scientific[2] teaching of the day, especially relative to the colored races in regard to the miscegenation, that is, the mixing of the blood of the black and white races. They say that this would deteriorate the white races, but the Bible infers that it would be just the opposite. Surely in the case of our Lord Jesus this is evident, for he had Negro blood in his veins; yet he was the fairest among ten thousand, of whom it is said even of his enemy and judge, Pilate, "Behold the man." He was indeed the holiest among the mighty and the most mighty among the holiest. Our Lord lifted the gates of Empires—He turned the river of human history—and He changed time to A.D.

For the children of God who still resist the truth and purpose of God, the spirit of Onan still lives; but the will of God shall be done and men shall know at last that all flesh is grass. Judah said to Tamar his daughter-in-law—who was a Canaanite woman as his wife was, "Return as a widow to your father's house

until Shelah my youngest son grows up," for he reflected—perhaps she shall also kill him like his brothers. Therefore, Tamar went and returned to her father's house. Now, as time went on, Shuah, the wife of Judah, died—and the Bible says, "Judah grieved for her." As time passed, Judah went up with Hirah, his partner, to shear the sheep at Timanth, and it was reported to Tamar that her father-in-law was going up to shear his sheep. So Tamar put off her widow's garments and concealed herself in her veil. Dressing in the attire of a harlot, she went down and sat at the well which is on the road to Timanth; for she saw that Shelah was grown up and he was not given to her as a husband. Judah saw her and thought she was a harlot, for she had hidden her face, so he turned from the road to her and accosted her as a harlot. Tamar said, "What wilt thou give me, that thou mayest come in unto me?" And Judah replied, "I will send thee a kid from the flock." She replied, "Wilt thou give me a pledge, till thou send it?" He said, "What pledge shall I give thee?" And Tamar answered, "Thy signet, and thy bracelets, and thy staff that is in thine hand." So Judah gave them to her, and she consented to him. Then she arose and put off her veil, dressed herself in widow's garments and went away. Thereafter, Judah sent the kid of goats by Hirah, his partner, who was to receive the pledge from the hands of the woman, but he could not find her. He therefore inquired of the men of the place, asking, "Where is the harlot, that was openly by the way-side?" But they replied, "There was no harlot in this place." So he returned to Judah and replied, "I cannot find her." Three months later it was reported to Judah, "Your daughter-in-law Tamar has prostituted herself, bring her here and burn her." And they brought

2. [Ed.] Lawson has "pseudo-scientifically."

her. But she produced the ring and staff, and said, "By the man whose these things are, am I with child," and she continued, "Discern, I pray thee, whose are these, the signet, and bracelets, and staff." Then Judah replied, "You are more virtuous than I am, for I did not give you Shelah my son." He therefore proceeded no further to examine her. "And it came to pass in the time of her travail, that there were twins in her womb. And when she travailed, one put out his hand. So the mid-wife tied a scarlet thread upon its hand, remarking, "This came out first." And it came to pass, as he drew back his hand, that, behold, his brother came out; and she said, How hast thou broken forth? This breach be upon thee: and his name was called Pharez. And afterward came out his brother that had the scarlet thread upon his hand: and his name was called Zarah."

Thus was born to Judah, by the two Negro women, the children who were the progenitors of the tribe of Judah. If any race have whereof to boast as touching things of the flesh, relative to our Lord Jesus Christ, the colored race has more: for they gave to the world the two mothers of the tribe of Judah—out of which Christ Came. If I may so say, they were the mothers of our Lord; for as touching the flesh, he was at that time in the loins of his father, Judah; to whom pertaineth the pre-eminence among the twelve tribes of Israel. To whom was given the adoption, and the glory, and the covenants, and the giving of the law, and the service of God, and the promises: whose of the fathers, and of whom as concerning the flesh, Christ came-who is over all, God blessed forever, Amen. (Gen 38; 49:8–13).

For fear that it may be reasoned that Judah had other children and out of the branch came Jesus, we will trace his genealogical descent. 1 Chron 2:3–15, where it is recorded; " . . . the sons of Judah; Er; and Onan, and Shelah; which three were born unto him of the daughters of Shuah, the Canaanitess. And Er, the first born of Judah, was evil in the sight of the Lord; and he slew him. And Tamar his daughter-in-law bore him Pharez and Zerah. All the sons of Judah were five. " So you see, Judah had no other sons other than by these two Negro women—three by his wife, and twins by his daughter-in-law. Matthew clinches this in his gospel of the genealogy of Jesus, chapter 1 verses 1–4. It reads: "The book of the generation of Jesus Christ, the son of David, the son of Abraham, Abraham begat Isaac; and Isaac begat Jacob; and Jacob begot Judah and his brethren; and Judah begat Pharez and Zerah, of Tamar." In studying the genealogy of Jesus, in St. Matthew['s] revised version, it is interesting that although Judah had no other children except by these two colored women, there were at least two other Negro women who gave their blood in the royal line and veins of our Savior, Jesus. Saint Matthew further says that, "Phares begat Hezron; and Hezron begat Ram; and Ram begat Amminadab; and Amminadab begat Nahshon; and Nahshon begat Salmon; and Salmon begat Boaz of Rahab" who was the next colored woman who gave her blood unto the royal line. She was of Jericho, which was the first Canaanite City captured by the Israelites under Joshua, and evidently a Negro woman; for unto this day the people of Jericho equal in blackness the darkest tribes in Africa. I will never forget while in Palestine, after having made a pilgrimage to the river of Jordan, that we passed by modern Jericho. And after buying some oranges of the natives, we proceeded on our way up the beautiful palm-tree shaded road leading towards the ruins of ancient Jericho—upward of a mile away. In passing, I beheld some black folks laboring in the vineyard to the left of the road and some working around a house. Upon inquiry of my guide, I asked, "Who are they?" He answered readily, "They are the people of Jericho; that is, the Aborigines—the people of the land." There remained no doubt in my mind concerning the assertion that Rahab, the harlot, who had the warm sympathetic heart for the foreigners who came to her house in Jericho to spy out the land, was a black woman. Perhaps it was this wonderful warm-blooded attribute that is innate in the heart of the black race—or Hamite, that the Lord desired to mingle with the highly developed spiritual and psychic emotional nature of the Shemites. When Israel settled in the land, Rahab, the harlot, was spared and was not given to the edge of the sword because she received the spies in peace. She was numbered with the children of Israel, and she married Salmon, who begat Boaz, who in turn married Ruth, the Moabite, who is a representative of the Anglo-Saxon—the Japhethic—branch of the human race.

But before we shall dwell upon this, we shall make mention of the fourth Negro woman who gave her blood in the anthropological development of Jesus. This woman is Bathsheba, the wife of Uriah the Hittite, whom David saw bathing one day and brought her unto the house while her husband was in the front fighting [in] the army of Israel in defense of the throne of David. David humbled her, and she conceived and sent word and told David, "I am with child. " David, in order to cover up his sins, sent for Uriah from the front—ostensibly to inquire how the battle was going but in reality to have Uriah go to his home unto his wife, so that he, David,

would be sheltered from the guilt of his sins. But Uriah slept at David's door. And in the morning he said unto King David, "The ark, and Israel, and Judah, abide in tents; and my lord Joab, and the servants of my Lord, are encamped in open fields; shall I then go into mine house, to eat and to drink, and to lie with my wife? As thou livest and as thy soul liveth, I will not do this thing."

Then the basest act of David was committed when he conspired with Joab against the life of Uriah: when he ordered that Joab should put Uriah in the front of the battle and the thickest of the fight, so that he would be killed. It so happened that Uriah was killed, and after his wife Bathsheba had mourned for him certain days, David sent and took her for his wife. Her first-born died; notwithstanding that David prayed that it should be healed. However, she bore him another child whose name was Solomon, who, after David's death, reigned as king in his stead. Solomon was reputed to have been the wisest man that ever lived. If so be the case, to the everlasting honor of the colored race, he was a Negro that is a half-breed. According to the laws of the South, and the standard of the Ku Klux Klan—of whom a lot of our white brethren seems to be under the influence, he was a Negro, for he had more than one-sixteenth Negro blood in him. And according to that standard, if our Lord would return to the earth again in the flesh, and would go down South incognito, he would be jim-crowed and segregated; for he himself had more than one-sixteenth of Negro blood in him. In singing to the bride of his love, Solomon Wrote, "I am black but comely." (Song of Sol 1:5).

Publuius Lentus, a Roman scribe, was said to have given this description of our Savior: "He was a man in stature of about six feet. His hair being wine-colored and overflowing the shoulders. His countenance, convincing to behold, yet with a note of tenderness and authority. He was the color of a filbert, a nut of reddish hue. Thus making Jesus neither white nor black." This record of Publuius Lentus is only to be found published in the ancient church histories.

There is No Denying of the Father in Baptizing in the Name of the Lord Jesus

There are many honest souls who are anxious to obey the voice of God and be baptized in the name of our Lord Jesus Christ, but they are intimidated by persons misconstruing the scripture which says, "He is Anti-Christ, that denieth the Father and the Son." (1 Jn 2:22).

There is no one who knows the word of God, and has been baptized in the name of our Lord Jesus Christ, that denies the Father and the Son. They acknowledge the Father and the Son in Christ Jesus. To acknowledge the Father and the Son does not necessarily mean to believe in "three persons in the Godhead."

The Fatherhood of God Manifested in the Flesh

The following portion of this article will be sufficient to convince any God-fearing person that they cannot deny the Father by being baptized in the Name of our Lord Jesus Christ.

"Whosoever denieth the Son, the same hath not the Father, but he that acknowledgeth the Son hath the Father also." (1 Jn 2 :23). We desire to call this question to the reader for prayerful consideration. While reading it "Father also" drew my particular attention. I believe it will help many to see God's purpose in these last days. The thought before us is, that He that denieth the Son (Jesus Christ) the same has denied the "Father also." Why is this; is it not because Jesus and the Father are one? (Jn 10:30).

There is no scripture that says, He that denieth the Father the same hath not the Son, but to the contrary, all scriptures seem to be opposite, by this I mean that all scripture identifies the Father in the Son. "God was in Christ reconciling the world unto Himself" (2 Cor. 5:19). "God was manifested in the flesh." (I Tim. 3:16). Therefore when one turns from Christ, he turns from God. He that believeth not on the Son, the same believeth not on the Father; but he that believeth on the Son believeth on the Father also. (Jn 12:44; 14:1). The Jews believed that God would take away their sins (Jer. 31:33–34) but, they did not believe that Jesus had anything to do with it; and Jesus said, "If ye believe not that I am He, ye shall die in your sins." (Jn 8:24). He that knoweth not the Son, the same knoweth not the Father, but he that knoweth the Son, knoweth the Father also. (See Jn 8:19, 14:7). To know Christ is to know God the Father, for the mystery of God the Father is in Christ (Col. 2:2.9). He that seeth not the Son, the same seeth not the Father; he that seeth the Son seeth the Father also (Jn 14:8–11, 12:44–45). To love God, one must love Jesus, for Jesus and God are one and inseparable. If the Father and Son are two separate persons, then we could love one and hate the other, as the Jews sought to do. If you do not love Jesus, you cannot love God, but you cannot love JESUS without loving God, for Jesus is God manifested in the flesh, i.e.: in a visible form. If the above scriptures are true (no one can honestly say they are not) why does not the same hold with the name used in baptism? Let us look at it from a scriptural standpoint as it were. He that baptizeth not in the name of the Son (Jesus) the same baptizeth not in the name of the Father; but he that baptizeth, or is baptized in the name of the Son (Jesus) baptizeth or is baptized in the name of the Father also.

By the scriptures, this is clearly proven from the fact that the commission given as recorded by St. Matthew: "to baptize in the Name of the Father and of the Son, and of the Holy Ghost." (Matt 28:18, 19) but, on the day of Pentecost and thereafter according to the Book of Acts, all of the disciples baptized in the Name of Jesus, the Son, proving that they recognized it to be the name' of the Father also. (See Acts 2:38, 8:12–16, Acts 9:18 with Acts 22:16, Acts 10:47, 48 with Acts 19:5.

All who are baptized in the Name of Jesus are baptized in the Name of the Father also, but those who have not been baptized in the Name of the Father. The only way to obey the command of Jesus in Matt 28:18, 19 is to do as the Holy Ghost authorized on the day of Pentecost, and carried out by the Apostles according to the Book of Acts. The only way a person can really "Deny the Father" is to fail to acknowledge that Jesus is the true and only living God (1 Jn 5:20; Jd 25). When you are baptized in Jesus' name you thereby acknowledge that the Father, Son and Holy Ghost "are one" (1 Jn 5:7), and that "In Christ Jesus dwelleth all the fullness of Godhead in a bodily form" (Col. 2:9). Be not faithless, but believe (Jn 12:44, 45:20; 26.38).

JAMES C. RICHARDSON JR. (1956–)

Apostolic Church of Christ in God

James C. Richardson is a lifelong member and son of one of the founding bishops of the Apostolic Church of Christ in God. He is also pastor of Mt Sinai Apostle Church in Martinsville, Virginia, the congregation his father, Bishop James C. Richardson, founded in 1935. The younger Richardson took over leadership the congregation and of the denomination upon his father's death in 1985. Richardson attended Howard University Divinity School where he received his Master of Divinity degree under such notables a James Tinney.

From With Water and Spirit

Water Baptism

"Unless you get baptized in Jesus' name, you don't have it the right way, according to the scriptures." This statement can be heard countless times in any Black Apostolic church. It is recited by ministers and laity alike with conviction, confidence, and enthusiasm. On various other doctrinal points, Apostolics can be lumped or labeled with other Protestants or other Pentecostals. But the Apostolic belief about baptism is a distinguishing doctrine. It is considered to be a primary Apostolic feature.

Strangely enough, Apostolics often use Matthew 28:19[3] as a point of departure because they feel an error has been made in the interpretation of the Matthew 28:19 passage. Apostolics do not interpret this as a textual formula for baptism. It is rather understood as a general command to do something.

Apostolics believe the command was fully obeyed for the first time during the events recorded in the latter part of the second chapter of Acts. Apostolics contend that Jesus' command to baptize

"all nations in the name of the Father and of the Son, and of the Holy Spirit" was carried out when they were baptized "in the name of Jesus" in Acts 2:38. While the Matthew text is not regarded as formulaic, the Acts 2:38 text is regarded as historical use of a formula:

> Let all the house of Israel therefore know assuredly that God has made him both Lord and Christ. This Jesus whom you crucified. Now when they heard this, they were cut to the heart, and said to Peter and the rest of the Apostles, Brethren, what shall we do?
>
> And Peter said to them, Repent, and be baptized everyone of you in the name of Jesus Christ for the forgiveness of your sins; and you shall receive the gift of the Holy Spirit . . . So those who received his word were baptized, and there were added that day about three thousand souls.

This text is primary for Apostolics, who believe the "name of the Father, Son, and Holy Spirit" is Jesus. Other scriptures also confirm belief in Jesus' name baptism. In the Book of Church Order and Discipline of the United Church of Jesus Christ (Apostolic), Bishop Monroe Saunders says this about baptism: "We baptize in the name of Jesus Christ because it is

---

3. [Ed.] Richardson quotes from the RSV throughout.

Apostolic in origin and practice (Acts 2:38; 8:12–17; 10:47, 48; 19:1–6).

". . . No other mode of baptism is to be found in the New Testament. For more than one hundred years after Pentecost, believers were baptized only in the Name, Jesus Christ."

Lest there be some doubt concerning the command that Jesus gave his apostles, Saunders adds this:

". . . In Matthew 28:19. we have a commission or a command given; in Acts 2:38, we have the command executed. In the former, the apostles were told what to do, in the latter, they did it."

In addition to the scripture in the second chapter of Acts, Saunders lists three others in the book of Acts. The second scripture is Acts 8:12–17. In this passage, Phillip, who had gone to Samaria to preach, was subsequently joined by Peter and John.

"But when they believed Phillip as he preached good news about the Kingdom of God and the name of Jesus Christ they were baptized, both men and women . . . Now when the apostles at Jerusalem heard that Samaria had received the word of God they sent to them Peter and John, who came down and prayed for them that they might receive the Holy Spirit; for it had not yet fallen on any of them, but they had only been baptized in the name of the Lord Jesus. Then they laid hands on them and they received the Holy Spirit."

This scripture is important for Apostolics because it demonstrates that the Samaritans (a mixed group of people considered as societal outcasts) were included as God's people along with Jews and Gentiles. And further evidence of Gentile inclusion is shown in the following passage:

"While Peter was still saying this, the Holy Spirit fell on all who heard the word

. . . Then Peter declared, can anyone forbid water for baptizing these people who have received the Holy Spirit? . . . And he commanded them to be baptized in the name of Jesus Christ."

Whereas some think Paul raises points of difference with Peter on tongue speaking, they are in agreement on water baptism.

> While Apollos was at Corinth, Paul passed through the upper country and came to Ephesus. There he found some disciples. And he said to them, "Did you receive the Holy Spirit when you believed?" And they said, No, we have never ever heard that, there is a Holy Spirit. And he said," Unto what then were you baptized?" They said, "Unto John's baptism." And Paul said, "John baptized with the baptism of repentance," telling the people to believe in the one who was to come after him, that is, Jesus. On hearing this, they were baptized in the name of the Lord Jesus. And when Paul had laid his hands upon them, the Holy Spirit came on them . . .[4]

These scriptures prove for Apostolics that baptism should and must be administered in the name of Jesus.

It is certainly clear that if water baptism is to be administered at all in the Christian church. the correct formula should be "in the name of Jesus Christ."

Apostolics view the words, Father, Son and Holy Spirit as titles denoting God's different relationships to his creation and his creatures. But all Apostolics agree that when the Apostles followed Jesus' command (Matt 28:19), they did baptize in the name of all three titles.

Apostolics understand the correct name to be Jesus. We note the following:

4. [Ed.] Acts 19:1–7, RSV.

"Father is not a proper name, nor son, nor Holy Ghost. Father expresses a relationship, also Son; and the Holy Ghost means the Holy Spirit, but does not mean His name but His nature. 'Holy' is an adjective meaning 'more excellence,' 'pure in heart,' and Spirit is a noun but not a proper name. So they that baptize in the (Trinitarian) formula . . . do not baptize in any name at all.

". . . Jesus said, "Go ye therefore and teach all nations, baptizing them in the name"—not names, but name (one) of the Father and of the Son and of the Holy Ghost, and if there is none other Name under heaven given among men whereby we must be saved but Jesus Christ (Acts 4:12), then if we have not been baptized in the name of Jesus Christ, then we have not been baptized in the name of the Father, Son and Holy Ghost."

In addition to the above words by the late Bishop R. C. Lawson, using in part Acts 4:12, Apostolics give other scriptures for Jesus' name baptism. Apostolics believe that salvation is only in Jesus Christ, and that Jesus is also the Lord.

Therefore God has highly exalted him and bestowed on him the name which is above every name, that at the name of Jesus every knee should bow, in heaven and on earth and under the earth and every tongue confess that Jesus Christ is Lord, to the glory of God the Father.[5]

According to Apostolic interpretation, the scripture in the second chapter of Philippians emphasizes the importance of the name of Jesus. Therefore baptism must be in the name of Jesus Christ. In addition to Paul's emphasis on Jesus in his epistle to Philippi, he also stresses the name of Jesus again in his epistle to the assembly of Colosse.

. . . Let the word of Christ dwell in you richly, as you teach and admonish one another in all wisdom, and as you sing psalms and hymns and spiritual songs with thankfulness in your hearts to God. And whatever you do in word or deed, do everything in the name of the Lord Jesus, giving thanks to God the Father through him.[6]

Apostolics take this literally to mean that almost everything must be done in Jesus' name. There is no question about the fact that baptism is certainly one of the things to be done in the name.

If one used the New Testament as a basis for belief, then baptism in Jesus' name is more accurate than the more traditional Trinitarian formula.

Jehovah of the Old Testament Is Jesus of the New Testament

Interwoven with the Apostolic belief of Jesus' name baptism is an even more controversial doctrine. Even as Unitarian-Universalists deny the doctrine of the Trinity, so do Apostolics. But the reasons are different. Whereas Unitarians do not accept the Trinity because they do not believe Jesus was divine, or God, Apostolics refute the Trinity because they believe Jesus is God. In other words, in the Black Apostolic church a major doctrine is that Jehovah-God of the Old Testament is Jesus Christ of the New Testament.

According to Morris Golder, the Trinity is a part of historical Christianity, the post-biblical ages.

"We repudiate and deny that the doctrine of the Trinity is substantiated by the word of God. It is true that it is a part of the great heritage of what is known as 'historical Christianity;' however,

5. [Ed.] Phil 2:9–11.

6. [Ed.] Col 3:16–17.

Apostolic Pentecostals do not accept all that Christendom has embraced historically . . . the 'doctrine of the trinity' must be read into the sacred text. The Bible is the book of 'One God' who has revealed Himself in many ways."[7]

The One-God idea has always permeated the whole of Black Apostolic church doctrine. There has always been just one God. He has, however, taken on or been known by different names at different times.

While God was known by other names in previous dispensations (i.e., Jehovah, Yahweh), in the dispensation of Grace his name is Jesus. And because God's correct name is Jesus, Apostolics call on him by that name. While non-Apostolics have accused this group of putting too much emphasis on the second person of the Trinity, Apostolics have not meant it that way at all. For Jesus is not the second person of a divine Trinity; Jesus is all.

To merely state this thesis as doctrine without biblical proof would, for Apostolics, make it false. Diligent efforts have been put forth over the years to point out parallel scripture from the Old Testament and from the New Testament which prove that Jesus is God. Bishop R. C. Lawson did one of the most thorough jobs in this regard. He compared over one hundred passages of scripture in the Old and New Testaments.

It is not necessary to duplicate the entire list, but a sample list of some of the scriptures will illustrate.

Jehovah God of the Old Testament is Jesus Christ of the New Testament

This is proved by the Creation

Gen 1:1; Is 44:23, 24, compared with St. John 1:1, 10.

Gen. 1:1. In the Beginning God created the heavens and the earth.

St. John 1:1, 10. In the beginning was the word and the word was God.

vs. 10—He was in the world, and the world was made through him, yet the world knew him not.

This is proved by His Incarnation

– Is 7:14, 9:6, compared with Matt 1:18–25.

– Gen 3:15, Ps 68:21; Lk 8:11; St. John 1:2–14; Matt 1:22–25; Gal 3:16.

– Isaiah 7:14. Therefore the Lord himself will give you a sign. Behold, a young woman shall conceive and bear a son and shall call his name Immanuel.[" (RSV)]

– St. Matthew 1:18–25.[8] Now the birth of Jesus Christ took place in this way. When his mother Mary had been betrothed to Joseph, before they came together she was found to be with child of the Holy Spirit; and her husband Joseph, being a just man and unwilling to put her to shame, resolved to divorce her quietly. But as he considered this, behold, an angel of the Lord appeared to him in a dream, saying, 'Joseph, son of David, do not fear to take Mary your wife . . . Behold, a virgin shall conceive and bear a son, and his name shall be called Emmanuel' (which means, God with us).

The two areas mentioned in detail give an idea of how Lawson constructed his parallel scriptures. For the rest of his chart, a shorter version will be given.

7. Golder, *"The Principles of Our Doctrine,"* 5–6.

8. RSV.

This is proved by the works that He did
– Matt. 11:2–7, compared with Isa. 35:3–10; Jn 9:1–4; 14:11.

This is proved by His crucifixion
– Zach. 12:1, 10, compared with Jn 19:31–38; Acts 20:28.

This is proved by His burial
– Psa. 74:12, compared with Matt. 12:40; Eph. 4:7–10; I Ptr. 3:18–21; 4:4, 5.

This is proved by His resurrection
– Psa. 68:1, 16–19; Eph. 4:7–12; Col. 2:9–11.

This is proved by His ascension
–Psa. 47:5–9, compared with Acts 1:9–11; I Thess. 4:13–17.

This is proved by His second coming
–Psa. 50:1–8, compared with I Thess. 4:13–17; Tit. 2:11–14; I Jn. 3:1–5; Zach. 14:3–6; Hab. 3:3–6; Rev. 1:7–8; 19:11–18; compared with I Tim. 6:14–16.

This is proved by prophecy fulfilled
– II Ptr. 1:19–21; Isa. 40:3–4, compared with Matt. 3:1–4, Jn. 1:19–27.

The preceding list . . . is taken from the *Discipline Book, The Church of Our Lord Christ*. Bishop R. C. Lawson, who founded the organization, wrote this book of doctrine and discipline . . .

This particular doctrine presents no major problem in dealing with the incarnation. Apostolics feel that since God found no one worthy to reclaim the world, he chose to do it himself. By impregnating Mary, God was able to assume some human form. He thus became Jesus in the flesh. This was done, however, without abandoning or sacrificing any of his divine nature or divine powers. While Apostolics will acknowledge that Jesus the Man was not omnipresent, there is no question but that he was omnipotent and omniscient.

It is believed that the physical body that Jesus used was a temporary "temple" while he lived on earth. The death, destruction, or termination of the physical body did not in any way limit Jesus because he still had the infinite spirit. And while the spirit dwelled in the body, it also existed outside of the body. Today it is that omnipotent spirit of Jesus that is God.

MARY MAGDALENA LEWIS TATE
(1871–1930)

Church of the Living God Pillar and Ground of the Truth

Though Pentecostal in doctrine and Holiness in piety, the Church of the Living God Pillar and Ground of the Truth, which Tate founded and over which she presided, understood itself as divinely ordained by God for special revelation regarding the nature of the church and of true Christian faith.

Tate refuted the Methodist and Baptist, and even other Pentecostal churches for carrying names that she perceived were unbiblical. Her rejection of oneness doctrine falls in line with her outright rejection of other tenets that fall outside of what she saw as special revelation God has given her for the last day's restoration of the church.

A Letter From Mother Tate Concerning Baptism in the Name of "Jesus Only"

P.O. Box 658
Nashville, Tennessee
1811 Heiman Street
North Nashville, Tennessee

Dear Friend,

Should you in life meet with people or persons who really believe or teach that all persons should be baptized in the name of "Jesus only," please give them to know with Bible proof, that this is a false report and a false belief, and those who believe or teach such are making wrest upon the sayings of Brother Paul and other [scripture] as spoken of in Second Peter, third chapter, verses 16 and 17. Now the broadest, truest, and greatest commandment given on baptism entrusted to man to perform was given and commanded through and by Jesus Christ Himself in St. Matthew 28:19.

The apostles had no commandment, neither instructions from God, neither Jesus Christ to baptize anyone in the name of Jesus only. The cruel unconverted Jews had with cruel hands naturally crucified Jesus because they did not believe that He was the Son of God and they believed He had no Father, but was only and by Himself. So when the apostles would get those unbelievers to really believe that Jesus was the Son of God and was not alone, then they saw it expedient to not lay their hands upon them for the reception of the Holy Ghost first, but to command that they first be baptized in the name of the same man that they had slain and hung on a tree. After then the apostles would lay hands upon them that they might receive the Holy Ghost and not before then. So the apostles commanded this among the Jews only, and to no one else, for there was no people so against Jesus as the unbelieving Jews. Now, let us ever be wise enough to understand the commandments given by Jesus Christ in St. Matthew 28th chapter, verses 19 and 20; also St. John 12:48 and 50. Be governed accordingly as Jesus promised to be with all ministers and among all people and nations.

Now, if we love Jesus we will keep His Word (Jn 14:23). "Sanctify them through thy truth, Thy Word is truth," (Jn 17:17). See also St. John 17:21–23; Acts 1:8; Acts 2:1–4; St. Luke 1:16; Numbers 6:1–4; Deuteronomy 14:2–10; and Titus 2:14–15.

All you who desire to hear me preach or have me lay hands upon you that you be healed or blessed in every way, bow down on your knees and offer a prayer unto the Father, the Almighty God, in the name of Jesus the Mighty God, for me to come to you. Then get up and figure my expenses and write me.

I am truly,
The Chief Apostle Elder
Bishop M. L. Tate
May, 1925

ROSA ARTIMUS HORN
(1880–1976)

Pentecostal Faith Church, Inc.

Though born the granddaughter of a slave, Rosa attended private school throughout her young life. She worked as a dressmaker in Augusta, Georgia, where she remained until the death of her husband, William Artimus, and where she discovered a local Pentecostal church. She soon became a member and very shortly she was evangelizing, before migrating to Evanston, Illinois, where she became an ordained minister under the ministry of Maria Woodworth Etter. By 1926, she had moved to Brooklyn, New York, where she established her first congregation. Horn was assisted in the ministry by her two daughters, Jessie A. Horn and Gladys A. Brandhagen. The three worked as a team, establishing congregations throughout the United States as well as foreign missions.

From her church in Harlem, Horn took on a number of battles within both the secular and religious world. She fought to keep, what she considered, houses of ill repute out of her community, taking local bar owners to court to curtail their activities. She fought with famed radio preacher Lightfoot Solomon Michaux and Father Divine over control of the broadcasting airways. Finally, she took on Oneness Pentecostal proponents, contending that their understandings of the Godhead and the necessity for baptism only in "Jesus's name" were unfounded.

Is Jesus God the Father of is He the Son of God?

The children of God are warned against apostates, who deny the deity of Christ and say that Jesus is God, the Father. Jesus is not the Father; Jesus is the Son of the Father. (Heb. 5:5) God said to Jesus, "Thou art my Son, this day have I begotten Thee." (1 Jn. 2:22) "Who is a liar but he that denieth that Jesus is the Christ? He is antichrist, that denieth the Father . . . and the Son." Jesus is the Son of God. I believe the Bible, don't you? The Word teaches that there is a Father in Heaven and a Son. (1 Tim. 2:5) "For there is one God and one mediator between God and men, the man Christ Jesus." That makes Jesus an Intercessor, interceding to the Father for us. Thank God, He is our intercessor and not the Father, but the Son. All right, Glory to God! Amen.

Away with [any skeptic] who says Jesus is God. His head is stopped up and needs to be blasted with the Power of the Holy Ghost; not a ghost, but Heaven's Holy Ghost. The words of John the Baptist (Jn. 1:34), "And I saw, and bear record that this is the Son of God." Amen.

When Jesus rebuked the devils out of the man (Luke 8:28), the devil cried out, "What have I to do with thee, Jesus, thou Son of God most high? I beseech thee, torment me not." The devils confessed that Jesus is the Son of God. Would you let the Devil be better than you, who say that Jesus is God the Father? Jesus is not God the Father, but the Son, as He said. Praise the Lord! (Jn. 14:28) Jesus said, "My Father is greater than I," and why do you contradict Jesus, by saying Jesus is the Father? Jesus is not God the Father; but He is the Son, as He said. (Jn. 14:23) Jesus answered and said unto him, "If any man love me, he will keep my words and my Father will love him and we will come unto him and make our abode with him."

"My Father and I" (plural) said Jesus, "will take up our (plural) abode with him." Is Jesus not speaking of His Father here? Thou child of the Devil, trying to confuse the Word of God. (John 14:24) "He that loveth me not keepeth not my sayings; and the word which ye hear is not mine, but the Father's which sent me[.]" The scripture shows that you don't love Jesus. Jesus said if you don't love Him, you wouldn't keep His sayings.

You not only fail to love him, but try to make Him a liar, but you can't do it; thank God. The Word is too plain. Jesus said His Father sent Him and you say Jesus Himself is the Father. I believe Jesus. God said, "Let every man's word be a lie and My the truth." I believe the Word of God, not you.

Let me warn you, dear children of God, who have been standing up for the truth. May God help you to stand firmly on the Apostles' Doctrine and "Have no fellowship with the unfruitful works of darkness, but rather reprove them" (Eph 5:11). (II Cor 11:13–15) "For such are false apostles of Christ. And no marvel for Satan himself is transformed into an angel of light. Therefore it is no great thing if his ministers also be transformed as the ministers of righteousness; whose end shall be according to their works." (I Jn 5:5) "Who is he that overcometh the world, but he that believeth that Jesus is the Son of God?" And the 7th verse says, "For there are three that bear record in Heaven, the Father, the Word and the Holy Ghost." Beloved, don't deny the Father and the Son, for I John 2:22 tells us, "He is an antichrist that denieth the Father and the Son."

Now to any innocent reader of this tract, who does not understand the doctrine of Jesus; if you are going to be baptized, you are privileged to ask how they baptize, for these [skeptics] baptize in the name of Jesus only, which is not scriptural. Jesus said in Matthew 28:19, "Go ye, therefore, and teach all nations, baptizing them in the name of the Father and of the Son, and of the Holy Ghost."

Peter on the Day of Pentecost, told the Jews and all who had not received Jesus, as they had only been baptized unto John's baptism (Acts 2:38) to be baptized in the name of the Lord Jesus; not to deny the Father, whom they had already accepted, but to believe in Jesus, also. If it is right to baptize in the name of Jesus only, in whose name did John baptize?

Beloved, be careful to watch your salvation. When you sin that puts you out from under the Blood of Jesus and you are susceptible to take on any spirit of delusion. God's Word says, "Because of the hardness of your heart, I will send strong delusion upon you, and you will rather believe a lie than the truth."

When Elder [Haywood] was turned out of the Pentecostal Church at Indianapolis, Indiana for his hardness and misbehavior, that is when he went into this terrible delusion, saying that God's name is Jesus, made himself a bishop and began to spread it before he died. Mark my words, his followers will say to you, "If God is Jesus' Father, what is His name?" They will answer for you, "His name is Jesus." Such delusion is absurd.

There is only one place under the lids of the Bible where God told His name to anyone and that was Moses. When the Lord sent Moses to deliver the children of Israel from Egypt's bondage, Moses said unto God, "Behold when I come unto the children of Israel and shall say unto them, the God of your fathers hath sent me unto you; and they shall say unto me, what is His name, what shall I say unto them?" And God said unto Moses, "Thou shalt say unto the children of Israel, I am hath sent me unto you. This is my Name forever, and this is my Memorial, unto all generations (Ex. 3:13–15).

Let no man beguile you of your reward, intruding into things that ye know not of vainly puffed up by your fleshly minds. Is this thing essential to salvation? No, but saving souls is.

In Proverbs 30:4, we read, "Who hath ascended up into heaven, or descended? Who hath bound the waters in a garment? Who hath established till he ends of the earth? What is His name, and what is His Son's name, if thou canst tell?" These questions are not hid from the people of God.

Let us be careful how we divide the Word of God, Paul said to Timothy, "Study to show thyself approved unto God, a workman that needeth not be ashamed, rightly dividing the Word of Truth" (II Tim. 2:15); and there is a way that seemeth right unto man but the end thereof is the way is death. "Search the scriptures," Jesus said, "For in them ye think ye think ye have eternal life and [there] are they which testify of me."

One of the things that is causing much trouble in the church of God today is hurrying the seekers through. I've seen them telling the seekers something to say real fast, such as glory, save me, save me, or hallelujah; (many times they don't even say hallelujah but lu, lu, lu) instead of teaching them to repent of their sins. Hence, the unsaved are being fellowshipped into the church as saved. There we have much trouble. No man can walk with God except the carnal mind has been taken away, for the carnal mind is not subject to the Will of God, neither indeed can be. The only remedy is to wait at the altar until the work is done. You won't need anyone to tell you. "Let he sinner forsake his ways," saith the Lord, "and the unrighteous man his thoughts and let them return unto the Lord and he will have mercy upon them, und to our Cod, for he will abundantly pardon." Godly sorrow worketh repentance and out of your mouth confession is made unto salvation.

Ah, beloved, if you would see Jesus, tarry before God, in humble heartfelt contrition, pouring out your soul. There, the tears of joy will begin to flow. One taste of God calls for another. You will know when the work is done and you won't have any more trouble with [your] old self, but you will have joy unspeakable and full of glory.

(Jude, beginning at the 17th verse)

"But, beloved, remember ye the words which were spoken before of the apostles of our Lord Jesus Christ; how that they told you there should be mockers in the last time, who should walk after their own ungodly lusts, These be they who separate themselves, sensual, having not the Spirit. But ye, beloved building up yourselves on your most holy faith, praying in the Holy Ghost, keep yourselves in the love of God, looking for the mercy of our Lord Jesus Christ unto eternal life. And of some have compassion, making a difference; and others have with fear, pulling them out of the fire; hating even the garment spotted by the flesh.

Here is another beautiful picture of the Father and the Son. In Revelation 4:2–3, John the Revelator said, "And immediately I was in the spirit; and behold, a throne was set, in heaven, and one sat on the throne. And He that sat was to look upon a jasper and a sardine stone: and there was a rainbow round about the throne, in sight like unto an emerald."

(Rev. 5:1–13 [KJV]) And I saw in the right hand of Him that sat on the throne, (God the Father) a book written within and on the back, sealed with seven seals. And I saw a strong angel proclaiming with a loud voice, "who is worthy to open the book, and to loose the seals thereof?" And no man in heaven, nor in earth, neither under the earth, was able to open the book, neither to look thereon. And I wept much, because no man was found worthy to open and to read the book, neither to look thereon. And one of the elders saith unto me, "Weep not: behold, the Lion of the tribe of Judah, the Root of David, (Jesus) hath prevailed to open the book, and to loose the seals thereof." And I beheld, and lo, in the midst of the throne and of the four beasts, and in the midst of the elders, stood a Lamb as it had been slain, having seven horns and seven eyes, which are the seven Spirits of God sent forth into all the earth. And He (Jesus) came and took the book out of the right hand of Him (God the Father) that sat upon the throne.

And who is this sitting upon the throne? God, the Father. Who is this who took the book out of the right hand of Him that sat upon the throne? Jesus, for He is the only Lion of the tribe of Judah the Son of the living God. "And when He had taken the book, the four beasts and the four and twenty elders. fell down before the Lamb, having everyone of them harps, and golden vials full of odors, which are the prayers of the saints." (Oh, thank God, the prayers of the righteous availeth much.)

And they sang a new song, saying, Thou art worthy to take the book, and to open the seals thereof: for Thou wast slain, (Jesus) and hast redeemed us to God (God the Father) by Thy blood out of every kindred, and tongue, and people, and nation: And hast made us unto our God kings and priests: and we shall reign on the earth. And I beheld, and I heard the voice of many angels round about the throne and the beasts and the elders: and the number of them was ten thousand times ten thousand, and thousands of thousands; saying with a loud voice, Worthy is the Lamb that was slain (Jesus) to receive power, and riches, and wisdom, and strength, and honor, and glory, and blessing. And every creature which is in heaven, and on the earth, and under the earth, and such as are in the sea and all that are in them, heard I saying, blessing, and honor, and glory, and power, be unto Him that sitteth upon the throne, (God the Father) and unto the Lamb (Jesus the Son) forever and ever.

chapter six

Black Pentecostals in Majority-White Denominations

CRAWFORD F. BRIGHT SR.
(1884–1952)

Church of God (Cleveland, Tennessee)

Florida native C. F. Bright was raised in the Primitive Baptist Church, where he was ordained as a deacon. He was ordained as a deacon in the Church of God in 1911 and began his preaching ministry in 1913. By 1916, he was ordained as a bishop in the Church of God and was appointed by General Overseer Ambrose J. Tomlinson to serve on the Questions and Answers Committee of the General Assembly, and as overseer of Pennsylvania in 1919, then of New Jersey in 1920.

Despite such overtures in a generally segregated denomination, Bright eventually left the denomination, claiming that "the colored would never be recognized with the whites." Within two years, however, he returned to the Church and God and resumed a fruitful ministry that saw him serving in numerous key positions within the Church of God Colored Work. By trade he was a successful carpenter, and his skill in this industry would serve the church of God well since he would be involved in building twenty-eight churches, including the Church of God Auditorium in Jacksonville, Florida, and the Church of God Industrial School and Orphanage in Eustis, Florida. Five of his twenty-two children became ministers.

Stick to the Church of God[1]

I want to sound a note of praise for His great Church this morning. Thank God I am one of her members today. I withdrew from the Church of God in Nov. 1920 but the Spirit did not seem to go with me and I failed to find glory all along the way. When I fully made up my mind that I would go back home to the Church of God the Lord began to bless and save souls for me. So I ran the first weeks meeting in the name of the Church of God in Baldwin, Fla. And three souls were saved, sanctified and "added to the Church" of God.

I think it was on the fourth of January, 1924, my wife and little son, C. F. Bright Jr., and myself were added to "the Church of God" again to stay till Jesus comes or calls. We have just returned from the West Coast District Convention of the Church of' God in Fla., where the Lord most wonderfully blessed us.

Dear ones I thank God for the Church of God and her government. Truly she is the only one of her mother. There is none like her.

I want to warn others not to let the devil fool you. Regardless of what others do, "stick with the Church of God." I thank God for our overseer, Brother David LaFleur, a real man of God. I thank Him for dear Brother Sapp, the pastor of the, Church of God at Sanford, where the convention was held. I also thank Him for many other dear ones we met while there. Glory to God! Hallelujah! I feel the glory now flooding my soul.

I thank God for the Bible training school and many other good things that

1. This article appeared in the *Church of God Evangel* 15/13 (March 29, 1924) 2. Courtesy of the Dixon Pentecostal Research Center, Cleveland, Tennessee.

he has given us in these last days. Oh how I love him and his Church, and I mean to stick to her and obey her government until Jesus comes.

May God bless all who read this is my prayer.

C. F. Bright
Rte 5, Box 32
Jacksonville, Fla

ROBERT HARRISON
(1928–2012)

Assemblies of God

Bright and talented, Robert Harrison was the grandson of Cornelia Jones Robertson, an Azusa Street Revival participant, an associate of Aimee Semple McPherson, and a fairly prominent Assemblies of God preacher and pastor. Harrison was converted at an evangelistic service while a student at San Francisco State College. Later, while he was attending the Assemblies of God's (AG's) Bethany Bible College, his professors recognized his giftedness and encouraged him to apply for ministerial credentials within the denomination. His 1951 application, however, was denied by the Northern California District because of his race, and he was counseled to seek credentials with a black denomination.

Harrison's giftedness did not escape the attention of more progressive Evangelicals, and in 1960 he was tapped to work for the Billy Graham Evangelistic Association. From that time until the mid-1960s Harrison worked prominently with that organization, undertaking evangelistic campaigns throughout the United States, Africa, and the Far East before being recognized by AG leadership, who, in 1957, apologized to Harrison for his past mistreatment and issued Harrison credentials as a licensed minister. Harrison went on to gain recognition in the AG and used that platform to push for greater racial justice and greater involvement of blacks within the denomination.

From *When God Was Black*

But What Can I Do?[2]

If you are white and a Christian and have read this far, I believe chances are pretty good that you really want to do something about the black potential for God in our midst.

Though there are plenty of racists in our churches, I believe there must be a great silent majority of people like yourself who honestly don't know what they can do. They are silent primarily because they are removed from the problem. They are not excluding blacks—they just don't know any blacks. They aren't the ones keeping blacks out of churches and conference grounds and seminaries and missionary conferences. Wrapped up in their own problems and their own enthusiasms, they simply are unaware of that great black exclusion.

This could not have been brought more forcefully home to me than at the World Congress on Evangelism in Berlin in 1966. Here was the leading evangelistic organization of our century calling the peoples of the world together to consider the lofty subject of "One Task, One Gospel, One Race."

There was much elaboration on this theme with position papers, lectures, and discussion groups. But the emphasis was almost exclusively on "one task" and "one gospel." There was no position paper on "one race."

Ostensibly we were there to discuss for at least one third of the time "one race." We were from all the races of' the world, and the matter of race was one of the crucial problems of that world. Yet the whole subject was virtually ignored. There were many at the Congress, myself included,

2. [Ed.] Bob Harrison with Jim Montgomery, *When God Was Black*, 144–53.

who believed that one of the greatest hindrances to the Gospel was the fact that we Christians didn't consider ourselves one race. We considered ourselves to be many different races and we tended to isolate ourselves along racial and national lines.

As the Congress was drawing to an end and we began to realize how lightly the subject was being treated, a number of Negro delegates got together and confronted Dr. Carl Henry with this omission.

I should say it was not just American blacks who were disturbed with the problem. Delegations from such places as India, South America, Africa and the Orient also felt the omission. As I have brought out elsewhere in this book, there is a growing revulsion among the emerging peoples of the world to the idea that white races are superior.

This certainly is a vivid illustration on the grand scale of what I have been talking about. The problem of the black Christian is so far removed from the white evangelical that even when he gets together for a World Congress to talk about one race, he inadvertently overlooks the whole issue.

The beauty of the whole situation, however, is that once confronted with it the Congress was quick to make a change. It was too late to include any position papers or discussion groups, but the Congress was preparing a final statement relating to its theme.

When we confronted Dr. Carl Henry with the omission, he immediately apologized for the omission and put us to work developing a statement about "one race" to be included in this final paper.

A number of us worked into the late hours. Some of those present besides myself were Jimmy McDonald, Dr. Howard Jones, Ralph Bell, the Rev. Lewis Johnson,

and the Rev. James E. Massey of the Church of God.

Our statement spoke to some of the injustices and sins of the evangelicals in their exclusion of minority groups. It addressed some of the issues relating to race and evangelism.

This part of the final statement really put a spotlight on the problem. I believe this was a tremendous victory. The results of the Congress were publicized around the world. The inclusion of such a strong statement about "one race" in the final paper has done much already to get people stirred up about what they can do. Some things have already been accomplished.

I take a great deal of encouragement from this. A great host of white Christians are ready to become involved, I believe, if they are just made aware of the problem and shown in a practical way what they can do.

Where can you start? Well, by reading this book you have already begun. Perhaps our biggest problem is one of an information gap between the white and black evangelical. By graciously taking time out to read my story, you have become much more aware of the real situation and the things that separate the two races. Perhaps for the first time you have become aware of the black brother as being a real identity.

There are many other good books on the market, both evangelical and secular. These can further enlighten you. You should subscribe to *Ebony* magazine, a black publication which can be picked up at almost any news stand. You'll find it to be a quality, entertaining and realistic periodical. It will keep you up to date with good articles and will review the books that will be most enlightening and helpful. Then share this information and literature with others. Get your friends to read the books and articles that shed light on the subject. Include in your discussion and training classes at church the place of the black Christians in world evangelism today. Get your pastor to speak on the subject. There is no substitute for this first step of a wide scattering of information.

Secondly, there is no escaping the Biblical pattern of righting a wrong by confession of sin. In many cases it might be primarily sins of omission and apathy rather than outright prejudice and racism. It should be personal confession as well as corporate confession by the local church, by denominations and by the Church as a whole in America. As you read on in this chapter perhaps more and more things will come to mind that need to be confessed.

Use a little imagination in your prayer and confession. The church has always been a minority and through the ages has been persecuted in one form or another. You should be able to identify with the black Christian who has carried the load of double minority persecution—being black and being an evangelical Christian.

Thirdly, I feel that the white Christian of America must once and for all flush from his mind those tricky theological rationalizations about the curse of the black man. The evangelical racist still uses the ninth chapter of Genesis to prove that the black man is cursed of God and therefore should be separate.

They preach that the curse of God was on all Hamites and that the Hamites were Negroes.

It's a ridiculous notion, of course, and would hardly deserve any attention except for the fact that some still preach it and many still have some residue of this idea in their minds.

If one takes a literal view of the passage he finds first of all that the curse was on Canaan, Ham's son, and not on Ham himself. Overlooking that, they then try to divide the peoples of the world into black, Oriental and white by saying that Ham was a Negro, Shem became the founder of the Oriental races, and Japheth the founder of the white races.

It's a wild theory at best and certainly not supported by careful scientific study let alone good Bible exegesis.

One shred of evidence that is referred to is that the Hebrew word for Ham means dark color or swarthy. This is interpreted to apply to Negroes.

But of course there are swarthy Greeks, Indians, Spaniards, Filipinos or any number of peoples around the world.

Even if it were true that the Negro race was cursed along with the curse of Ham, what do we do with the work of Jesus Christ on Calvary which obliterated all curses and all sins? The whole idea is just too much to swallow. I hope the thinking Christians of America will bury this wild hypothesis.

An even more absurd attempt to drag segregation out of the Bible comes from Paul's message at Athens recorded in Acts 17:26. It says, "And he made from one every nation of men to live on all the face of the earth, having determined allotted periods and the boundaries of their habitation."

Even if this verse did support segregation, how anyone could get out of this that just Negroes should be segregated is beyond me. If we're going to segregate on the basis of this verse, we're going to have to segregate our Swedes and our Italians and our Greeks and our Jews and our Orientals and everyone else in America.

Furthermore, let's stop calling the black Christian "our dear colored brother," as if he were a separate category of Christian. It's quite apparent what color I am. I can't hide that. I can even be kidded about it. But when I am categorized as being another kind of a Christian, then we are missing the great, beautiful thing that Jesus Christ brought: There is a oneness in Christ that overshadows all other differences.

After being informed and after confessing and cleansing our minds of all stupid racial prejudices, then the white Christian must in the fourth place, begin to *do* something. I have often found in talking with people that they imply that because they can't do everything, they can't do anything. What they really must mean is that they *don't want* to do anything. They don't want to become involved. Why go out of the way to look for trouble?

Jesus could have said that about all of the races. Why become involved in humanity? What would it bring him but sorrow and pain and grief?

There is no way we can serve the Lord effectively without becoming involved. And there is no way to help the Negro serve the Lord effectively without becoming involved.

The least you can do is to insist on a series of exchanges in your church. Think what it would do for the church of Jesus Christ all over America if the white churches invited black pastors and black singers and black converts to give their testimonies. The lines of communication would be opened. Understanding would begin. Even love would blossom as blacks and whites found the great unifying factor of love for Jesus Christ being a common bond that surmounts all other obstacles.

And by the way, don't *just* invite black musicians. That only perpetuates the stereotype that blacks are very musical. There is more to us than that.

Exchanges will help the black realize that he has something to give as well as something to get. But there are other activities typically held in white churches that the blacks need to experience. The next time your church holds a missionary or Bible conference you ought to invite delegations from black churches to attend and provide a bus to pick them up if necessary. Their experiences in these areas are so limited that they wouldn't know where to start on their own. But by observing and participating in what you are doing, they will quickly learn and will begin doing the same in their churches. It will be all the better if you have blacks participating on the platform in these conferences to help your guests identify with the program.

You will have some opposition to this in your church. But somewhere along the line someone must be willing to stand on conviction and do what is right and necessary. The time for mere talk has surely long since passed.

Another thing you can do is to begin putting pressure on Christian schools and seminaries, conference grounds and missionary organizations. If a host of white Christians began doing this, each in his own circle of influence, the tide would be irresistible.

You can take that step farther. Many such institutions are now eager to include blacks but don't know how to contact them or how to get them to attend. This was the question in a group of leaders with whom I was talking at Mt. Hermon. They wanted blacks at their conferences but the plaintive question always was, "How can we get them here?"

Whites must actively seek the participation of blacks. We blacks are so ignorant of what is commonly available to the white Christian that you are going to have to make an effort to inform us. Then you are going to have to make a determined effort to convince us we are really wanted.

Every black Christian in America has had dozens of experiences where he has been offered something but only in politeness. He must not only hear that he is welcome, but he must see demonstrated that he is definitely wanted.

In many cases this might even involve subsidizing blacks. The history of excluding blacks has been too long and too deep for you to simply sit back and say that any black can come who wants to. Think what it would mean if you as an individual or if your local church sponsored some black young people to a summer conference. It would undoubtedly make a great spiritual impact on their lives as well as help them and the white campers become acquainted in a natural setting. In knocking about the grounds for a week together, black and white kids would discover just what normal human beings the people of each group are.

If this were done on a wide scale throughout the country, we would soon see blacks pouring into our Christian schools, into pulpits around the country and into evangelistic and missionary organizations. The great black potential would begin to be developed for the cause of Christ.

Right now and certainly as more and more black Christian leaders are being trained, every evangelical organization should have a strong recruitment program to include Negroes. If each of these organizations used any part of the ingenuity they have put to work in getting the white Christian to part with his dollar in meeting this issue, we would see the black church coming to life.

Another thing, I have honestly written that the point of what I am saying is not to get churches integrated. This is a side issue. But it still is a tragic thing to see the white churches fleeing from the inner cities as black Christians move in. When the neighborhood starts turning black, the white Christian can't get out of there fast enough. Then, having abandoned his ministry, the white Christian wants to sell his church to the black Christians moving in. This only perpetuates the conditions excluding Negroes from the challenge and training and inspiration they would get in white evangelical circles.

Frequently, this means selling the church to a "liberal" black church. If you would ask the pastor if he believed in the virgin birth, or miracles, or the resurrection and so on, he would say that he did. But if you began asking members if they had ever personally committed their lives to Jesus Christ for salvation they would not understand. The Gospel as such has never been clearly presented to them. The only invitation they have ever heard from the pulpit is the pastor saying, "The doors of the church are now open." By this he means to say that everyone ought to be a church member and you are now invited to join.

"Give me your hand and God your heart," he says. Anyone coming forward to join the church either by "profession of faith" or baptism is immediately voted in by a motion from someone in the congregation and a raising of hands. I have never seen anyone turned down.

By "profession of faith" the new member means that he gives mental assent to the historical Jesus. He believes all that the Bible says. But it is an historical belief. The truths of the Bible are usually related to social justice and not spiritual life. He does not deny the cardinal doctrines but at the same time he does not know about a personal relationship with Jesus Christ.

When your church flees the approaching black tide and sells out to a black congregation, this is the spiritual ministry you are leaving behind. Aren't you proud of yourself?

How beautiful it would be if instead of this the white churches of our cities would follow a suggestion I made to an Assemblies of God Church in east Oakland. They left the black neighborhood as it enveloped them. Nothing wrong here. But instead of abandoning the church, my suggestion was that they sell it to the mission board of the denomination. They in turn could develop a black church with a black pastor who was strongly evangelical and would really meet the spiritual needs of the community. We can't begin to say we are going into all the world to preach the Gospel if we deny this wonderful message to the very ones moving into our neighborhoods.

Your church may not be in such an inner city community—most congregations have already fled to the suburbs (something that needs confessing?)—but you can still "mother" a church in ghetto areas. Again, the Assemblies denomination has begun to really think about this. In a top level meeting gathered specifically to talk about the black church problem, it was suggested that if every district of the denomination provided buildings and black pastors for one ghetto church, the denomination would immediately have forty-seven new congregations. It is such creative thinking that is going to make a difference in the problem we face.

There is just no end to the amount of things you and your church can do if you'll just apply some ingenuity and brainstorming creativity to the problem. All the bases, from ghetto Sunday schools and vacation Bible schools to helping sponsor black pastors to missionary tours, can be touched.

Somewhere along the line someone is going to have to stand up and be counted. There is too much at stake to let ten million black Christians continue to drift when we could see their potential energized in a tremendous way in the cause of Christ and world evangelism.

Once Around Jericho[3]

Now let me say something to my black brother. Obviously there is not going to be any real change if we expect only the white Christian to make all the efforts necessary. There is much we can do and should do and must do if we are going to realize the potential in our black churches.

I think we have to change our attitudes. We must come to the full realization that when God is black, God is *God*. He can do the same mighty exploits through us that He can through anyone else.

In this light we must stop feeling sorry for our black skin which brings injustice and discrimination. Isn't God bigger than these? If He can feed a multitude, heal the sick, raise the dead, overcome the devil himself, do you think for a moment that He can't overcome any apparent disadvantages of our blackness and all it represents?

So our black skin brings us lower paying jobs, poor housing, inferior education for our children. Jesus suffered worse

---

3. [Ed.] Bob Harrison with Jim Montgomery, *When God Was Black*, 154–59.

than these, yet He changed the course of the history of the world.

And this same Jesus lives in us.

We are going to have to change our attitudes about our responsibility to the world about us. We have been discriminated against and the white man owes us a lot in the secular sense. But as born again children of God we owe Him a lot, too.

The time has come for us to stop using the excuses that we can't go to the white Bible school or to the white conference grounds or go out as missionaries with white societies or join other white evangelical organizations, or even attend a white church if that is the place where you can get the best training to serve Jesus. If these institutions are the places we must go to be fully equipped for the work of the ministry then we must knock on their doors until they let us in. The tide of history is on our side. They are going to have to let us in, but we're going to have to do the knocking. We can't all wait until some enlightened white Christian comes to our door with a big scholarship and begs us to attend his school. The responsibility is ours just as much as it is his.

Man, take a look at my life again. Sure, I can sing and I learned to preach. But you have some abilities and talents I don't have. Look at Romans 12, and I Corinthians 12, and Ephesians 4 and you'll find that God has given gifts to *all* His people.

I had to fight—and I didn't always win—to have the chance to use my gifts and you probably will too. One school wouldn't take me and another wouldn't let me preach in their denomination. Finally they said I could preach but I couldn't become an ordained minister. I quit fighting for a while, but God opened some doors so that I could get after them again. Now, as a direct result of that fight, a black can

go to any of their schools. I was their first ordained minister but they now have twenty-five and are begging for more. A few years ago they were ignoring blacks but now they are meeting frequently to talk about nothing but what they can do to help us get the training and challenge and experience we need to make something of ourselves.

Those first years as pastor in Fillmore were no cup of tea either. But I did the best I could in the situation where God put me, and it wasn't long before I was singing and preaching in Europe and Africa and Asia and Latin America. Then God opened up doors with Billy Graham and Overseas Crusades and formerly lily-white pulpits in conference centers and churches and schools.

God might not have the same program for you. The point is that He can and wants to develop your abilities to the very highest for His glory. If you're willing to take a chance and pay the price He'll do just that.

I'm not promising, of course, that everyone is going to make us feel entirely welcome and comfortable. But the Father didn't promise that to the Son when He sent Him into the world either. We are followers of Jesus first and blacks second or third or fourth.

And I'm not promising that some big white daddy is going to pay all the bills. Our young people are going to have to sweat and sacrifice and work and borrow to attend the camps and schools that are going to prepare us for service. Our pastors and our churches are going to have to raise scholarship funds and raise support for a host of black missionaries going out to the corners of the world.

I know our people will respond to the challenges of our day if some will just take the leadership. Rev. Ernie Johnson, then with Overseas Crusades, and I hold a capsule missionary conference in the San Francisco Revival Center not too long ago. Rev. Don Green, pastor of the 250 members, realized that his black congregation knew little about missions but wanted to do something about it.

We started with a Friday night rally, held a men's breakfast Saturday morning and a ladies' luncheon Saturday noon, and then emphasized missions in all departments and the church service on Sunday. It was thrilling to see the response. They had stretched their faith and set a goal to raise $5,000 for foreign missions. When their faith promises were counted, they had raised over $8,000.

One 65-year-old member said that he thought that missions was just for women. "At the men's breakfast I realized it was for men, too," he said as he made his faith promise. The whole congregation was turned on by the opportunities of service and involvement in foreign missions. The church pledged $100.00 a month to my ministry, promised to fully support a black missionary nurse to Haiti, and plans to send their pastor on a missionary tour.

Pastor Green's church is not a special case. The congregation consists of many domestics and others getting by on minimum salaries. But when the needs and opportunities and challenges of foreign missions were presented, they couldn't wait to get involved.

We need to see hundreds upon hundreds of missionary conferences like this in our churches across the land. You may have to join with a white church the first time to learn what to do and to get some of your top leaders enthused, but it will be well worth the effort.

I think the time is coming when we blacks are going to have to start our own black Christian institutions.

I've been saying, for instance, that it is becoming more and more of an advantage to have a dark skin when going to the emerging nations of the world as missionaries.

But get this picture: You go to a country as a missionary. You convince the nationals that God is God of the brown man, too. Then the head of your mission visits the field. The man who makes the decisions, who handles the purse strings. His skin is white. Now what are you going to tell your nationals?

It was my pleasure to help start and serve as a board member for the Fellowship Bible Institute in San Francisco which now after ten years of operation has about fifty students. Dessy Webster, the founder and president, found an old house which he had rebuilt to serve as a school.

We need a lot of Dessy Websters who have vision and faith enough to start with whatever they have available.

There is much more we must do. I hope I've said much of this by my life and my testimony and hope you've gotten the picture. Now that you've read this book, go out and *do* something. Go out and *be* something. God is black, and God is *God*.

As I write this final chapter I feel a deep sense of guilt and frustration. In this last word I've been addressing my remarks to "white Christians" and to "black Christians" and thereby perpetrating the very idea I abhor.

In Jesus Christ we are not two groups but one.

Paul speaks of Christ's followers as making up a body.

This body of Jesus Christ is made up of black parts and white parts and brown parts and red parts and yellow parts. The white parts of the body of Christ cannot say to the black part, "You are only black, I have no need of you." Neither can the black part say, "Since I am only black, I don't have to take my responsibility in the body of Christ."

This cannot be any more than the eye can say to the hand, "I have no need of you," or the head to the feet,, "I have no need of you" (I Cor 12:21).

In this book I have had to refer to "white Christians" and "black Christians" simply as a practical matter to be understood. But my dream and my prayer is that someday we will be able to say these words about "black" and "white" Christians:

> On the contrary, the parts of the body which seem to be weaker are indispensable, and those parts of the body which we think less honorable we invest with the greater honor, and our unpresentable parts are treated with greater modesty, which our more presentable parts do not require. But God has so adjusted the body, giving the greater honor to the inferior part, that there may be no discord in the body, but that the members may have the same care for one another. If one member suffers, all suffer together; if one member is honored, all rejoice together.
>
> Now you [black, brown, white] are the body of Christ. (1 Cor 12:22–27 RSV)

When Christians everywhere finally realize that we are one body, we won't have to talk anymore about what happens when God is black. All of us will coordinate together as one beautiful body, each having the opportunity and accepting the responsibility for going into all the world and preaching the Gospel to every creature.

The walls have come tumblin' down in my life, but for the whole black church we've only been once around Jericho. We 'have twelve more laps and a great shout to go before the enemy is defeated.

May Christians of all colors join together to bring the victory. For the enemy is not the white man or the black man but the devil himself. Let us together be more than conquerors for Christ.

DORETHA O'QUINN
(1951–)

International Church of the Foursquare Gospel

Doretha O'Quinn is an ordained minister in the International Church of the Foursquare Gospel. She began attending a Foursquare church in 1965. Her forty-five years of involvement has included 40 years of ministry. In addition to being a member of Foursquare's board of directors, she serves on the National Church Committee and the Urban & Multicultural Committee.

After O'Quinn earned a BA in theology at Life Pacific, she later became a trustee of the institution. She went on to earn her PhD in intercultural education at Biola University. O'Quinn taught and worked as an administrator at a number of educational institutions, including in the public school system and in Christian schools, and at Azusa Pacific University before assuming the positions of associate dean and associate professor at Point Loma Nazarene University. Currently O'Quinn serves as vice-provost of multiethnic and cross-cultural engagement at Biola University. She also sits on the board of directors for the International Church of the Foursquare Gospel.

From *Silent Voices, Powerful Messages*

Let Their Works Speak for Them and the Strength of Their Faith Live On in Us

A few years ago I had the honor of teaching what was called the New Foundation Class from *This We Believe*, the Foursquare curriculum used for new members to teach the doctrine, history and beliefs of the Foursquare Church. As my students asked questions and reviewed pictures from several of the books documenting Foursquare history, a particular young woman asked, "After hearing about the history of this denomination and looking at these pictures, I want to know if there was any involvement of African-Americans that contributed to or influenced this denomination?"

Immediately I said, "Yes there were," and briefly recalled the names of those [early African American pioneers]. I was awakened the next morning at about 3 a.m. with a strong sense of God's call to write about the remarkable lives of the early African-American pioneers of the Foursquare Gospel movement . . . to the stories of the beginnings of the African-American Foursquare Church and those whose lives had the greatest impact on the Church's history for African-Americans . . .

The stories . . . encapsulate the influence and contributions of African-Americans both in advancing the full Gospel of Jesus Christ and in advancing the growth and development of the Foursquare Gospel Movement in spite of many challenges, and at times, oppositions. It is my firm desire to give sound to the African-American Foursquare pioneers' silent voices and powerful messages left behind for all who serve in the Foursquare Church today to hear.

Just as the Foursquare movement began in the city of Los Angeles in Southern California, so did the African-American Foursquare Church. Aimee Semple McPherson began her ministry with an unwavering strong conviction about the inclusion of people of all ethnicities. This was demonstrated by the tremendous courage she showed in holding tent meetings in the southern states in the early 1900s that welcomed African-Americans (then called "colored") and "whites," together. "Sister" McPherson also held tent meetings exclusively for African-Americans which, in fact, was illegal at the time. When she opened Angelus Temple in 1923, she encouraged people of all ethnicities to openly participate in ministry there. She founded LIFE Bible College, calling on African-Americans and women to enroll. Such a thing was practically unheard of at the time. African-Americans did attend in impressive numbers.

Those African-Americans who graduated from LIFE Bible College during the 1920s and 1930s went on to be actively engaged in ministry activities such as quartets that sang on the Radio Station KFSG (Kall Four Square Gospel), prayer counselors in the 500 room of Angelus Temple for 24-hour intercessory prayer, altar workers for services preached by Sister McPherson and any other capacity needed. It was during the 1930s that the first African-American who entered LIFE Bible College graduated. However, [Pearl and Wardell Tolliver] did not begin the first African-American Foursquare Church until 1942. This signified the beginning of a new community of churches within the Foursquare movement.

The experiences of these great pioneers reveal the depth of their sense of call, commitment, obedience and understanding of God during very difficult times in society for African-Americans . . . and individual stories of amazing personal and spiritual strength, of remarkable accomplishments, of racial challenges and of incredible oppositions . . . personal accounts of the ministries of these early "true pioneers" . . . Their relationship with God empowered them with enormous abilities to find alternatives to the blatant racism encountered. The unique strategies they discovered for church growth were centered around great amounts of personal time spent meeting the needs of the members and building the church community as one family. The early pioneers . . . were true to the beliefs of the Foursquare doctrine. They taught and developed their congregations to support and consistently uphold the standards and the Foursquare doctrine as a way of life. God always set the direction for these strong leaders who were totally committed to the Word of God. They built a church network interconnected in terms of support and encouragement and trust throughout the duration of their leadership.

Each in his or her own way contributed to the growth of the Foursquare Church, both financially and in sheer numbers. They taught their congregations the value of community as the church family. Empowerment for service was at all levels—young children, teens, adults and seniors. Fulfilling what they knew to be the will of God and meeting needs of the community were at the heart of the ministry of these early pioneers. Aimee Semple McPherson, [was the] founder of the Foursquare movement, whose unfailing commitment was that her ministry provide inclusion and acknowledgement of gifts and abilities of African-Americans. Her willingness and desire to be inclusive by her lifestyle and behavior are documented in her writings. Sister McPherson did not compromise God's Word even in the face of laws that forbade her to open her meetings to African-Americans. Sister McPherson publicly acknowledged

God's love was for all, that at the foot of the cross all men were the same.

Along with Angelus Temple, Sister McPherson founded LIFE Bible College where students were trained in methods that helped them understand and study the Bible in order to teach others. The African-American students developed a kinship and a support system for each other as they began their churches. LIFE Bible College training not only gave them resources for developing sermons for public ministry, doctrine and spiritual formation principles, but also instructed them in business strategies such as accounting and bookkeeping, ministry development, property management and ethics in business through accountability. They also learned endurance, self-motivation, community preservation and a strong sense of commitment to God and His commitment to them.

Following Sister McPherson's death, the leadership in the Foursquare denomination became resistant to assisting African-American churches and began erecting walls of hidden prejudice and discrimination. Rather than allow these walls to become detours to their inclusion and involvement, these pioneers began home meetings that were soon to birth African-American Foursquare churches, unlike white churches that began in church buildings. Within two to three years of each other, two of the first African-American Foursquare churches opened in storefront sanctuaries.

Two of the first African-American pastoral husband and wife teams, Rev. Pearl and Wardell Tolliver and Rev. Curtis and Alma Hammond, were all graduates of LIFE Bible College. Rev. Pearl and Wardell Tolliver opened the doors of the first African-American Foursquare Church in a small home meeting on Hooper Avenue in Los Angeles, California, in 1942. The Hammonds opened their church shortly after. Sister McPherson was still alive when the Tollivers began their church in a small home.

Wardell was very supportive of Pearl and the powerful ministry she possessed. Read their story and learn the personal accounts from members who served with them. Understand through reading their life experiences the characteristics of true heroes. Learn the historical accounts of their church struggles. The pastoral teams embraced the obstacles and transformed them into stepping stones to victories. Hooper Avenue is now pastored by Rev. Donald T. Paredes.

Curtis and Alma Hammond began their ministry in the 1950s in a home in Compton, California. Their ministry to children was an effective way to reach the parents and to develop their church. This church is on the property purchased by the early members of Carver Foursquare Church and is now pastored by Rev. Horace and Brenda Doby.

As Sister McPherson's accomplishments as a strong woman of ministry captured the nation's attention, they also captured the attention of a young woman by the name of Rev. Johnnie L. Smith who became the first female Foursquare African-American pastor.

She was a student of Sister McPherson and a graduate of LIFE Bible College. "Moma Johnnie" taught us that her strength was in perseverance. Moma Johnnie's uncompromising trust in God, her prayer life, confidence and wise investments all demonstrated her remarkable leadership. Married, she had the strong support of her husband who was not in public ministry, but their pastoral care enhanced the lives of many in the inner city of Los Angeles. After graduating from LIFE Bible College, Moma Johnnie was sent by the Foursquare denomination to Monrovia, California, in 1948 to pastor a church. By her own words, "Nothing was growing in Monrovia," so she returned to Los Angeles to begin in her home, then on to a storefront on 48th and Avalon called Avalon Zion Foursquare Church, later moving to the current location on 55th and Avalon. The church remains on 55th and Avalon, pastored by Rev. Frank Holley.

Dorthy Hall, a protégé of Moma Johnnie, [showed] courage in using the strategies learned under Moma Johnnie's leadership as a female African-American pastor. Shortly after graduation from LIFE Bible College, Dorthy accepted an assignment to pioneer the first African-American church in Houston, Texas. Dorthy began this church in her home and later built the Way of the Cross Foursquare Church. She was not exempt from racial prejudice but her perseverance and willingness to confront the issue caused a heart-to-heart change.

Dorthy's ability to pastor a church while coping with tremendous personal health challenges, financial battles and other oppositions originated in the character of a brave and courageous woman who understood the power of God. Prior to her passing in June 2001, Dorthy remained the pastor of Way of the Cross Foursquare Church of Houston, Texas.

One of the Foursquare movement's largest ministry outreaches is to foreign countries or what is commonly called the "mission field." There has been only one African-American appointed as a Foursquare missionary to full-time service, after graduating from LIFE Bible College. Her name was Rev. Lucile Marie Johnson. Hers is a story of one of the greatest African-American challenges observed in this denomination. The story of Marie's resiliency, fortitude and faith to withstand the delay of her assignment is a story of long-suffering and patience to fulfill such a heartfelt passion for her ministry. For me, the opportunity to discover Marie's influence and contribution to the Foursquare movement resulted in one of the most exciting discoveries I could have made, one that is humbling.

This woman, so filled with passion, loyalty and determination, was related to my husband, Michael. His mother was Grace Bunche, the sister of the renowned and highly respected Ralph Bunche, Jr. Marie Johnson was their first cousin. What an honor and a challenge for me to hold on to such an incomparable mantle.

Rev. Payne LeVais tells his personal story of literally giving up everything to go to Puerto Rico without Foursquare support because God told him to do so. I was personally challenged by the willingness and commitment of one man's passion to give up everything to follow God's leading. His courage to sell all his possessions and move his family to a foreign country without any financial support evidenced his total commitment and faith in God. Rev. LeVais was allowed to maintain his pastoral position of First Foursquare Church of Compton while in Puerto Rico, until a change in Foursquare leadership required he return home or lose his church. Marie and Payne LeVais were among the first African-Americans to go to the mission field.

During one of the most intense racial climates since the Civil War, Marvin and Juanita Smith accepted a pastoral position at South LaBrea (later named West Adams) Foursquare Church, a church on the verge of being racially segregated from its community. The story of the Smiths is nothing less than an exciting account of two of the most creative and innovative pastors to serve in the Foursquare movement. This pastoral couple whose marriage was made in heaven stood together in ministry against hell. Their numerous accomplishments were always partnered with challenges and obstacles. They were a team in every sense of the word. They functioned so complementary to each other that it was difficult not to admire them just for their example of a married couple in ministry. They had an enduring love for people, a passionate desire to empower members of all ages for leadership and a willingness beyond measure to believe God and work hard to achieve the impossible. The fruit of their labors resulted in major church growth, building expansion, national and international travels, numerous church ministries, development of non-profit organizations, a Bible training institute and other ministry developments.

Their story will create and strengthen any aspirations you may have for learning the benefits of empowering people, and will cause a desire in you to know them and learn how they brought about such tremendous accomplishments. You will come to know their God who gave them such great vision! Since the Smiths' pastorate of West Adams Foursquare Church, there have been two pastors and two church name changes. It is as though the name of West Adams Foursquare Church is spoken synonymously with Marvin and Juanita Smith.

LIFE Bible College was the beneficiary of one of the most dynamic scholars ever to grace its portals—Dr. Paul L. Hackett. For many years, Dr. Hackett was the sole African-American professor at LIFE Bible College. Even so, he was primarily responsible for the largest enrollment of African-Americans and Anglos

during the late 1960s, 1970s and 1980s. Dr. Hackett was an inspiring teacher, a knowledgeable theologian, and taught God's Word with compassion. He traveled the United States and Canada, preaching and teaching in Foursquare churches and representing LIFE Bible College as a recruiter. The prejudice and racism that he experienced as an African-American professor while teaching at LIFE Bible College, he used as effective teaching tools to educate students and colleagues about racial issues and bridging race relationships. It is the testimony of many Anglo students that it was because of Brother Hackett that they attended the college.

The term "brother" was an endearing term to him since he spent so much of his life being in a cross-cultural setting. He was considered a brilliant man when it came to teaching the Scriptures. He made the Bible come alive! It goes without saying that many African-Americans attended because of his influence. Dr. Hackett faced one of his greatest losses during one of the years he taught at LIFE.[4] True to his teaching gifts, he used this loss to teach his students a great lesson of personal courage and strength. His actions after this tragedy made a lasting impression on the lives of many Foursquare pastors. His love for the Word and his students, and his unique ability to ardently train future ministers in the Foursquare denomination and other churches had great impact for God's kingdom, bringing about the birth of many of today's Foursquare churches, especially [those that are] African-American.

The contribution and influence of these great leaders that commissioned

---

4. [Ed.] Dr. Hackett's wife, Dorothy, was diagnosed with colon cancer and subsequently died, leaving him with four children to raise. See O'Quinn, *Silent Voices, Powerful Messages*, 177–78.

me to preserve their stories. Their courageous and enduring dedication not only advanced their local church, but leadership among African-Americans in the Foursquare movement. The early pioneers you will read about in this book were true to the beliefs of the Foursquare doctrine. They taught and developed their congregations to support and consistently uphold the standards and the doctrine as a way of life.

Their stories are a direct result of this promise from God, "God is not unjust; he will not Forget your work and the love you have shown him as you have helped his people and continue to help them. We want each of you to show this same diligence to the very end, in order to make your hope sure. We do not want you be become lazy, but to imitate those who through Faith and patience inherit what has been promised." (Heb 7:10–12)

A New Foursquare Community is Organized

I recently attended a seminar session on the "History and Philosophy of Community Organizing." As the presenter proceeded to identify the seven characteristics of a community organizer, I said to myself, "That's it, that's exactly what these pioneers were 'community organizers' of the African-American Foursquare Church in Los Angeles." Even though these terms are new in our culture today, this was God's mission. Community organizers begin at the grassroots level and are typically silent voices because they are not large in number and it is the commitment to what is to be accomplished that produces powerful messages. These incredible pioneers were Silent Voices with a Powerful Message.

To organize a community, one must know the interest and needs of the people and engage them in the process. They must understand the rules or guidelines to effectively operate within the system that needs to develop (for our pioneers it was the Foursquare Church) and adjust the rules to meet one's community needs. In addition, one must not only understand the rules, but play by them.

Each of these pioneers learned the Foursquare Church system through their studies at LIFE Bible College; in their own individual styles, they developed the vision God gave them in conjunction with the principles they learned to effectively reach their unique communities. The seven characteristics of a community organizer are power, ability to build relationships, identifying self-interest, ownership by participation and involvement, not doing anything for anyone they can do for themselves, empowering people and agitation.[5] I would add an eighth that would become first on the list for each of these pioneers and that is: Answering the call of God in one's life.

They Were Called by God

Each of our pioneers publicly acknowledged the call of God in their lives and the results were evident. The call was to become the first African-Americans involved as pastors, missionaries and teachers in the Foursquare Church. They responded first by understanding His call and then by developing a relationship with Him. For these pioneers, developing the relationship involved prayer, reading the Bible and acknowledging [the call] to others. The preparation for fulfilling their

5. Jim Field, "History and Philosophy of Community Organization."

specific responsibilities after answering the call began by attending LIFE Bible College. Following their preparation, each knew they had met the requirements of the Foursquare Church and took that as authority to begin. The powerful example, affirmation and encouragement of Sister McPherson had a great impact and influence on the ministry of the Tollivers, Sis. Pauline Duvalle and Moma Johnnie.

Power but not Empowerment

The ability to change the lives of people comes from power. These pioneers acknowledged that their ministries were the result of the power of God. Their ability to achieve what they did, in the face of obstacles and oppositions to external empowerment and inclusion, left only the internal power to make their accomplishments reality. While they were not necessarily empowered by those who led the Foursquare movement following the death of Sister McPherson, confidence in God and the principles they learned assured them of the internal power that again and again led the way to success.

Such understanding of God's call enabled them to triumph over those who opposed them and who constantly threw up road-blocks. They boldly confronted the issues causing opposition when necessary; on other occasions, they chose an alternative which often was in the best interest of the people they led and fulfilled the plan of God. Their spiritual power was the source of their great strength. They believed in themselves, one another and the power of God to work in them. These early pioneers recognized a great principle that revolutionized their ministry and could do the same for today's African-American Foursquare Church.

Waiting for man's empowerment becomes a great limitation; obedience to God's power in you, in spite of opposition and obstacles, is freedom, growth and success in ministry.

These Pioneers Built Relationships with Their People

Our pioneers took the time to get to know their people and their needs in their ministries. Church functions were solely to bring their congregations closer and build community. Most of their ministries began in homes and with the younger generations in that children became the focus of these pioneers. The greatest investments were made in building the lives of children even though they were not the tithers. Reaching out to children resulted in bringing many families into the church. They kept the interest of the people first during the times when segregation laws presented prohibitions in this nation and in parts of the Foursquare Church.

The church mission and program development of the early pioneers involved building the lives of the people served based on what they learned while spending time with them. The education received at LIFE Bible College prepared these pioneers to be good teachers and trainers. Their effective teaching and training were the primary reasons that the churches grew to the extent they did. The church growth produced a need to train, develop and empower new leaders within the congregation to work with the increasing opportunities in the church and community. Those who could afford to further their leadership in the Foursquare movement enrolled in LIFE Bible College.

The influx of African-Americans attending LIFE Bible College was a direct result of [the work of] Dr. Paul Hackett which, in turn, was a direct result of his spending time in churches, answering personal questions of young African-American high school students and sharing great teaching which they could also expect at the college. Relationships built among the African-American Foursquare churches provided frequent community support when addressing problems or concerns, especially matters of racism and prejudice. These pioneers created a cohesive support system when there was overt racism or prejudice experienced at public events. Their inner strength and faith in God often allowed them to overlook, forgive or use alternative strategies that define them as true pioneers. They saw their ministries as a support to one another, rather than a threat.

The early African-American Foursquare churches fellowshipped together, ate together, participated in special events together and often supported one another. Pastors took the time to build relationships with one another through holiday events, special services and integration of their congregations. They lived and understood unity, love and compassion, all of which resulted in ongoing growth of their churches.

What They Accomplished

Their accomplishments can be characterized as similar to that of today's definition of a community organizer's self-interest or personal goals. However, as a bit of contrast, their self-interest was encased in God's interest which focused on building people of all ages. This interest found in each of the lives of these pioneers was building faith in God's Word, building hope and building perseverance for

success in the lives of people who had often experienced rejection. They empowered members in their congregations to make God's vision a reality through teaching, training and providing opportunities to become leaders and developers of their personal ministry. Their greatest instruction to those who followed them was articulated by the examples the leaders showed in their personal lives. They worked successfully within a system that often changed the rules which meant defeat at times. Their members learned from the action of these pioneers that there was more than one solution to what seemed to be almost impossible situations. They exemplified and brought an internal strength to the people they led, not only by the words they spoke but by their lifestyle. And it was a two-way street. The commitment of the members was one of phenomenal support when it came to building new facilities, development of new ministries, obtaining financial support and other areas of need. Yet one of the greatest accomplishments for our pioneers must be their unfailing investment in the lives of their members, and at the same time the continual denial of their own personal self-interest or goals. Each of these pioneers exhibited a total commitment to fulfillment of the interest of God (spiritual development and maturity) in the lives of the people they led.

Personal Involvement and Participation Meant Ownership by the Congregation

These African-American spiritual heroes were as involved in the development of the churches they served in as the people they led. If there were buildings to build, food to cook and other responsibilities to be completed, they worked alongside the people. They expected the people to "own" their role as a community and church partner and participant by demonstrating their responsibility and involvement in church development through their fundraising efforts, church building projects and other social functions. [They often used] personal pronouns such as "us," "we," and "our," signifying their personal ownership of the church, in particular, ownership of the responsibilities within the ministry. The spiritual development of children was the responsibility of all adults. The training and development of new leaders was everyone's role.

Involvement and inclusion of new members (children or adults) was to happen through members of the congregation. Church growth was not taught by consultants in seminars but by members in the congregation reaching out to their immediate community and speaking about their personal relationship with God and their respective church[es].

These early pioneers knew the secret of what it took to build a church. They recognized that people were the church and the building only accommodated the people as the numbers required.

They only built buildings when the people needed more space because of growth. Investing in people and what was important to them were always clear to the early pioneers because they sought out God for direction and they knew He knew the needs of the people. The faith of the early pioneers and their confidence in God was central to everything they set out to do. The results followed.

These characteristics transformed their congregations and caused members to respond as owners of the ministry of their churches.

They Dealt with the World as It Was, Not as They Wanted It to Be, "They Kept it Real"

The early pioneers' relationship with God was real. God spoke to them and they acted upon His directions. There was prejudice, injustice, racism, exclusion and it was not hidden. This was the world as it was during their leadership from the 1920s through the 1980s. What appeared to be decision-making delays or standstills, exclusions from missionary opportunities, and token positions at LIFE Bible College were real-life experiences for these early pioneers. Conditions improved through the years but the reality was, in the Foursquare denomination, African-American pastors held few positions of authority to make decisions other than in their local churches.

Each of these leaders would naturally have wanted to be offered leadership opportunities at the board levels or decision-making levels. But they realized it was not to happen. Even though there were a few attempts to choose one or two African-Americans for certain positions, it seemed to some African-Americans to be genuine inclusion and value. Knowledge, experience, expertise, skills—these were the qualifications for leadership that these African-American pioneers wanted as the basis for advancement opportunities in the denomination. This was not to be, so they worked in the real world, their local churches. There were results: growth and development in personal relationships with God, spiritual development, personal ministry development, new students in LIFE Bible College and even TV ministries. Their reality was empowering people to embrace a personal faith in God for a successful life.

Their accomplishments were not recognized. It forced the most successful pioneer couple to work outside the exclusively designed Foursquare denomination's institutional system, and inside God's vision to cause their reality to outgrow the accomplishments of the denomination both nationally and internationally. The struggles experienced were not what they expected, much less how they wanted to build their churches. But they learned through dealing with their world as it was that people were the community God called them to, not an organization or building. In my opinion, the lack of inclusion, representation and empowerment of the newest community at every board or administrative level of the Foursquare movement during the days of these great pioneers was a travesty, and it continues to adversely impinge on effectively bridging cross-cultural relationships with African-American Foursquare churches today.

They Didn't Expect the Foursquare Denomination to Build Their Ministry, They Worked Hard

"Don't do anything for anyone that they can do for themselves" is a definition of empowerment. The early pioneers did not expect or depend on the Foursquare leadership to build their churches or contribute to their work. They received their direction from God and followed his plan. Even though they had every right to expect the denomination to support their work with resources and other provisions, they realized these resources were among them and moved forward.

The early pioneers had an ideal model in the life of Sister McPherson. They applied her strategies to the work

of the small churches and they were very effective in bringing about the growth of each of the churches. They believed in themselves and the people being the vessels God would use to build their churches and ministries. They remained focused on and pursued together the goal and vision they were given by God.

Their extended community of churches meant developing relationships with other African-American denominations, yet they built their own church community. Their growth in every area was the result of them following the plan God gave them for their churches. Their' obedience was always rewarded.

Looking Ahead to the Future for These Pioneers Meant Experiencing Agitation

The early pioneers spent their ministry being agitated. Agitation is the ability to help others see differently and help them grow. In the beginning of their ministry, agitation involved members of the congregation. The early pioneers spent most of their lives helping people grow. It took hard work to create within the people they led the ability to see life differently. However, this ability was what it took to empower the people to build each of the churches, pursue missions and attend LIFE Bible College. These pioneers lived life with daily agitations that forced them to see and often think differently to fulfill the Will of God.

Their agitation always involved looking ahead to the future. They could not remain static in the work they were called to do.

The African-American churches in the Foursquare movement today are being sustained by the silent voices and powerful messages of these little-known legacies—work hard, endure incredible challenges but[6] overcame them by their unwavering commitment to God, and unconditional love for people.

Their ability to begin and build Foursquare churches among members of the African-American community in Los Angeles makes them great pioneers. Each of them died in ministry. They worked alongside the people until God called them to rest. The people they influence today, remain in ministry with the expectation that their story will agitate the Foursquare denomination. Thus making the 21st century a period of reformation in leadership. There must be inclusion and empowerment of African-American leadership and development at all levels of decision-making. Therefore becoming inclusive and empowering Sister Aimee Semple McPherson made it very clear through her actions and words that African-Americans are precious people and, "There is no difference between them and us in God's sight; all must meet on the common footing—the Blood of Jesus. All must be baptized into the one body by the same Spirit."[7]

It's time to let the words spoken to us in the message of our founder become the catalyst that moves us to pursue making God's Word a reality to honor the Kingdom of God and bring Him glory.

We should now be challenged to raise our voices together (all races) with questions of how the Foursquare Church leadership will approach its ethnic communities. It is time to take inventory of every area of its organizational structure as it relates to ethnic pastors and engage them in productive dialogue about the need and strategies for a new paradigm of multi-ethnic leadership in the Foursquare denomination at all levels. If this cannot happen, we will be forever the houses divided by unequal parts that will soon be reduced to its lowest term. Let the silent voices resonate powerful messages that speak to us in as many ways as possible to make a difference for future generations. Let us become the Church envisioned by Sister McPherson in 1923, for all nations, races, colors, gender and creeds, proclaimed in the message set in a marble tablet in the center columns of Angelus Temple affixing the Foursquare Church's focus and mission in the minds and hearts of people who entered its doors as "Dedicated to the cause of Inter-Denominational and Worldwide Evangelism."

The Fruit of the Labor of the Early Pioneers Came . . . Forty Years Later in the Foursquare Church

The labor of the early pioneers was not in vain. Some strides have been made, yet there is still more work to do. Approximately 40 years after the first African-American pastors Rev. Wardell and Pearl Tolliver opened the doors of the first African-American church, Dr. Paul L. Hackett was appointed to the first leadership position on the Executive Council in 1980 until 1992. A few years later, the first African-American female, Rev. Marie Trimble, was added to the same council. Rev. Trimble fulfilled her term on the council and currently is the pastor of Trinity Foursquare Church in Lynwood, California. Rev. Naomi Beard was appointed to the International Board of Directors from 1996 until May 2001. She has completed her term and is now

---

6. [Ed.] O'Quinn has "and but overcame them . . ."

7. *Bridal Call* 9 (February, 1918).

working independently as a seminar and conference speaker for women.

Dr. Ricky Temple was the first African-American appointed to the Foursquare Cabinet, 1995–1999. During his tenure of service on the cabinet, he became a strong voice that expressed many concerns, not only for African-American pastors. His greater emphasis was the importance of developing strong relationships between all churches, reflecting a move toward becoming a genuine church family throughout the denomination. Dr. Temple often became a lone ranger in his efforts to communicate many of the cross-cultural concerns that addressed the hard task of embracing and inclusion of all family members and their needs.

Though his voice is still sounding in the walls of the ICFG [International Church of the Foursquare Gospel] corporate office and he is highly respected, Dr. Temple and the Overcoming by Faith Church he pastors in Savannah, Georgia, is no longer a Foursquare church. In one of our many personal interviews, Pastor Rick defined this transition to leave the Foursquare denomination as an opportunity to "redefine family as one with the same vision and the same blood but a different focus." The congregation was one of the largest African-American churches in the denomination. His departure from the Foursquare Church was painful for many, yet defining for all.

From 1988 to 1997, Rev. Naomi Shivers became the first African-American to serve as secretary to the third president of the International [Church of the] Foursquare Gospel, Dr. John Holland. She later became the dean of the Angelus Temple Institute of Ministry.

Dr. Juanita Smith and Dr. Paul Hackett served as the first African-American divisional superintendents. Currently there are six African-Americans serving as district superintendents. There are 10 districts that are supervised by district supervisors in the United States that oversee the operations of the Foursquare Churches in the United States. At the time of this writing, there are no African-Americans holding these positions. There are no African-Americans that hold an executive office or who serve as administrators at the Corporate Office. There are currently no African-American missionaries.

Rev. Arthur Gray was the first elected African-American to the International Board of Directors of the Foursquare Church. He was selected by the pastors of the Foursquare churches from the Southern California District. In conjunction with Dr. Temple and Rev. Naomi Beard, his involvement on the board of directors has assisted in the development of the Multicultural Office with a focus on the needs of the ethnic churches. He has also assisted in the development of understanding official bylaws and the relative meaning of property ownership as it relates to all Foursquare pastors but primarily to those of color.

Finally, the denomination has held annual conventions throughout the United States with many Foursquare leaders as speakers that began in the early days of Foursquare. The first African-American Foursquare pastor that was invited to be a plenary speaker was Dr. Paul Hackett in the mid-1970s. Since then, there have been eight other African-American Foursquare pastors that have been invited to be plenary speakers [including] Dr. Ricky Temple, Rev. Marie Trimble, Rev. Naomi Beard, Bishop Clarence McClendon, (who pastored the largest African-American Foursquare church during the 1990s), Rev. Arthur Gray, Rev. Parnell

Lovelace, Rev. Rosa Wijesieiwardena and Rev. Lamont Leonard.

A multi-ethnic desk has been established in the international office with a full-time staff member, Ken Bringas. Rev. Rosa Wijesieiwardena has been elected by the African-American pastors to serve as liaison in this office one day a week to address the concerns unique to specific needs of African-American congregations. She receives a stipend in support of these services from the international office.

There are many committees that meet and plan on behalf of pastors (male and female) women, children, youth, singles, married, and other community needs of the Foursquare Church. Most do not represent the specific concerns of the African American Foursquare Church at this time. Everyone in the Foursquare family must be willing to assess our ministry goals together and seek to work together to become intentionally inclusive at all levels.

Many of the early African-American pioneers did not live to see or experience the personal fruit of their labors in African-American involvement in leadership. However, there is no doubt in my mind that the Silent Voices they provided have resulted in the Foursquare Church leadership hearing and acting on their Powerful Messages. We now have approximately 73 churches pastored by African-Americans and there is still much work to be done in order to fulfill the founder's vision for the Foursquare Church and the Great Commission.

Resolution on Human Rights[8]

Church of God (Cleveland, Tennessee)

WHEREAS the gospel of our Lord Jesus Christ is relevant to the problem of human rights; and,

WHEREAS the issue of human rights focuses upon the integrity of our democracy; and,

WHEREAS Christian obedience to the law of love requires a concern for one's neighbor is plainly enjoined in Scripture; and,

WHEREAS no Christian can manifest a passive attitude when the rights of others are jeopardized;

BE IT RESOLVED that the Church of God continue to create a climate of informed and spiritual opinion, and,

8. [Ed.] From the Minutes of the 50th Church of God General Assembly, 1964. Copyright Pathway Press. Used by permission of the Church of God Publishing House/Pathway Press.

BE IT FURTHER RESOLVED that we identify a basic premise on which concerned opinion must rest. That premise, undergirded by the dignity and worth of every individual, assures all Americans the right to full citizenship. In particular this means that no American should, because of his race, or religion, be deprived of his right to worship, vote, rest, eat, sleep, be educated, live, and work on the same basis as other citizens; and,

BE IT FURTHER RESOLVED that Christian love and tolerance are incompatible with race prejudice and hatred; and,

BE IT FURTHER RESOLVED that the Church of God—recognizing that moral problems are ultimately solved by changing the heart of the individual by the power of the Holy Ghost, resulting in a love for all men—supports that which assures all people those freedoms guaranteed in our Constitution; and,

BE IT FURTHER RESOLVED that the church be urged to continue to practice the love and brotherhood it preaches.

Resolution on Racism and Ethnic Disparity[9]

Church of God (Cleveland, Tennessee)

WHEREAS the Church of God from its inception has contended to be inclusive of peoples regardless of gender, cultural background or race; and

WHEREAS the 50th General Assembly in 1964 adopted a resolution on human rights affirming the worth of every individual; and

WHEREAS every race bears the image of God and has its origin in Adam who is the Father of all mankind; and

WHEREAS in Christ Jesus there is neither Jew nor Gentile, slaves nor free men, men nor women, but we are all one in Him; and

WHEREAS the Resolution on Leadership and World Vision in the 1990 General Assembly Minutes commits the church to be "international . . . transcending culture, race, nationalism, and politics;" and

WHEREAS we are beholden to a Christ-like example and lifestyle, one of acceptance, affirmation, and unconditional love;

THEREFORE BE IT RESOLVED that this International General Assembly recognizes all members of the body of Christ as equal in function and consequence, and every race and ethnic distinction a valuable and necessary field for the winning of souls and the furtherance of the kingdom of God upon this earth; and

BE IT FURTHER RESOLVED that we commit towards the elimination of racism and bigotry, corporately identifying racism and bigotry as sinful hindrances which prevent us from truly realizing brotherhood and Christian love within and outside the body of the international church and the many peoples and races which it reaches and encompasses.

9. [Ed.] From the Minutes of the 68th Church of General Assembly, 2000. Copyright Pathway Press. Used by permission of Church of God Publishing House/Pathway Press.

Statement of the General Presbytery of the Assemblies of God Regarding Social Concern

General Presbytery of the Assemblies of God

THE ASSEMBLIES OF GOD recognizes with growing solicitude the grave crises existing in every segment of our contemporary society. In order to relate our church meaningfully to its social responsibilities to men as well as its spiritual obligations to God, we make the following affirmations:

As members of the evangelical Christian community, we believe that the Church has a unique and indispensable contribution to make in the current efforts at improving human conditions. We oppose the social ills that unjustly keep men from sharing in the blessings of their communities; and we abhor the moral evils that destroy human dignity and prevent men from receiving the blessings of heaven.

As sons of God as well as citizens on earth, we reaffirm the Biblical view that man is a sinner and inclined to evil by his nature; that crises in human affairs are produced by selfishness and pride resulting from separation from God; and, that the spirit of alienation, rebellion, and racism is a universal human weakness reflecting the native spirit of fallen humanity.

Because of this Biblical view of the human race, we neither believe that alienations are healed by devised confrontations between those alienated, nor that revolution is the key to social progress. Community-betterment projects and legislative actions on social improvement may alleviate the symptoms of a fundamental human problem (and by all means they should be prominent in our society); but the human solutions to social problems are not enough. Man's greatest need is his need of God; and without God he can hope for no just and equitable society.

It is here that the Church makes its most significant social contribution. This contribution is not of goods and services only, however urgent may be the need for economic justice. And this contribution is not all good will and recognition merely, however alienated and oppressed any people may be. A sin-sick world needs the salvation of God. The first and foremost obligation of the Church to society is to preach publicly in every community the Biblical gospel of the Lord Jesus Christ.

We of the Assemblies of God intend as citizens to make our influence felt where concrete social action is justified in areas of domestic relations, education, law enforcement, employment, equal opportunity, and other worthwhile and beneficial matters. However, we reaffirm our deep conviction that the greatest need of man is for personal salvation through Jesus Christ, and we give this spiritual need its due priority. It is only as men become right with God that they can truly become right with one another.

As a community of Christians we labor to *win* men, not merely to move men. We are called to accomplish our objectives not by coercion, but by conversion. It is not in dashes and confrontations that we manifest God to the world, but it is in demonstrating the power of the Holy Spirit to change men's lives.

In these matters the world does not write our agenda. Nor do the circumstances of our times dictate our mission. These are given to us by God. Our calling is to be faithful to Him.

WE THEREFORE PLEDGE to humble ourselves before God, to pray, and to seek the power of the Holy Spirit to change the lives of men; and

WE FURTHER PLEDGE to give ourselves in the Biblical way to meet today's challenge by a renewed dedication to proclaim the fullness of the universal gospel of Jesus Christ both at home and abroad without respect to color, national origin, or social status!

WE FURTHER PLEDGE to exert our influence as Christian citizens to justifiable social action in areas of domestic relations, education, law enforcement, employment, equal opportunity, and other beneficial matters.

chapter seven

Women in African American Pentecostalism

LILLIAN SPARKS

Mt. Sinai Holy Church of America

Nothing is known of Sparks except that she was a member of Ida Robinson's Mt. Sinai Holy Church of America and had, therefore, imbibed the early egalitarian stance that Robinson espoused. She may have been among the several women that Robinson took under her personal tutelage, not only training them in biblical literacy, but also grooming them to become leaders in the Mt. Sinai organization. Sparks, who pastored a congregation in Pensacola, Florida, eventually became a bishop.

Women's Rights

There's neither Jew nor Gentile,
To those who've paid the price;
'Tis neither Male nor Female,
But one in Jesus Christ.

I am going to tell you friends
Without the slightest doubt,
A day is coming very soon,
When your sins will find you out.

A day is coming very soon,
When sin you cannot hide:
Then you will wish you'd taken
The Bible for your guide.

You'll wish you had let women alone
When they were trying to teach.
You'll be sorry you tried to hold them
   down,
When God told them to preach.

Come, dear brothers, let us journey,
Side by side and hand in hand;
Does not the Bible plainly tell you
Woman shall co-ordinate the man?

The hand that rocks the [cradle]
Will rule the world, you know;
So lift the standard high for God,
Wherever you may go.

Some women have the right to sing,
And some the right to teach;
But women, called by Jesus Christ,
Surely have the right to preach.

Some men will call you anti-Christ,
And some would rather die:
Than have the Spirit poured out,
When women prophesy.

To prophesy is to speak for God,
Wherever man is found;
Although lots of hypocrites,
Still try to hold them down.

So be steadfast in the Word of God,
Though fiery darts be hurled;
If Jesus Christ is on your side,
He is more than all the world.

ELIZABETH J. DABNEY
(1903?–19??)

Church of God in Christ

In 1926, C. H. Mason sent Elizabeth and E. H. Dabney to Philadelphia to help Orzo Thurston Jones Sr. begin a ministry there. After working with Jones for three years and seeing hundreds come to Christ, the couple planted a new congregation in a dilapidated building in North Philadelphia, and Elizabeth promised God that if God would send revival to their church and neighborhood, she would pray at an appointed time each morning for three years.

She kept her promise, and at the end of the three years of enormous hardship and spectacular growth, people began contacting her from around the country, requesting prayer. Hundreds of people from all over the globe visited the church, and many came to Christ. Responding to requests from servicemen and women, foreign missionaries, and others, the church distributed more than seven million handkerchiefs over which Dabney personally prayed. After learning of her work, Mason began sending Dabney across the country to minister.

From What It Means to Pray Through

My Covenant Ends

One morning I arose early after I had completed my home duties. I was impressed to go to church earlier than usual. I lived thirty-one block[s] from the church, and had to board two trolley cars.

The Lord was with me as never before. I felt victory in my soul; it was real joy unspeakable. I was pure and clean in my heart; thanksgiving, praises and adoration ascended unto Him. The wheels of the trolley seemed to be praying with me; my cup ran over; I fought bravely to restrain the tears. The trolley car was so crowded; I did not want any demonstration. I did not realize it was the end of my covenant.

When I unlocked the church door, the glory of the Lord met me and pulled me in; as usual I greeted Him with, "GOOD MORNING, JESUS!"

He said to me, "Go back home." His voice was not as it had been; I was amazed, but I did not demonstrate. I ran as fast as I could trying to make it to my prayer altar.

Midway [down[1]] the aisle, all of my strength left me. I fell on my knees; His voice sounded again like an angry man, "GO BACK HOME!" I looked forward to the ceiling, and inquired of Him what crime had I committed that offended Him. I was brokenhearted. It seemed to me as if I was in the deepest trouble, and sorrow, I had ever been in in my life. His manner was not what I had expected. I thought as far back as I could go into the past. I could not find a thing to explain His displeasure at this hour; absolutely I had done all that I could, and given all that I had. I wept bitterly, I wrung[2] my hands with grief; I knew the end of all things was at hand for me. Suddenly my strength came, I leaped and ran forward trying to make it to my prayer altar before nine o'clock, but

---

1. [Ed.] Dabney is missing a word here.
2. [Ed.] Dabney has "rung."

He uttered those words like thunder and many waters, "GO BACK HOME." By this time I was helpless; I fell near the altar, my handbag went one way and my Bible the other.

I felt like someone who had suffered a stroke. I screamed and cried as loud as I could. I asked Him what had separated our fellowship, what had disrupted our communion, what changed His attitude toward me. I told Him the people would molest me now; surely they would slander me as never before. I never would be able to show them what good I had derived from walking with Him. I asked Him to observe my record. If I had displeased Him, I was willing to make it right. 1 said, "Please tell me, dear God, what happened?" He said, in a calm voice, sweeter than anything I had ever heard, "*Your three years are up. You have prayed through into my glory.*" My strength came; it seemed as if the world lifted from my poor shoulders. I thought how wonderful it would be to rest in my home, in my bed again. I thought how sweet it would be to eat another square meal at my own table; I thought of the pleasure of being relieved from the hunger pains I had suffered while going through. Oh! Friends, I was hungry many times. I was so much in need of food, the devil told me to lick some of the dust from the cracks in the floor and swallow it, but I did not. I was so thirsty I felt like sucking the back of my hand to moisten my mouth which was dry and hot, but I did not.

When I realized that this was the end of my covenant, I just could not understand; I laughed for joy. I looked at the piece of paper I wrote at the river bank; there it was, three years ago I had said, yes, to God.

I staggered to my chair where I always prayed. I requested the Lord not to send me home, but grant me the privilege to stay in the building all day and make love to Him. By this time the building was full of His glory I could feel His everlasting arms around me. He told me He did not want me to stay there; He wanted me to go home. Naturally, I obeyed Him. When I got off the trolley on Fifty-Sixth Street, near where I live, there was a great change in my soul, and in the world around me. The heavens, the tree tops, the house tops, everything was praising God in these words, seemingly the sunshine joined in the great refrain, "*You have prayed through into my glory.*"

The children had been dismissed from school for recess, they waved greetings to me, but I was too full to respond; therefore I ran as fast as I could trying to make it to my house.

"The heavens declared the glory of God; and the firmament sheweth His handiwork."— Psalm 19:1.

When I opened my door, the Lord pushed me in the house. The door closed behind me; I became afraid, my bones began to tremble; I started up stairs; but His presence met me on the steps. It was under my feet; it was in the hall. I rushed into my room, I may as well have entered into the door of heaven. I told the Lord to please let me be satisfied with what He had given me. I wanted to go into the street. My son was in school; my husband had gone to eulogize the dead. I had no help. I told the Lord I had gotten myself into a terrible predicament by praying so long. This did not alter His affection or manifestation; the waves of glory were sweeping over me continually. I was like a helpless ship on a tempestuous ocean. The carpet on the floor was like glass; I tried to adjust myself by holding on to my bed; it was like ice and made my hands slip off. I staggered near the dresser and put out my hands to grasp it for protection; it moved out of my way. I staggered like a drunken woman.

The Lord commanded me to sit down. I could feel His arms around me like a dear father, or a grand-father. He said unto me, "My servant, you made a covenant with me three years ago. You vowed to keep it praying and fasting. You have kept your vow; you did not break it; this day I come to bless you, raise your hands, and say 'Yes' unto your God."

I praised Him until the fear disappeared. Singing and music broke out in my soul. I sang about my furniture, my rug, the draperies, even the flowers that were in the dress I wore. My, I thought this was worth suffering for. I never experienced such a glorious afternoon in my life. This feast lasted until four o'clock that afternoon. The unction lifted. The Lord said unto me, "Go into your basement; I shall meet you there." I pleaded earnestly with Him not to send me to the basement, for I always disliked basements. For some reason I never cared for bungalows; they were always too near to the surface of the earth. I told Him I was ready to die, but I did not want to die in the basement, neither was it my desire to pass into the beyond before my husband returned home. I had saved a sum of money for my son's education (his father did not know this); therefore, I asked Him to let me live long enough to adjust these matters, then I would be ready to yield up the ghost.

The Lord shook me and commanded me again to meet Him in the basement. I went over to my desk to write the information and leave it where my husband would see its contents, but my hands were so heavy I could not lift the pen, they felt as if weights were on them.

I felt the hands of the Lord pushing me out of the door. I had a new pair of patent leather pumps I had never worn; I put them on my feet and went to the basement as a convict would walk to the electric chair to be executed. I did not know where the Lord would meet me. When I came to the furnace, a light came out of the coal bin which overshadowed and blinded my natural vision.

A spigot turned on in the ceiling and the oil of the Lord ran upon me until I was encased about eight inches thick. It was like being placed in a closet. I was to that place I could not think, all human help had disappeared; my flesh and self never offered resistance—this was a glorious scene. Satan knew the Lord was preparing me for this prayer battle. He told me I would strangle to death; I had always especially feared death by strangulation or by fire. When he reminded me of this I tried to raise my hands to protect my nose, but there was no response. I was absolutely helpless; I just said; "Amen" to God in my heart. I lifted my head heavenward and submitted to Him for His will to be done. When this ceased, the Lord appeared before me with a paper in His hand. He said,

> You made the covenant, you vowed; you did not break it; this day I have anointed you with the gift of soul-saving, wherever you shall go and pray, souls shall be delivered out of bondage. Both men, women, girls and boys.
>
> Thou shall not add unto my program. The day you add socials, styles and finance to help yourself: I will lift my anointing from you. While you pray, I will send finance to help my suffering pastors and the church. I will also take care of you. Thou shall see it, behold, I tell you it shall come to pass, while you are praying, all nations shall come and pray with you. Do not be selfish, be wise; be faithful, be kind and

diligent. If you obey, I will make thee a blessing unto the people.

With a few other instructions He passed off the scene. By this time, it seemed as if I had entered into "His Guest Chamber of splendor and delight." A band of music came out of the coal-bin and I shouted until the heels came off those new shoes. It was the sweetest music I had ever heard. It seemed as if I was shouting so high I had a platform in the air. A few minutes after five o'clock this anointing lifted; I ascended the steps with those heelless new shoes on my feet. When I entered the living room, my husband came in.

Then I remembered it was for him to be blessed for kingdom building, it was for his edification and the saving of souls that I had suffered.

I ran as fast as I could, with my arms outstretched to meet him, but I fell at his feet. I was unable to relate the story unto him. He was acquainted with the responsibility I had endured. He knew what soul-breaking, heart-rending pains I had suffered, trying to make life worthwhile for others. He picked me up and carried me upstairs to our bedroom. He knew it was too much for a human being to undergo, therefore, he thought the end had come. He accused himself and wept over my still, cold, lifeless body.

He laid his hands upon me, and asked the Lord to heal my body, and restore life and strength; when he touched me I was so charged with the presence of the Lord it knocked his hands away. He tried to help me the second time, but he experienced the same thing.

Then he decided, if I was dead, the glory of God was in it. Joy filled his soul. He praised the Lord and shouted. When I reacted he was very happy. I related to

him the story; I called his attention to the piece of paper he had in his pocket recording the covenant I had made at the river bank. I told him, "as I live my three years expired today." He could not believe it, but when he saw the contents of the paper it verified my statement. We rejoiced together; he was interested and delighted to know I would be able to live a normal life again. He had been so despondent after beholding the way in which I had suffered, just for the Gospel's sake and for his ministry to be a success. He said he had been to the mission more than a hundred times to make me go home and give the idea up, but each time the Lord encouraged him to let me go to the end of my journey.

I was new altogether, a soldier completely equipped to work in the army of the Lord, praying for everybody everywhere, "holding on for their deliverance, and facing the issues of life as they would be presented unto me in this great prayer ministry." I thought, since I had experienced the presence of the Lord in such a wonderful way, I would not have to be bothered by Satan and his forces as I had been. But I am persuaded the more the Lord blesses an individual, the greater are the demands and suffering. I told my husband to permit me to dress, and to carry me before "a theater, a ballroom, or a saloon that night and let me pray." I had so much of the Lord's material in my heart and soul I wanted to see how it would be manifested. I thought of how wicked the people were and this would be an opportune time for prayer to be offered. He prevailed [on] me to be satisfied and go to church and let the people know how much patience the Lord had given me to walk with Him. There was a time in that building that night. My husband permitted me to conduct a three weeks' revival;

he went to Uniontown, Pennsylvania, to visit an old friend, Elder Carr. I was very happy to have him leave me, for the first time, and go far away. I wanted a test meeting or, in other words, I wanted the Lord to show me how the prayer revival would be conducted.

God's Approval and Manifestation

One afternoon I went to church; I placed six chairs before the altar, I knelt in prayer alone. High school girls passed the building, and heard me praying and groaning. They thought we were having an afternoon service and were impressed to come in. This had to be God's leading; I was there alone and I was groaning within myself very softly. Some of them left, but five decided I was so pitiful and sad they would pray with me. The Lord saved those five girls that afternoon, and demonstrated to me how He would work while I prayed for everybody everywhere.

After this, the devil continued to use unwise individuals to press the charge of witchcraft against me.

The attack was so humiliating; I almost decided to give up the life of prayer and live an isolated life away on a farm somewhere.

One day I visited a convention; the accusation I received was so disgraceful I almost collapsed, but I endured for the Gospel's sake. It hurt my husband's heart to see me mistreated for nothing so he sent me to Fairfield, Maryland, for a rest.

I tried my best to be quiet, but, Pastor Parker said, the Lord had sent me there to pray. I told him I was almost afraid to conduct a prayer meeting; the people were so bitter against me for praying. He would not accept this; therefore, I prayed in his church. The Lord saved

seventeen souls. Fear came over me; I told the pastor I would have to lose the meeting at once. It rained hard that night, but God touched the hearts of the people; they gave me forty-two dollars as a love token, and I prepared to go home. I was so excited, I forgot I had a telephone in my home, therefore, I sent my husband a telegram to meet me at 30th Street Station. When he greeted me, he knew I was in distress.

He knew the vacation did not refresh me, neither had I received any strength to carry on. I told him I did not know what happened, that I had prayed and the Lord had saved a goodly number of souls; I was very sorry it happened, but the Lord surprised me. He comforted me by saying, "God has blessed you, and no man shall be able to defeat you in your work."

The next day as we were sitting at the table, the telephone rang; it was the voice of Pastor Kelsey, of Washington, D.C. He was despondent because his tent service had been unsuccessful. He requested Elder Dabney to send me at once, but he refused, thinking I was too tired in my body. My heart seemed as if it was melting within me. I excused myself from the table; I ran upstairs as fast as I could. I fell on my knees and wept bitterly before the Lord.

My husband ran after me; he lifted me up and asked me if I really wanted to go. I told him, "Yes." My insurance was paid; I just felt like I wanted to die in Washington, D.C. He called Pastor Kelsey, and gave his consent to send me to Washington on Sunday morning. He packed my baggage, purchased my ticket, and put me aboard a special train. When the train left 30th Street Station, my heart was praying so loud, I could not hold my head up. I never heard such intercessory lamentation before. The words were so godly and sympathetic for everybody, and conditions throughout the world, I was spellbound and cried all the way. The passengers were so in sympathy with me, they manifested it, but I dare not utter a word to anyone. I felt more like having a prayer meeting than ever before. When I arrived in Washington, I called a cab, and went to Pastor Kelsey's home. When he and his dear wife greeted me, they were amazed at the expression on my face. They knew how lovely my home life was, but they realized that something had occurred somewhere. They took courage and asked me what had happened. I told them how God had blessed my soul to enter into this divine fellowship with him, how the attacks of the enemy were rained upon me from everywhere and I felt it was more than I could bear. But they are blest with that spirit of consoling God's people.

When they told me what the Lord said in His Word concerning "living godly," it oiled the wheels of trust in my soul, it stirred the gift that was within me to press forward for God even if I died. The sun was shining bright; the birds were singing, the trees were in bloom; the very atmosphere seemed to send out a welcome to my soul. The tent would seat over a thousand. When we walked under the canvas, I heard rain falling upon it like hail. I asked the pastor if he heard it; he said he did not, but he felt the presence of God in his whole body, even his legs were saying, Amen. That evening he presented me to the people; as soon as the Lord led me in prayer, two sinners came forward and fell at the altar. God saved them and the soul-saving feast started. I am unable to tell you in English language how great the presence of the Lord was with me, but He worked.

So many sinners were saved we had nowhere for the seekers. I opened the prayer service on Sunday night; by Thursday of the next week sixty souls had been saved. I was so amazed, I told the Lord if He sent Bishop Mason before the week closed, I would be confident and satisfied to work for Him, regardless of what the future presented.

The next morning, at ten o'clock, Bishop Mason called; he was at the Pennsylvania Station in Washington, D.C., enroute to the Pittsburgh conference. The pastor rushed to the station, and related to him how God had sent spiritual bread to the city. Not only that, but, He had supplied every financial need. Bishop Mason prayed in the station, and sent him back with the message for me to "Keep on Praying"; the outpour would be greater. In fourteen days, the Lord saved "ninety-five souls." A few weeks thereafter, Pastor Kelsey baptized nearly all of those converts in the Potomac River, and a large group of them joined his church. Then Pastor Kelsey and his wife told Bishop Mason, God's hands were upon me. It was their desire to see the Lord's work carried on in my life; they did not want the prayer ministry abused, nor my life crushed. Undoubtedly, what they said touched his heart, concerning me.

Late one night, a telephone call came from Pastor Carr stating, Bishop Mason wanted me to meet him in Baltimore, Maryland, the next afternoon. This was another battle for me; the devil told me that Bishop Mason wanted to rebuke me as others had done. That was a miserable night; I did not sleep; I could not turn back into the world; Oh! This was more than I could bear.

I was so excited and nervous; my husband was afraid to drive his car to Baltimore. One of the brothers carried us.

When we arrived in Baltimore, I was so weak in my body they had to lead me into the church where Bishop Mason was waiting. I trembled like someone who had a chill. Bishop Mason showed a great concern; he wanted to know if I was ill in my body. After Elder Dabney related the story to him, he understood the situation in every detail. Like a father, he drew near unto me and took my hand, and the Lord led him out in prayer. I could hear my soul saying, "all the days of my appointed time I will wait until my change comes."

Then he read the Scripture: "yea everyone who lives godly in Christ Jesus shall suffer persecution." He told me not to pay any attention to the devil and his attacks, but to press forward; God had greatly overshadowed and blessed me with the spirit of prayer, like unto his ministry. He told me it was his long, long prayer request answered. He realized he was growing older; he could not carry the spirit of prayer on other side with him. He had prevailed with the Lord to put it upon some of his children in the Gospel.

It came to pass, everywhere I went, the Lord confirmed His work by saving over a hundred souls, in each revival.

All nations met me. Many came because of that wicked report the devil branded me with in the beginning. As the time passed on, they tried to contaminate Bishop Mason's mind with these same evil thoughts, but he rebuked them sharply for their carnal minds, and unbelief in God. He told them the Son of God was branded with the same thing. The revival fire broke out; the spirit of the Lord groaned in the very depth of my soul. I could hear the Lord telling me continually, "I am going to bless you more." This blessing shall become greater. As we met together, there was no discrimination, no denomination, no class, color nor creed. Then the Lord made known unto me what He said when He blessed my soul;

all nations should come and pray with me while I was praying.

There was a deep concern in my soul, and a righteous desire to see all of God's people together; not worshiping in one building, of course, but that they should be united together in Word and in purpose; that we would all speak the same thing, and walk by the same rule.

Whereas we would be able to do constructive kingdom building, and convince the sinners that there is something better than merely living in the world separated from God. When I call your attention to the mountain of prayer, and the Christian growth, it inspires my hope knowing of a truth, those who walk with God do not decrease in value, but they increase, as they learn their daily lesson in the school of knowledge, and wisdom from God. Too much cannot be said concerning spiritual progressiveness in consecration and prayer. Preaching is essential; it always has been. The Gospel is the power of God unto salvation unto everyone that believes.

No soul can hear without the preacher; he cannot administer God's ordinances and law, nor is he able to feed the flock of God, unless he has been sent by God. Teaching is necessary; heaven is won in no other way. The Bible must be taught to be obeyed; for the salvation of our children, and our children's children, depends upon the correct teaching of the Bible. It is a treasure which can only be unlocked by the art of teaching; in order to teach, the tutor must know his native alphabet, above all, his spiritual guide book. But one God-heard answered prayer, will explore, undermine, root up and shake the entire universe.

It will undermine the natural foundation of individual minds; it will place their feet on the solid rock. It will make a way for the Gospel minister. It opens the ground for "His Gospel to plow" the Word. It will send the Word piercing through stony hearts; it will sail across the ocean faster than a plane can go; it will take the hand of a lost soul and unite it with the hands of our lovely Saviour.

One day Bishop Mason sent me to Los Angeles, California, at the request of Bishop Crouch, the pastor of Thirty-third and Compton streets Church. He, and his dear wife, made it possible for all nations to come and pray with me in that great revival. The meeting was so great, he wired Bishop Mason and my husband to come at once and behold the glory of the Lord. While Bishop Mason was there, he met a friend; Miss Faye Bress. She told him there was a longing in her heart to meet a woman after the old biblical type of prayer, as there was during the days of yesteryear, when the gospel fire burned in Los Angeles and stirred the world. He invited her to visit the services at Compton Street on Sunday afternoon. I did not know she was interested in the type of woman that I am, nor the work I am engaged in. As a general rule people do not appreciate a woman who prays always. They rather class her with what they call the back number.

I left Los Angeles the next day for Philadelphia; Bishop Mason felt so sorry for me. He requested Miss Bress to send me a letter of greetings to comfort my heart when I arrived home. I received the letter; it encouraged and lifted my spirit. Miss Bress is an unusual type, she loves God with all her heart. She is a student of the Scripture, a Christian lady, with an appealing personality; she is full of good work, but she never likes for anyone to give her credit for anything.

When I went to Norfolk, Virginia, to pray, Pastor Williams, his dear wife and Brother and Sister Raddick were glad for me. But it seemed as though I was like John when he was put out on the Isle of Patmos. I did not appeal to some of the people. They were looking for a tall, stout, old woman; when they found out I was small in stature, they were very much displeased, but the Lord convinced them it was not in the age or size. He sent a prayer revival and stirred the city. When God spoke to Samuel, he was very young, but this did not hinder the manifestation from being revealed unto the priest. Many times individuals turn away a prayer-answered blessing because the representative fails to meet the public ideal and approval.

The Lord told me if I would go to church at four o'clock each morning and pray, He would show me His glory in the morning time. I was under such a burden for souls to be delivered, Miss Bress felt it in Los Angeles, and took it upon herself to send me a special delivery letter every other day. I answered each one; I tried to express my feelings, the obligation of the work I was doing, and the sacrifice I had to make in order to please God in this prayer life, and ministry. I had no idea I would ever see my name on the headlines of papers, and magazines, neither had it entered my mind once that Miss Bress would publish excerpts from my personal correspondence. The Lord led her, I say it was the Lord; I have every right to believe it was in His divine plan for her to send this Gospel unto the many anxious inquirers who were languishing, conversing over what God did for Peter and John and the church in the early days. But they thought all of the praying people were dead, and the Gospel was suffering for prayer warriors, in a day like this.

Miss Bress relates the story of how God moved upon her after she had read my letters. He told her to make carbon copies and send them to each pastor, and request them to read it to their congregation.

She did not do this alone; she called her friends together, Miss Serby, Miss Stover and Miss Davis, who are Bible School teachers. They decided it was too good and too impressive to keep in Los Angeles; they would contact Mr. and Mrs. Moore, who are publishers of tracts and papers, and see if they could make arrangements to have this carbon letter published in some of the Christian magazines and papers.

Mrs. Moore contacted the Editor of the *Pentecostal Evangel* and his staff. They decided to publish the article under the name, "WHAT IT MEANS TO PRAY THROUGH." It stirred so much interest they requested the article to be made in tract form. I did not know anything about it until one night I went to church, after I had returned to Los Angeles on my second trip. I found on my chair an *Evangel* and the tract. When I read it, I almost collapsed. I told Miss Bress I know my enemies would rail upon me greater

than ever before. She only said, "Darling, the mouth of the Lord has spoken it and it has come to pass; it has gone too far for me to call it back."

As a result, more than three million letters are in my possession from all parts of this world. Many other noted magazines and Christian papers published the same article, which has caused this great Christian prayer publicity.

So many inquiries have been received for information concerning what I did to contact God: and what it means to pray through, that I am writing this book for no other purpose than to let you know what it means.

In all of my dealings, Jesus is the center of attraction; no other person or thing shall be magnified in my life. I glory in the cross of Jesus. Humble is the way that leadeth unto everlasting life; at his feet shall be the highest place my soul shall go. I have found it to be the pinnacle for His children. All exhortations, elevation and honor will be bestowed upon each individual who will learn this one lesson, "humble is the way."

ROSA ARTIMUS HORN

Pentecostal Faith Church, Inc.

Was a Woman Called to Preach? Yes!

God said, "In the last days, I will pour out of my Spirit upon all flesh, and your sons and your daughters shall prophesy (preach)," etc. (Acts 2:17–18). Prophecy covers the past, present, and future tense, unfolding the blessed Word of God, and is profitable for doctrine, (preaching) for correction, (preaching) for reproof, (preaching) for instruction, (preaching) in righteousness" (2 Tim. 3:16).

Did not God tell Ezekiel to prophesy (preach) to the dry bones in the valley? And the dry bones came together and received life. Go, ye women and prophesy (preach) to the dry bones, that they may hear God's Word and live. Time is almost out and millions and billions of souls are being lost.

Men, don't take time to fight the women. You need to use every moment of your life and all the breath that God gives you for the saving of precious souls.

Note that when God said your sons and your daughters shall prophesy (preach)[,] that meant man and woman. You can't hinder the woman anyhow, for the prophecy of Jeremiah 31:22, 606 B.C., is now being fulfilled, which saith, "For the Lord hath created a new thing in the earth, A woman shall encompass a man." That's the Word! Are they not doing it? They are filling the pulpits and not only filling the pulpits, but bringing in precious sheaves for the Master, for He is coming soon.

Did not the Lord say that He would pour out His spirit upon all flesh in the last days? Yes, the last days, saith God, the last days. When you see the women preaching in the pulpit, preaching in the house, preaching in the streets, preaching everywhere, these are some of the signs of the last days, the last days saith God; healing the sick, raising the dead, casting out devils, speaking in other tongues, living holy without spot or blemish; these are some of the signs of the last days. Yea, the Lord Jesus will soon descend with a host of angels on clouds of bright glory, to catch away His waiting Bride. Are you ready to meet Him and [bring] your sheaves with you? If not, get ready, stay ready, be ready when Jesus comes.

To whom did Jesus give the first message? Did He not say to the Marys at the tomb, "Go and tell Peter and my disciples to meet me in Galilee?"

Instead of obeying the Word of God given to them by the women, those disciples were standing around talking and Jesus, passing by two of the men, asked them "what conversation have ye among yourselves and are sad?" Not knowing it was Jesus who spake with them; they didn't believe He was risen, as the women told them; they answered Jesus, "Are you just new in Jerusalem and have not heard how they crucified Jesus of Nazareth?" Jesus said, "Oh thou fools and slow of heart to believe," etc. Previously, Thomas[,] one of those men[,] said, "Except I can see the nail prints in His hands and thrust my finger into His side, I will not believe."

Surely the Lord has called the women, under the Law and under Grace and he uses them whenever he needs them.

Was it not 1336 years B.C. that we find Deborah, a woman judge, a ruler in Israel[?] The first three judges were Othniel, Ehud, and Shamgar. Deborah and Barak were the fourth and fifth judges. Barak was Deborah's assistant. At the time to go to battle, Barak said, "I will not go except thou go with me," and Deborah said, "I will go but the honor will be given to a woman this day." When Sisera, the Captain of the Canaanite Army, fled, he was slain by Jael, another woman in Israel, and so God gave Deborah and Barak victory over their enemies and Israel had rest for forty years.

Did not Hilkiah the priest and Ahikam, and Achbor, and Shaphan, and Asahiah go unto Huldah the prophetess (a woman preacher) who dwelt in the college of Jerusalem to inquire of her what thus saith the Lord? She said, "Thus saith the Lord, I will bring evil upon this place, as I have said," etc., "but concerning the King of Judah which sent you to inquire of the Lord, say ye to him; because thine heart was tender and thou hast humbled thyself, etc., I will bring thee to thy fathers in peace" (2 Kings 22:14–20). Another message from God to a man by the mouth of a woman; 624 years B.C. and 684 years before Paul's letter to the church concerning [Phoebe] (Rom. 16).

Paul said, "I commend unto you [Phoebe] our sister, a servant of the church which is at [Cenchraea]: That ye receive her in the Lord as becometh saints, and that ye assist her in whatsoever business she hath need of you: for she hath been a succourer of many, and of myself also." She took his place, in other words; a woman assist[ant] pastor. Paul said a servant in Christ, not a cook.

Oh, yes, God bless the bravery of the woman, I say too, help her, obey her. Paul, the Chief Apostle said obey her, assist her. Woman messenger, above all the obstacles and hindrances; run, carry the glad message to whosoever will receive it. Why, God has even said that a little child shall lead them. Many times I've seen little boys and girls of all ages, preaching the unadulterated Word of God, another sign of His soon coming.

Did not the Lord say, "I will write my law in the fleshly table of their hearts and stamp it in their minds?" Again He saith, "I shall be in them and I shall walk in them and I shall talk in them."

Not the spirit of you, oh man, whoever thou art. In Psalms 147:10, God said, "He taketh not pleasure in the legs of a man." Again the Lord saith, "Not by power nor by might, but by my Spirit and if any have not the Spirit of God, he is none of His." Not the man, the woman, the boy or the girl, but the Spirit of God walking in that clean, sanctified, pure heart, without spot or wrinkle; bringing victory and honor and glory unto His Holy Name. Oh, hallelujah! Glory to God!

What about the church in the house of Priscilla and Aquila, man and wife preaching God's Word[?] Paul said also to receive them in the Lord; not to cook or scrub, but in the Lord.

What about Philip, the evangelist, the man who was caught away by the Spirit of God out of the eyesight of the eunuch and the next time he was seen was at Azotus (Acts 8:38–40)[?] He walked closer to God than we have been able to yet, but keep on striving. This Philip had four daughters which did prophesy (Acts 21:9). Prophesying is preaching as I told you before. Come on Ezekiel and help me now.

Here is a beautiful type of God using the women in the ministry. When Israel was in great distress because the ark of the Lord had been captured by the Philistines, who was it that brought back the ark after it had been in the country of the Philistines for seven months? They didn't tie oxen to the cart which was the custom then as is today, but in I Samuel 6:7–15, we read how the men tied two milk kine to the cart and shut up their calves at home. Nobody said, why are you hitching up those female cows instead of male oxen? They were in great distress and only those pure, clean female cows could answer the purpose.

And they laid the ark of the Lord upon the cart, and the kine took the straight way to the Bethshemesh, and went along the highway, lowing as they went, and turned not aside to the right hand or to the left. Take note, those women cows didn't turn to the right hand nor to the left, but they led those five lords of Philistines the straight way. No man directed the kine where to go, but those five men watched and followed the ark. No one was driving them, but God led those female milking cows and they brought the ark of the Lord back home, into a wheat field. The reapers of the wheat harvest looked up and saw the ark and rejoiced.

The kine stood with the ark right by a great stone in the field. There those Philistine lords made restitution to the Israelites. The stone is a type of our blessed Saviour; yes that great stone that was hewn out of a mountain, tearing down the kingdoms of this world, the Rock Christ Jesus, oh Hallelujah!

Take note, women preachers, the kine stood the ark by the great stone and they also left their little ones willingly; shouldering the ark. The five men watched the kine as they went the straight way by the way, and followed them. Glory! Preach the Word.

Let me say to the women whom God
    has called.
Go Carry the Word to one and all!
And God will give you a great reward[.]
Cry aloud, don't take down,
The day will soon be gone,
God will bless you on that glorious
    morn,
For all the golden sheaves you've won.

EARLINE ALLEN
(1923–)

Church of God in Christ

In 1941, Earline Allen, a lifelong member of the Church of God in Christ, worked with her husband, Bennie, to found Greater Emmanuel Church of God in Christ in Houston. Today she is the director of Education of that congregation and dean of the Greater Emmanuel Bible Institute, which she founded in 1985. Allen was born into a musical family, and her siblings were accomplished secular musicians. A gifted organist, Earline, however, contained her music to the church. In the 1950s she was known as "the songbird of Texas" within the COGIC denomination and was in demand as a soloist and choir director.

She began theological studies after losing her singing voice following throat surgery. Pursuing courses first at Southern Bible Seminary and Mt. Hope College, Allen enrolled in a graduate program at Houston Graduate School of Theology at age 77, completed her studies with her class and received her Doctor of Ministry degree in 2002. Allen has published several books related to the history and polity of the Church of God in Christ.

From *Go Tell My Brethren*

Closing Argument

It has been well established that sin entered the universe by a woman, and what is sin? It is transgression of the law of God that was broken by Eve, the mother of all living, [who] listened to Satan who came to her in the form of a serpent and tempted her to break the law of God. As a result, all have sinned and come short of the glory of God (Romans 3:23). Yet, it has also been well established that it was woman who made it possible for mankind to be justified freely by grace through the redemption that is in Christ Jesus (Romans 3:24). It was a woman who gave us the Savior of the world to redeem us from all unrighteous.

God, being omnipotent, omniscient, and omnipresent could have chosen another way (after all, He is the Great Creator), but He chose a woman to bear His son. She was highly favored. The angel came in unto Mary and said, "Hail, thou art highly favored, the Lord is with thee: blessed art thou among women" (St. Luke 1:28). This tells us that God used the woman to initiate the plan of Salvation through the birth of the Lord. He also uses women to share that plan through gospel messages. How can we mortal creatures allow ourselves to be prejudiced against women in ministry when a woman carried the Living Word in her body? Cannot a woman carry the written word?

When Jesus spoke in St. John 15:16 and said, "you have not chosen Me, but I have chosen and ordained you, that ye should go and bring forth fruit, and that your fruit should remain; that whatsoever you ask of the Father in My name He may give it to you." He not only spoke to His disciples, but to all who have been chosen by Him. Many are called but few are chosen (Matthew 22:14). The big debate for years has focused on the question, does God call women?

In his book on the ordination of women, Paul K. Jewett says, "ordination presupposes that there is a theological dimension to one's entry into the Christian ministry: one is called of God to the office, one does not simply choose to be a minister as one would choose to enter a profession." And this bears on the question of women's ordination. The question is Does God call women, as He does men to be ministers in His church?" Those who are opposed to women's ordination answer, "of course not" and they rebut the charges that this answer is obscurantist (that which or one who opposes human progress or enlightenment). In that, emancipated women have excelled in all other professions, by pointing out that this very factor of calling means that the ministry cannot be equated with a profession like medicine, law, or teaching.

This worthy and needed clarification, however, can hardly be the last word on the subject. Granted the ministry differs from the professions that only God can call a person to such a task, why should he only call men? Why should he not also call women?

In every major ecclesiastical tradition—Eastern Orthodox, Roman Catholic and Protestant—it is recognized that there is an office of ministry and that ordination is the only way in which one is inducted into that office. One is set apart for and enters upon the Christian ministry by way of ordination. However, one may conceive of ordination—and there are differing theological viewpoints—there is a consensus that ordination is (ordinarily) necessary if one is to function as a minister in Christ's church. With the authority of one divinely called to the task, ordination constitutes among other things, the church's confirmation of this divine call, and thus it certifies, as it were, one's right to serve as a minister of Jesus Christ.

The above statement comes from the pen of Jewett, the author of "The Ordination of Women." During the writer's research it was clear that Paul Jewett had done an in-depth study on the ordination of women and shared many views in his argument from the Nature of the Office.

He shares with the reader the following viewpoint. In the oldest tradition of the West, that of the Roman Catholic Church, and to a lesser degree in the Anglican tradition, ordination, is a sacrament, involving an outward visible sign, wherein is bestowed an inner spiritual grace empowering one to perform the duties of the ministry. This grace is said to imprint on the recipient indelible character. The term "character" means the divinely given power of strength to perform the task of ministry. His power is said to "be indelible" in the sense that it is given the ordained once and for all in and through the sacrament of ordination. In other words, ordination, like baptism, is not to be repeated. In the sacramentalist tradition, then, the objection to the ordination of women takes the form of asserting that women are by nature incapable of receiving priestly "character." The ordination of women, in short, is an impossibility.

In current debate Roman Catholics and Anglicans who oppose ordination of women, are following the tradition of the centuries in saying that woman is incapable of receiving priestly or Episcopal "character." Yet they insist that such incapacity implies no inferiority as was assumed in other ages. What God has made woman to be, and what He intends for her to do, simply mark her as other than the man; they do not make her less than he.

The scholarly writings of Jewett affirm the fact that Christian churches teach in one way or another that God must give his enabling spirit to those on whom hands are laid in ordination if they are to have the inner spiritual strength to serve Him effectively as ministers of the church.

Therefore, to argue from the nature of ordination that women cannot hold the ministerial office implies that they are incapable of receiving that divinely given spiritual endowment symbolized by the laying on of hands in ordination.

The general consensus of all those who protest the ordination of women is the woman's incapacity for ministerial orders is due to her subordination to the man in the god ordained structures of life. Whether one has the Roman Catholic view or the Protestant view, in both traditions it is the woman's relationship of subordination to the man that disqualifies her for ordination.

Turning from the argument on ordination of women, it is needful to discuss the attention that Jesus gave to women.

It was no accident that the Virgin Mary was the mother of Jesus. It was a matter of choice. God chose Mary to give the world a Savior. It was a matter of choice that Jesus chose the women to be the first to witness His resurrection (Matthew 28:9), and then gave to them a message to the brethren. Of course, they did not believe the women, and called what they had to say, idle tales (Luke 24:11). Because of unbelief in a male dominated society today, women are yet segregated and denied the privilege of entering into the rank of the office of ministry that comes with ordination.

The writer's review and research of the Roman Catholic, Anglican and Protestant's argument on the ordination of women gave clearly defined views on this important issue. The conclusion that was reached is the Christian Minister is God's representative and the shepherd of His flock, which is the church, and such a task implies a spiritual authority, which by Divine appointment belongs to the man and not the woman.

The subject of the study for this project deals with non-ordination in the Church of God in Christ in which this writer has been an active member for sixty-three years. The non-ordination problem has caused many dynamic, valuable and efficient women to leave the denomination and begin independent ministries, or they join non-denominational ministries who ordain women to preach and pastor.

As research and investigation was done from books, magazines, journals and other sources on the question of ordination of women, it was interesting to find not only was the Church of God in Christ struggling with this issue, but other denominations, such as the Southern Baptist[s] and Lutherans, were also involved in heated debates on this controversial subject. The Southern Baptist[s] proposed a change to a document called the Baptist Faith and Message—to declare that the office of pastor is limited to men as qualified by Scripture.

Carolyn Weatherford Crumpler, a former executive director of Women's Missionary Union, the major women's organization within the Southern Baptist Convention, said she would not support the proposed revision. "I think it's a misrepresentation of scripture," said Crumpler, who is also a former moderator of the Cooperative Baptist Fellowship, a network of theologically more moderate congregations in the denomination.

Sarah Frances Anders, a retired sociology professor who is moderator of the Cooperative Baptist Fellowship, said that in 1964, the first Southern Baptist woman was ordained as a minister since the Civil War, but that women found a job as a pastor in another denomination, the American Baptist Churches. Since then, she said, about 1,600 Southern Baptist women have been ordained, although many are chaplains, ministers of music or supervisors of education programs. She said about 100 were associate pastors in Southern Baptist congregations. This report was given to Naples news on January 2, 2001. The proposed change of the document to be voted on by the 15.8-million-member denomination would propose the barring of female pastors.

Meanwhile the Lutheran Church–Missouri Synod says what Lutherans believe about the ordination of women. They base their argument on I Corinthians 14:33–34, 37. "Women should keep silence in the churches. For they are not permitted to speak, but be subordinate as even the law says." Again in I Timothy 2:11–12 it reads "I permit no woman to teach or have authority over men; she is to keep silent." I Timothy 3:1–2 states, "Now an overseer must be above reproach, the husband of one wife . . ." Titus 1:5–6 states, "if any man is blameless, the husband of one wife . . ."

The Lutherans argue that the church, which wishes to remain faithful to the Word of God, cannot permit the ordination of women to the pastoral office. They declare, when asked why some churches ordain women as pastors, the reason is based on differing attitudes towards the Scriptures. They make a great case for their view on the ordination of women.

The investigation of the issue of ordination of women further revealed that churches lost congregations after declaring wives should "submit graciously" to their husbands. Martha Phillips, interim pastor at Mount Vernon Baptist Church in Arlington, Virginia, where former Vice President Al Gore is a member, said, "I think more churches will leave." While the Baptists are struggling with congregations leaving, the Church of God in Christ

struggles with its women in ministry leaving the denomination.

To summarize the continuing debate the following authors all discuss the gender problem in ordaining women:

B. M. Ashley, *Justice in the Church: Gender and Participation* (The McGivney Lectures of the John Paul II Institute for Studies on Marriage and Family 1992) Catholic University of America Press (1996).

[Elizabeth] Behr-Sigel, *The Ministry of Women in the Church*, Oakland Pub. (1990) This is an analysis by an Orthodox theologian.

M. Chaves, *Ordaining Women: Culture and Conflict in Religious Organizations*, Harvard University Press (1997)

R. T. France, *Women in the Church's Ministry: A Test Case for Biblical Interpretation*, Eerdmans Pub. (1997)

S. J. Grenz & D. M. Kjesbo, *Women in the Church: A Biblical Theology of Women in Ministry*, Intervarsity Press (1995).

Shirley Stephens, *A New Testament View of Women*, Broadman Press (1980)

J. C. Melton, *The Churches Speak on—Women's Ordination: Official Statements from Religious Bodies and Ecumenical Organizations* [(The Churches Speak Series)], Gale Research (1990)

E. P. Mitchell, [e]d., *Women: To Preach or Not to Preach[;] 21 Outstanding Black Preachers Say "Yes,"* Judson Press (1991)

P. S. Nadell, *Women who Would be Rabbis: A History of Women's Ordination, 1889–1985*, Beacon Press, (1998)

These all conclude that it is obvious that, early in the 21st century, the only significant institutions in North America which will still deny equal rights to women will be portions of the Christian Church: Roman Catholicism, Eastern Orthodoxy, and the conservative wing of Protestantism. These groups base their decision to discriminate on their interpretations of Biblical passages. They view the Bible as prohibiting female clergy.

These writers suggest that, as gender discrimination becomes as abhorrent to the public as racism, these denominations will be under increased pressure to conform to the non-sexist secular standard, by judging candidates for ordination on the basis of knowledge, personality, commitment, ability, and so forth, but not gender. Gender discrimination will be viewed by many as a millstone around the necks of conservative denominations. It will present a serious barrier to the evangelization of non-Christians. Whenever religious institutions are perceived by the general public as operating at a lower ethical level than the rest of society, religious conversion becomes more difficult to promote. In *The N.T. View of Women* by author Shirley Stephens, she states: "The Jewish Oral law declared that the testimony of one hundred women was not equal to that of one man." [3 "]The first-century world did not consider women to be reliable witnesses. Except for rare cases, their witness was not accepted in court. Women could not even serve on juries. How, with this prevailing attitude, would Jesus choose a woman to be the first person in Samaria to spread the news that He was Messiah? Why did Jesus make His first appearance after the resurrection to a woman? Why did He select women

to be the first persons to pass on to others the news of that great event?"[4] It was His choice.

It is easy to see why Paul said, "let your women be silent in the churches, I suffer not the woman to usurp authority over man" (1 Timothy 2:11–12). Paul was bound by Jewish Oral law that said women were not reliable witnesses. The Oral law stated a strict Jewish rabbi would not talk to a woman in public, even if he met his own wife on the street. The oral law said, "Let no one talk with a woman in the street, no not with his own wife."

To discuss the problem further from a theological standpoint, Jesus was a man of purpose. He had a specific purpose in mind when he talked to the Samaritan woman. He broke down the barrier of segregation between Jews and Samaritans and also the barrier of men against women. But someone must have put the barrier back up of men against women, for today in the 21st century; it is easy to see the gender problem in the church world more than in secular society.

Prominent women pastors, such as Dr. Ernestine Cleveland Reems, left the Church of God in Christ to establish her own dynamic ministry in Oakland, California, because female pastors were rejected in Church of God in Christ (COGIC). She has now been consecrated as a Bishop. She maintains high respect among COGIC leaders.

Now one must realize as well known as she is, and admirable as she is, and having clout with the city officials of Oakland, it is a great possibility that other women will follow her. She has a great personality and truly knows the work of the ministry. Her father, "Dad Cleveland," was a Bishop

3. [Ed.] Stevens, *A New Testament View of Women*, 57.

4. [Ed.] Ibid.

in the Church of God in Christ in Oakland, California.

Someway and somehow these discriminatory practices must be addressed before more women leave. The women spoken of earlier are dynamic in their presentation; they are anointed speakers who earnestly seek God for direction daily to perform their ministries. They are prepared academically and professionally as theologians and biblical authorities, they have earned status in administration. They can represent any Christian Denomination, but they love the Church of God in Christ. COGIC must not judge their ministries and severely criticize them because they are female.

Conclusion

For more than 100 years God has shown favor to the Church of God in Christ as an agency for spiritual and social change in the life of our nation. Through Bishop Charles Harrison Mason's involvement the COGIC was in the heart of the Azusa Revival of 1906 that changed the spiritual landscape of America. During two world wars the Church of God in Christ was consistently loyal to the nation, while at the same time fulfilling its prophetic role of advocating for peace and justice. When blacks migrated in large numbers from the rural south to the north, east and west, the churches and storefronts served as refuge centers of help and hope. Further, the church rose to the challenge of representing the Kingdom of God during the devastating depression years and turbulent upheavals of the Civil Rights Movement. Some spiritual observers believe in this new millennium, there may be challenges and changes, turbulence and trouble of greater magnitude than in the

previous century. Therefore, at this time, it is appropriate that the church examines both its doctrines and practices in light of the Scripture. The Church of God in Christ today has its greatest opportunities to evangelize the nations and minister to the masses that are at our doorsteps. Everyone who is saved and ordained by God must be enlisted in this urgent harvest of souls—Will the women be permitted to share in this ministry of reconciliation or will they be silenced by the personal opinions of those who lead?

The writer of this book has attempted to convey to the reader that the church doctrine on ordination (the established vehicle whereby male believers are given authorization to conduct the spiritual and administrative affairs of the church) is rooted in beliefs, history, and traditions.

The major factor that precluded women from ordination was belief. Belief dictates one's behavior.

The dictionary defines "belief" as a state of habit of mind in which trust or confidence is placed in some person or thing. Sara Little in her book, *To Set One's Heart*, says that for a belief to be of any significance, it must be a component in a belief system. She went on to say that a belief system is a set of related ideas (learned and shared), which have some permanence and to which individuals and/or large groups exhibit some commitment. When ideas get shared and repeated, time and time again, they soon become a belief, consequently it gets sustained, reformed and embodied by faith communities. It is important that those individuals in the faith community know what they believe and why they believe it. Beliefs are thoughts. They can be true or false. Most things are usually implicit and taken for granted such that they are not challenged even by fair thinking, right minded individuals. The consequences of unexamined assumptions are institutionalized racism, sexism, ageism, and other cultural bias. Negative ideas imprison and it is difficult, if not impossible, to break out of perceptions. It gets cemented in place by what people say and re-say. These sayings and acts are often handed down from generation to generation, known as tradition.

Tradition was another factor that contributed to the COGIC's founding fathers' position on Female Ordination.

Jesus entered the historical scene at a time when the culture was heavily male dominated. Women were little more than possessions and had few legal rights. They were seldom educated and were forbidden to be taught the Torah (Hebrew word for "law"). They were not to be spoken to on the street, even by their husbands. But Jesus came speaking to women and interacting in ways that clearly indicated that He valued them as individuals for their personhood, not for their cultural roles.

The Bible tells the church that Jesus announced that He came to set men free. He brought about a new order. He that the Son sets free is free indeed. In Galatians 3:28, Paul says "there is neither Jew nor Greek, there is neither slave nor free, there is neither male nor female, for you are all one in Christ Jesus."

Jesus came to make a difference, to set all mankind free. Events throughout the scripture let believers know that Jesus broke down traditions. Whenever they can believe these events, behavior will change. Some beliefs, rules and patterns have been perpetuated until they have to live with them.

BLONDELL ROBINSON

Church of God in Christ

Blondell Robinson served as a chaplain in the Georgia Mental Health Institute in Suwanee, Georgia, and the M. D. Anderson Cancer Center in Houston, Texas. She worked as a teacher in the Houston public schools while she pursued her doctorate at Texas Southern University. After serving for a period as an ordained missionary,[5] Robinson completed her Master of Divinity degree at C. H. Mason Theological Seminary and was ordained to the ministry by her pastor, Bishop John D. Husband

Personal Views on the Ordination of Women in the Church of God in Christ

The ordination of women in the Church of God in Christ has not always been an issue of concern. Traditionally, women in the church have just accepted the position that women were not going to be ordained. Women knew their place and didn't dare venture beyond that boundary. However, the trend is shifting with more and more women accepting their call into ministry. In addition, they are being educated and entering seminaries across the country. Women are accepting the position that they deserve ordination and have earned a right to it.

Women who are graduating from seminary need ordination to further their careers in ministry. Ordination is also required for entry into the military or to serve as an institutional chaplain.

Prior to me accepting my call into the ministry, and before I decided to go to the seminary, I too, like so many other women in the Church of God in Christ, never thought about or even considered the idea of being ordained. I held a position as an ordained Missionary and I was quite comfortable with that. An Ordained

Missionary is the license endorsement given to women in ministry. It was not until I went to the seminary and after being exposed to the many types of ministry that I began to have an interest in ordination.

I was ordained in 1988, by the late Bishop John D. Husband, my pastor and a member of the General Board of Bishops. I approached him about ordination because I needed it to complete a class requirement for graduation. I served as a chaplain at the local county hospital. Bishop Husband was also a member of the Board of Directors of the Charles Harrison Mason Seminary. The Interdenominational Theological Center (ITC) is comprised of six mainstream Black Denominations, the Church of God in Christ being one of them. Bishop Husband was familiar with women needing ordination for institutional ministry. The idea of women needing to be ordained was not new to him. He did issue me ordination papers. However, he made it quite clear to me that it was only to be used for the purpose of fulfilling my graduation requirements. I accepted it, however, I also realized that it was patronizing.

I had asked our late Bishop Robert Earl Woodard, Jr. his views about ordination of women. I had informed him that I was interested and I wanted to know his position concerning the matter. In

---

5. One of two positions reserved for women. The other is ordained evangelist.

retrospect, his answer to me was vague and discouraging. He stated that he would support whatever position the national church supported. I could not be in disagreement with his statement. However, I do know for a fact that many accepted and embraced [women ordinands] in some places, and not in others. The decision to ordain women appears to be left up to the jurisdictional bishop.

Another argument that men often use to defend their position is, "women should not usurp authority over a man" (1 Timothy 2:12). I agree with the scripture wholeheartedly. I do not believe that a woman (or a man) should usurp, meaning to seize, hold, or take by force without legal right, authority over another, such as power, position, or rights.

One of the most discomforting thoughts about the ordination of women is that for me it is a clear and painful reminder of how African-American men and women were treated throughout history, especially during the time of slavery, reconstruction, and beyond.

Black men and women survived the horrible institution[6] of slavery and its aftermath. We had experienced time and time again what it felt like to be discriminated against, mistreated, abused, wrongly accused, misused, underpaid, overworked, looked over, passed over, walked over, and the list goes on. All these overt acts of prejudice were perpetrated because of the color of our skin; today similar acts of discrimination are resurfacing in the church, very covertly under the disguise of ordination of women. The shoe that once held blacks down, that was worn by White America, is now on the foot of the Black man holding the Black woman down in ministry.

I believe that all of this is rooted back in our history of slavery. The Black man has never had power or control of the Black woman. Power and control of the woman was solely in the hands of the White slave masters. Not only did the slave master control the Black woman, but he controlled the Black male as well. Black manhood was never acknowledged. He was consistently denied dignity and respect. Now that slavery has been abolished, controlling a woman's right to be ordained in ministry gives power to the Black male. He now has power and authority that history has repeatedly denied him. Several years ago I was somewhat bitter about not having a recognized ordination. Today I still do not agree with the idea of women being denied ordination. However, I have come to the realization that man does not determine my call to ministry. I know beyond a doubt that God called me into ministry. I have always been supportive and passionate about women in ministry. When I was a little girl, I knew of only one woman preacher. I admired her because I thought the idea of a woman preacher was wonderful. I can only imagine what it was like for her back then because it is bad enough for women in ministry today. I would love to one day be ordained publicly, but if it does not happen, I know that I have been validated by God and I am quite comfortable with that. I do believe the Church of God in Christ will revisit this issue in the not so distant future. This may not happen until the daughters, granddaughters, mothers, sisters, cousins, and aunts, of these great men of God who acknowledge a call to ministry step up and say, "Pastor, I want to be ordained."

6. [Ed.] Robinson has "institute."

JERRY RAMSEY III
(1942–)

Church of God in Christ

Jerry Ramsey, an ordained elder in the Church of God in Christ (COGIC), served as pastor of Bible-Way COGIC in Everett, Washington, for twenty years, before resigning to establish Old Path In-Reach Ministries, a research, publishing, and training organization in Gloster, Mississippi. Ramsey has published several tracts on COGIC history, doctrine, and practical issues.

The Ordination of Women: Right or Wrong?

The Ordination of Women and Those Who Support Them

You may wonder what are the philosophy, ideology and rationale behind this great thrust towards the ordination of women. At this time I am unable to cover all of the numerous religious groups in America and Canada with their various doctrines and creeds. According to *The Encyclopedia of American Religions*, there are over sixteen hundred religions and spiritual groups in the United States and Canada. More than four hundred and sixty-four religious creeds, confessions, statements of faith, summar[ies] of beliefs and articles of religion that are currently acknowledged by many of the churches of today. I will deal with a few of the philosophies that have led and/or is leading to the justification for the ordination of women and in doing so attempt to raise the status of women to the equality of that of men in callings and administration.

As we critiqued several books on the subject, we saw how much bigger this issue really is. It is obvious that the foreknowledge of God certainly was in action when Paul wrote to Timothy in I Timothy 2:11–15 and the church at Corinth in I Corinthians 14. He relates what he is teaching back to the beginning to incidents that occurred between Adam and Eve in the third chapter of Genesis. Notice in particularity in [1] Timothy 2:14, "For Adam was not deceived, the woman being deceived was in the transgression." The Apostle Paul does the same thing in writing on the ministry in the church in I Corinthians chapter 11. Again, he ties his teaching back to the creation of mankind, thus making it almost impossible to deal with these passages without dealing with creation.

Let's take a book entitled *Rethinking I Timothy 2:11–15 in the Light of Ancient Evidence*[,] by Richard and Catherine Kroeger. The book looks at different philosophies, and ideals, and poses questions in an attempt to discredit the verses that were emphasized in I Timothy 2:11–15 . . .

If there is one verse in the Bible more than any other which is used to disbar women from proclaiming the Good News of Jesus Christ and exercising their talents for his glory, it is I Timothy 2:12. On the basis of [this] verse, women are denied a vote in church affairs, rejected as teachers of adult Bible classes, kept home from the mission field, disenfranchised from the duties and privileges of leadership in the body of Christ, and forbidden the use of their God-given talents for leadership.

The explanations given by the writer of the book I quoted from are not at all applicable to 1 Timothy 2:11–15. Thank God that we, both male and female, of the holiness movement are quite aware, as convinced by the fact that the women in holiness have been very active in the ministry of Christ.

Their talents have never been discouraged in any area of worship, praise service, nor ministry. Do not be sidetracked by questions and propaganda that are totally irrelevant to the subject in question. Remember the question before us is, "is The Ordination of Women Right or Wrong?" *In other words does the Bible support women in pastoral positions?* Remember the pastoral position is a position of authority. It is obvious that one can teach without usurping authority over another, but one cannot be the pastor without usurping authority over the entire church. The issue here is pastoring, not talents, not abilities, not even gifts, but rather a calling and a divine appointment.

[Earlier in this work] the author goes back to Genesis 1:26–28, and attempts to argue as fact that Adam and Eve were created equal in Genesis 1, and that the double standard did not come until Genesis 2. It is obvious that Genesis 1:26–28 is actually a summary of the creation and Genesis 2:18–26 gives the details.

It is true that Eve was not put under the direct authority of Adam until Genesis the third chapter. However, it does seem reasonable to assume that by virtue of the fact that Eve was made for Adam and from Adam that her subjection to him would have been automatic. But when Eve did not automatically give him that respect and honor, God commanded it so. The author goes on the show the leadership ability of women, quoted primarily from the Old Testament. They spoke of the virtue and wisdom of these women, their resourcefulness, ability to lead and their prudence and courageousness. I too applaud those women whose expertise God recognized und utilized.

To show the contradiction between 1 Timothy 2:14, which speaks of the woman being first to transgress, and Roman 5:12–19, that speaks of sin passing upon the whole world through the first Adam. It is true to say that Adam was the carrier of sin. It was through the seed of the man that the earth was replenished. Paul's statement in Timothy merely addresses the fact that of the human family, Eve was the first to disobey God and thus was the first to sin. In light of the fact that Jesus is made like unto the first Adam who for his love for fallen humanity became like man so that he might redeem him[, i]t would be safe to say that Adam also loved Eve to the extent that he was also willing to become a partaker of Eve's sin without which there would have been no possibility for her redemption.[7] Which comes through childbearing and Christ redemption. No child born to the human family was born without sin since they were from the seed of Adam. Jesus being the only human born sinless, was not born of the seed of the man, but rather was born of God, who was Holy, through the seed of woman, who was not the carrier of sin.

The [author points] to the necessity to understand inspiration, the action by which God gives the Word to humanity, and interpretation, the human process by which we define its meaning. They noted

7. [Ed.] Ramsey has, "In light of the fact that Jesus is made like unto the first Adam who for his love for fallen humanity became like man so that he might redeem him. It would be safe to say that Adam also loved Eve to the extent that he was also willing to become a partaker of Eve's sin without which there would have been no possibility for her redemption."

that God used ordinary people such as farmers, fishermen and shepherds to reveal his message. On the other hand, we the receivers can compare our response to a work of art created by an artist. We must respond with our own imagination, knowledge and creativity to what we see before us.

This is the fallacy of the whole matter, and the great misunderstanding of most of the theologians and scholars who are attempting to exegete the Word of God. Firstly, they have compared a divine inspiration with a human work of art. Secondly, they have attempted to understand a divine inspiration through the natural phenomenon, such as imagination, knowledge and creativity, which is a no-no in dealing with divine revelation. 1 Corinthians 2:14 says, "But the natural man receiveth not the things of the Spirit of God; for they are foolishness unto him; neither can he know them, because they are spiritually discerned." You see God, the inspirer of the Word, is also the God who interprets the same Word by His Spirit. In 1 Corinthians 2:11–12, it says, "For what man knoweth the things of a man, save the spirit of man which is in him? Even so the things of God knoweth no man, but the Spirit of God. Now we have received, not the spirit of the world, but the Spirit which is of God; that we might know the things that are freely given to us of God."

In the second book *The Ordination of Women*, by Paul J. Jewett, a professor of systematic theology at Fuller Theological Seminar[y], an attempt is made to show that God is neither male nor female, and that Jesus being incarnated could have been either. He asks the question . . . , "does it really matter whether we say he or she, father or mother, son or daughter, when speaking of the Godhead?" He goes on to attack the Apostle Paul for using

terms that tend to be female in nature, such as the words *nourish* or *cherish*. There are times that he ascribes only the usage of female.

The argument in this book suggests that it is at least necessary to question the agenda of the Godhead and the writings of the Apostle Paul, in order to justify the ordination of women.

A third book of a similar title was done by Raymond Tiemeyer. It was a report authorized by the Lutheran Church and this also questioned the maleness of God. On page 10, the author makes the statement that God's male contention was not only judged weak[, but] it was rejected by all Lutherans who took part in the council's study. He goes on to question why all the apostles were male and whether Jesus was establishing a precedence to say that women should be excluded from the Apostleship. The strength of his argument is that if this is so then no Gentile could ever be an apostle, since none of the apostles were gentile brethren.

If the Biblical rendition of God as male was an accident, or God did not intend in any way to establish precedence, somewhere should this have been revealed. Jesus apparently was influenced by the scriptures dealing with God in creation, to have appointed all of his apostles male. He went on to say in the scriptures that his apostles were all given to Him by God. So the question now would be, "why would God[,] not being influenced by culture or a male chauvinist attitude, choose all males to be apostles?" If Jesus had anything to do with it, the question would be "why did He not include His mother or some of the other women to whom He demonstrated had such love and respect?"

It also seemed that the Apostle Peter was also influenced by God in choosing all male apostles. In replacing Judas, he failed to consider the women who had proven themselves faithful. It is also ironic that the Apostle Paul, who was taught by revelation, according to his explanation of his teaching, should have received no revelation that women should be included in the apostleship or pastoral ministry. However, not only did he not ordain any but he actually taught that it was being ungodly. We see therefore that this practice of God in choosing all male apostles, and Peter's choice of a male replacement for Judas is substantiated and greater solidified by the revelations of the Apostle Paul, for now it's not just practiced, but also taught.

With regard to the second part of the question as to whether Jesus was establishing a precedence to exclude women from the apostleship, I'd like to call your attention to the fact that the Holy Spirit who called the Apostle Paul to be an apostle also gave him the revelation that gentiles were now equally accepted as that of Jews. Now I know that it was the Apostle Paul who said that "there was neither Jew nor gentile, bond nor free"; but you must understand that it was the same Apostle Paul who forbade women to usurp authority over men, as a matter of fact taught against them being elevated to that position. It does not seem at all logical or indicative of Paul's response to God or to revelation from him to diametrically oppose and practice something different.

The Lutheran Council went on to question whether God had ordained an eternal, unchangeable subordination of women to men, or whether instead he is actually changing the order of creation by His constant action in history? It is this questioning of the authenticity of the revealed Word of God that is so dangerous to the church today.

But it is indicative of the mentality that the Bible revealed that would be taking place in the end time. It is from this mentality that which we receive the winds of doctrine and the uncertainties of truths, which leaves the church in a gray area.

What he says in 1 Timothy 2:11–15 was contradicted with that of 1 Corinthians 11. In 1 Timothy 2, the Apostle Paul says that "the woman should not teach nor usurp authority over the man." But then Paul supports women praying and prophesying in 1 Corinthians 11. What is misunderstood, is that in Timothy, Paul speaks specifically of teaching and authority, which makes reference to pastoral ministry[—]to teach with authority, to teach as a pastor with authority of, or over, or exercising authority over both male and female. While in 1 Corinthians 11 he speaks of prophesying and praying, a totally different ministry in the church.

The Apostle Paul addresses the silence of women in the church in 1 Corinthians 14:33–36 which says 'let the woman be silent in church and if she desires to know anything let her ask her husband at home." This has traditionally been explained as having to do with the business of the church.

The problem with this age-old explanation is that now with the liberation of women, and the change of mentality in the hierarchy in the church, we are attempting to give women representation in the areas of business and administration. She is no longer silent in this area. If we move the landmarks, just as it became necessary for Israel and Judah to justify themselves, we are also put in a position to have to justify ourselves. This is the dilemma, [toward] which the church is now racing.

This same process of debates, different philosophies, ideologies and rethinking of Biblical texts took place before we lost the handle on the marital issue.

As you know, marriage is now in total chaos. Few now address the question as to who is mine. Most energies now go into making it work, regardless to whose you are or whose you are not. Every major doctrine concerning marriage[,] in the moving of the landmark, follows the same process.

It should be noted that many theological seminaries endorse the books that we looked at. These are the schools that many Church of God in Christ preachers in particular have been educated at and have been consequently influenced by such propaganda as taught by the scholars of those reformations.

There is another book written entitled *The Churches Speak on Women's Ordination*, by Gordon Melton. This book gives a synopsis, the stand taken by many of the churches are and their arguments concerning the ordination of women. Those of you that are not convinced or are not quite sure what your decision should be on the subject might be advised to acquaint yourself with this particular book on the subject.

The question of the ordination of women in the Pentecostal Holiness groups [has] never been much of a problem, for where the Holy Spirit moved there was no need for philosophizing of the scriptures. The Holy Spirit revealed its meaning and of course greatly used women in those days, during the Acts of the Apostles, and throughout the New Testament scriptures. In the sectarian churches, seminarian studies were necessary before one could be ordained.

By keeping women out of theological seminaries, it thus kept them from qualifying for ordination. In many of the Pentecostal churches theological training was not necessary for either men or women, so the Holy Spirit could and did use any person He desired.

Many of the brethren in the Pentecostal Holiness movement are now substituting education and protocol for the actual move of the Spirit in revelation and vision.

Consequently, we have become victims due to the fact that there are very few, if any, theological seminaries that have come from the Pentecostal persuasion, which have written their own curriculum and prepared their own scholars. So by frequenting other schools, we get our learning from these areas.

It is unique that God through revelation brought Bishop Mason out of the theological seminary to found one of the largest Pentecostal groups in the world, the Church of God in Christ . . .

Summary

We started thus book with the question, is the ordination of women right or wrong[?] *The answer is*[,] *wrong.* However, men in their wisdom chose to debate, what was, and what is the mind of God on this issue. The conclusion of what they have learnt perhaps could be best said by Dr. I. Celeb Rosado of the Seventh Day Adventist[s], in an address he made in 1984, in defense of the ordination of women. In his concluding statement he said, "The Bible does not contain the absolute will of God, men wrote what they perceived God to be saying from their cultural and patriarchal perspective. The Bible is not God's pen."

Let me point out this fact that the theologians have left the Christian Church in shambles, in its very best a grey area. This is the same thing that the secular educators' constituency did to our education system. In the mid 60's the educators in our public schools began to distance themselves from the traditional moral values of the church, home and community. To do so, they came up with the teaching called situation ethics. In these teachings, they staged situations that would question the moral values that had traditionally been set in concrete. The moral values of our church, home and community had been derived from the influence of the Holy Bible. Some of these values were thou shall not steal, thou shall not bear false witness, thou shall not kill, thou shall not commit adultery, thou shall not covet [thy] neighbors manservant or his maidservant or his ass, not any of his possessions. These principles had become the moral values upon which our society was established. They proceeded to attack all of these values, which had been held as absolutes, by providing situations wherein one felt that there were exceptions to every rule. They presented the exceptions as if the absolute mentality concerning these things as far as being absolute, was destroyed. Therefore every decision would be made based on the circumstances rather than based on an absolute dogma concerning a moral value. As matter of fact, the exception became the rule.

The mentality had an effect upon our respect and of course the chain of command. For instance, they also taught that the parent had to earn the respect of their children. Of course this mentality also took over the family where husbands had to earn the respect of their wives, and law enforcement officers had to earn the respect of the community. In other words, there was no longer an absolute respect irregardless to the mentality or behavior of those who we respect.

This is not indicative of the teaching of the Bible. The Bible specifically says to children, "obey your father and mother that your days may be long." God did not qualify parents whether they were good, bad or indifferent. By the same token he says to husbands, "husbands love your wives, even as Christ loved the Church." Again, he does not qualify whether the [wife] is good, bad or indifferent.

Many times we were chastised not for what we stole, but for stealing, not for what we did, but for lying[—]that the principles of not lying or not stealing or not killing would be clearly recognized as the moral standard that was being set.

As a direct result of theologies espoused by our theologians, secular educators and psychologists; our churches, homes, educational system, community and country are all trying to operate in grey areas. There are no more absolutes that dictate our moral values, Christian standards, social behavior, family values and educational standards. These have resulted in . . . child pornography, violence on television, violence in our communities, splits in our churches, illiteracy in our school systems, homosexual[ity] and the ordination of women.

The big question facing us now is—will we accept these as norms for the twenty-first century or will we return to the faith of our founding fathers?

The church may be the only home for this civilization and the Bible and its authenticity, the only hope for the church. If the Bible is proven to be wrong as the theologians propose, then there is no hope for humanity.

The church condemned President Clinton for supporting Gay Rights. The church will be just as guilty if it supports the ordination of women. The Bible will not provide for either!

RANDOLPH G. GOODWIN
(1917–2002)

Holy Temple Church of Our Lord Jesus Christ of the Apostolic Faith

Goodwin was born in Columbia, South Carolina, and was one of ten children. He migrated to New York where he was converted and called to preach in 1947. For several years, Goodwin worked with Bishop Sherrod C. Johnson of the Church of the Lord Jesus Christ of the Apostolic Faith. Johnson died in 1961, and his vice president, S. McDowell Shelton, prevailed in court for the right to preside over the organization. Dissatisfied with Shelton's leadership, Goodwin led one of several congregations that pulled out of the body over the next year. In 1962 he founded Holy Temple Church of the Lord Jesus Christ of the Apostolic Faith from his Bronx, New York, congregation. Goodwin led that body for nearly forty years, until his death in 2002.

Goodwin wrote a number of tracts defending essential doctrines of Oneness Pentecostalism. He also was responsible for the reproduction of a number of tracts that Sherrod Johnson, his mentor, had originally produced. As his stance on women demonstrates, Goodwin's writings portray the most fundamentalist strand of Oneness doctrine and leave little room for compromise.

Can a Woman Preach or Teach the Gospel of Christ?

Concerning women preaching: It wouldn't be any conflict with me to ordain women to preach, if I had Bible qualifications for a woman to preach, I would be willing to ordain women. But I never read where Jesus ordained and sent a woman out to preach the gospel.

When Paul gave the qualifications in Titus 1:5, notice it applies to men: "For this cause left I thee in Crete, that thou shouldest set in order the things that are wanting, and ordain elders in every city, as I had appointed thee: If any (6) be blameless, the husband of one wife, having faithful children not accused of riot or unruly." So notice that the qualifications here for ordaining applies to a man.

A woman cannot be a husband. The scripture says, "The husbandman that laboureth must be first partaker of the fruits." (II Tim 2:6) This could not be a woman.

The scripture also says in 1 Timothy 5:1, "Rebuke not an elder, but entreat him as a father." A woman cannot be entreated as a father. The seventeenth verse says, "let the elders that rule well be counted worthy of double honour, especially they who labour in the word and doctrine." This applies back to II Timothy 2:6, "the husbandman that laboureth must be first partaker of the fruits." So, I hope you have gotten a little light on this subject. Remember Jesus ordained twelve apostles, and they were all men.

In 1 Peter the fifth chapter, Peter states, "The elders which are among you I exhort, who am also an elder, and a witness of the sufferings of Christ, and also a partaker of the glory that shall be revealed." Peter himself was ordained by Jesus Christ and was an elder. So, since he was an elder, likewise all the apostles that he ordained were also elders.

There is no Bible that stands behind a woman teaching or preaching or usurping authority over men or the church.

(1 Tim 2:11–12) "Let the woman learn in silence with all subjection. But I suffer not a woman to teach, nor to usurp authority over the man, but to be in silence."

1 Peter 5:2, "Feed the flock of God which is among you, taking the oversight thereof, not by constraint, but willingly; not for filthy lucre, but of a ready mind."

A woman can sing, praise God, clap her hands and dance a praise to God. But, when it comes to preaching and usurping authority over the man, that's when she is to keep silent.

"The husbandman that laboureth must be first partaker of the fruits." A woman cannot be a husbandman.

She can do other works in the church, such as; praying, fasting, ministering to the sick, giving out literature and telling the people where to come and hear the word of God by the husbandman that preaches the gospel and labors in the word and in the doctrine.

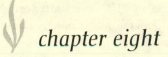

chapter eight

Neo-Pentecostal and Charismatic Movements

JOSEPH GARLINGTON
(1938–)

Covenant Church

Bishop Joseph Garlington, a frequent Promise Keepers speaker and Integrity Music recording artist, is pastor of Covenant Church, a multicultural megachurch congregation he founded with his wife, Barbara, in Pittsburgh, Pennsylvania, in 1971. Garlington, son of Oneness Pentecostal Bishop John Garlington, one of the founders of the Church of God of True Holiness, has made racial reconciliation and the primacy of authentic worship his major themes and has emerged as one of the most recognized and sought out black preachers among white evangelicals.

From *Right or Reconciled?*[1]

Stand Up and Be Reconciled

Jesus has called us to be light and to be salt. Light illuminates and rules the darkness, and salt affects everything it touches. Salt also provokes thirst. If you take the living Christ with you and begin to live among unsaved people, then sooner or later they will get really thirsty. God has given you and me the same ministry that Jesus had, and that is the ministry of reconciliation (2 Cor. 5:18–20). Unfortunately, we don't act like it.

All my life, the church taught me that friendship with the world is enmity with God, so I thought I couldn't have any friends who weren't Christians. We spent all our lives witnessing to Christians, and Sunday after Sunday, we thought we all needed to get saved again. (It's called "being born again, again.") We had countless altar calls for people who "weren't saved enough" this week so they could come and get saved all over again. Since none of us

knew any sinners, we couldn't invite them to church and none of them got saved.

When Jesus came to earth, he had the reputation of being a friend of sinners (see Matt. 11:19). What would happen if someone heard that you were a friend of sinners? The first thing your Christian critics might say is, "Birds of a feather flock together, you know." Nevertheless, God was in Christ reconciling the world to himself. That's what Paul tells us in the Epistle to the Galatians. Pay special attention to the final verse.

> Tell me, you who want to be under the law, do you not listen to the law? For it is written that Abraham had two sons, one by the bondwoman and one by the free woman. But the son by the bondwoman was born according to the flesh, and the son by the free woman through the promise. This is allegorically speaking for these women are two covenants, one proceeding from Mount Sinai bearing children who are to be slaves; she is Hagar. Now this Hagar is Mount Sinai in Arabia, and corresponds to the present Jerusalem, for she is in slavery with her children. But the Jerusalem above is free; she is our mother. (Galatians 4:21–26, NASB)

According to this Scripture, we have the same mother. I don't care whether you

1. Material from Joseph L. Garlington, *Right or Reconciled?: God's Heart for Reconciliation* is used by permission of Destiny Image Publishers, 167 Walnut Bottom Road, Shippensburg, PA 17257; http://www.destinyimage.com/.

are German, Italian, Brazilian, French, Zulu, Hottentot, Norwegian, Spanish, Irish, or Martian we have the same mother in Christ. Male or female, once you receive Christ Jesus as Lord and Savior, we have the same mother. Isn't that amazing? We have the same mother, and we are all free, whether or not we realize it.

Everything changes when God comes to you and says, "You have a new mother. Your mother is my heavenly Jerusalem, my kingdom, and it is above. That means you are free, and you can no longer make decisions after the flesh." Your decisions about life and death, and love and hate, must be made in the Spirit from this point on.

Don't make the mistake of thinking that I'm talking about politics or some social program or agenda. This is a message on what we must do with the ministry of reconciliation. What has God given us? What has he called us to be, and how can we fulfill our calling in the world without fumbling for answers?

The Holiness of Reconciliation

We are living in a day with increased tension between men and women. Ethnic and racial strife is inflamed all over the globe. The church of Jesus Christ continues to be unnecessarily divided because of denominationalism and sectarianism.

I can live with the pain of racial rejection, gender rejection, or religious rejection, but the only way to truly overcome is to become a minister of reconciliation. The only truly authorized medium of this message is the church of Jesus. If we don't do it, we will live with the consequences of our disobedience. The church must rise above her identity in ethnicity and gender, above denominationalism and sectarianism, and get on with the business of making disciples of all the nations. It's going to take the whole church to reach the whole world, and that world is cross-racial and cross-cultural. If we don't do it, the consequences are even more frightening than one would want to contemplate.

When I was born again, whether I liked it or not, you became my brother or sister. Chances are that if I had met you in those early days, I wouldn't have liked you at all, but there wasn't anything that I could do about it. The truth is that when I first surrendered to Jesus, I hated white people. I was born and raised in the public housing projects of Buffalo, New York, to a family that was essentially poor (although we didn't know that we were poor).

My life experience made me think that it was okay to feel such hatred toward white people. One day the Lord confronted me with it, and I said, "Lord, I really don't want to feel this way." At the time, I was preaching as a guest evangelist for a church in Los Angeles. This large black congregation had a total of three white members. When I finished my sermon, a little white lady with gray hair and a beautiful smile came up to me. I was cradling my Bible in one hand and I had my other arm down at my side, and this little lady just put her arms around me and pinned my arms to my sides. Then she began to say, "I just love you, Brother Garlington."

I said, "Praise God," but at the same time I was doing my best to break free. That woman had a steel grip on me, though, and she wasn't about to let go. She said, "You remind me of my son." I thought to myself, *You are lying. I know I don't remind you of your son.* She kept right on holding me. I was still wearing the clerical robe I'd worn for the service, and the perspiration I'd generated during the ministry time was making me feel cold. Then that woman started crying and telling me that she wanted me to be her son, and my kindly response was a silent but urgent prayer, *God, get me out of here!*

The woman just kept hanging on to me and telling me how the message had ministered to her. All of a sudden I felt something begin to seep out of me. When the lady finally let go of me, I realized that I felt differently about her than before she had come up to me. In fact, I felt differently about other white people too. I began to understand that this woman really was my mother in this New Jerusalem. I remembered the Scripture passage where Jesus promised us, "And everyone who has left houses or brothers or sisters or father or mother or children or fields for my sake, shall receive many times as much, and shall inherit eternal life" (Matt. 19:29). I have mothers all over the world, and they come in all colors. When I see them today, I don't view them according to the flesh because I don't know them that way anymore.

Neither Jew Nor Greek

"For you are all sons of God through faith in Christ Jesus, for all of you who were baptized into Christ have clothed yourselves with Christ. There is neither Jew nor Greek, slave nor free man, male nor female, for you are all one in Christ Jesus. If you belong to Christ, then you are Abraham's seed, and heirs according to the promise" (Gal. 3:26–29).

Paul tells us that in Christ "there is neither Jew nor Greek" (there are no racial distinctions), "there is neither slave nor free man" (there are no socioeconomic class distinctions), and "there is neither male nor female" (there are no gender distinctions).

Jesus came and essentially said, "I'm here to make some changes, but most of all I'm here to show you that the Father has a different attitude toward the world than that of the Pharisees." Many of us have been stuck with Pharisees all our lives (and some of us have even been Pharisees). You can spot a Pharisee by the telltale signs of hypocrisy. Pharisees don't like anybody and they don't appreciate anybody. No matter what or how often you do something good, that kind of Pharisee will find something wrong with it.

Pharisees pray like this: "God, I thank you that I'm not like other people. Thank you for making me better than that poor street person, that alcoholic, and that rotten lost person." The honest truth is that we *are* like them! Countless numbers of Christian men act like misogynists, or women haters, while saying they don't hate them. Millions of Christians hate millions of other Christians because they have different skin colors, eat different foods, or say different words over their communion wafers. We need to take personal responsibility for what we have done to one another. First we need to repent and get right with God so we can be reconciled to one another. Then we can reconcile the world to God as well.

We need to turn to one another and say aloud from our hearts, "I need you." We need to see each other as significant parts of the body of Christ, and without each part fulfilling his or her God-given call and destiny, we will all be impoverished.

We don't seem to understand that the Holy Spirit doesn't have a black church or a white church any more than he has a Korean church or an accountant church. We all belong to Christ's church, and we are called to model on earth what already exists in heaven. What exists in heaven? John has to describe the scene in Technicolor: "After this I looked, and before me was a great multitude that no one could number, from every nation, tribe, people, and language, standing before the throne and in front of the Lamb. They were wearing white robes" (Rev. 7:9).

You and I are praying that this reality will come to earth every time we pray the prayer Jesus taught us to pray in the Gospels, "your will be done on earth as it is in heaven" (Matt 6:10). Do we know what we are actually praying when we say this? We are saying, "Lord, get rid of or change every church that doesn't have a rainbow!" God loves to mix his colors into a brilliant portrait of unity and harmony in the love and grace of Jesus. Sometimes we don't want to mix with other colors, cultures, and nationalities, but God says, "That's an order. The love of Christ compels you."

Does He Have to Do It Here?

If you've been in Jesus long enough, you are discovering that there are some wonderful people who just happen to be white, and that there are also some wonderful people who just happen to be black. You have probably noticed that there are also some really mean people who just happen to be black, and there are also some really mean people who just happen to be white. Their meanness doesn't stem from the color of their skin. It's the product of their sin and fallenness. Dr. Mark Chironna says that there are only two races on the earth: "One is racing towards heaven; the other is racing toward hell. Which race are you in? One is a marathon and the other is a sprint."

The stronghold of racism isn't a human problem; it is a human symptom of a spiritual problem. We need to tear down the stronghold that has successfully invaded and wrecked human lives and divided the church for centuries. All of us who call upon the name of Jesus, regardless of our color, nationality, or gender, need to declare and claim our freedom in Christ, so we can offer it to others without shame or apology.

Here is the issue that God puts before us as ministers of reconciliation: Do we need to repent for our racism or for our families' racism? I believe that God is asking each one of us to tear down some ungodly altars from the past. This is a demand placed on every believer, regardless of color, ethnicity, culture, or racial history. When the prophet Daniel was interceding and standing in the gap for his nation, he realized that there was some sin that hadn't been dealt with in the purpose of God. He began to pray, "we have sinned and done wrong. We have been wicked and have rebelled. We have turned away from your commands and laws" (Dan. 9:5). Now, the record shows that Daniel himself was a righteous person, so why was he repenting for acting wickedly and rebelling? Daniel was taking spiritual initiative and personal responsibility for the sinful actions of his people. Perhaps you and I should do the same. Maybe we have come to the kingdom for just such a time as this.

It doesn't make any difference what color you are if you are part of the body of Christ. The reality is this: The Bible says, "If you keep on biting and devouring each other, watch out or you will be destroyed by each other" (Gal. 5:15). Somebody in the body of Christ has to take some initiative for reconciliation, and that "somebody" is you and me.

JOHN RICHARD BRYANT
(1943–)

African Methodist Episcopal Church

In the mid 1960s young African Methodist Episcopal seminary graduate, John Bryant was serving in the Peace Corps in Africa. While there, he became intrigued by the possibilities of "spirited" worship when he encountered a "realm of the Spirit," that he sensed "could not be explained away." He saw people healed, going into trances and exercising spiritual power—all "without the [Western] notion of Jehovah God or Jesus Christ."[2] The experience led him to reexamine Christian Scripture, to discover what it had to say about the spiritual dimension that was largely overlooked within traditional African American Methodism. For Bryant, this search led to the conviction that "in Jesus Christ everything the Bible said could be accomplished," and the Holy Spirit is "the power base of Christian theology . . . who can 'liberate and empower.'"[3]

This third-generation AME preacher was born in 1943 in Baltimore, Maryland. He was the son of Harrison Bryant, and he eventually assumed the pulpit that his father once held at historic Bethel African Methodist Episcopal Church.

I Believe in the Holy Ghost

Text—John 16:7

Jesus expresses Himself to His followers at the time in which He is about to leave. He tells them that after He's gone things are going to be tough. He tells them in the 14th and 16th chapters of St. John what to expect. He said[,] I want to tell you about it now so that when it happens it won't take you by surprise. He said, "When I'm gone some of you are going to have troubled hearts." He said, "When I'm gone they're going to drive you out of the synagogue and many of them are going to drive you out under the influence of their supposed righteousness." After I'm gone they're going to kill you, put you in a lion's den, make you stand defenseless before gladiators." After I'm gone, you're going to have to worship me in secret sometimes.

But then He turns on them and He says, but it will be worth it. You're going to want me to go because when I go I'm going to fix something for you that's going to make it all worthwhile. What in the world could Jesus have been talking about? What could ever take the place of Jesus— The Healer? What could take the place of Jesus—The Anointed? Jesus—The Savior? What could take the place of Jesus—The High Power and Defender? What in the world could it be?

There's much grief that we feel now anticipating His leaving—possibly making His leaving expedient for us. Jesus answers the question. He says when I go, I'm going to give you something. What could He possibly give that would make it expedient when folk are gone? Reject us, despises us and hate us when we are going to have to live without him? What could He possibly give us? Will He be giving us money? That couldn't be it because money can't buy salvation. Would He be giving us military might so that we could be able to overthrow the Roman oppressors? No, because bombs and tanks and

2. Gaines, "Revive Us, Precious Lord," 39.

3. Ibid.

missiles cannot kill sin. What will He be giving us?

Would He be giving us another king in the likeness of David who slayed his ten thousand and led the nation to a position of power in the family of nations of the world? No, because David does not know how to lead men in to the Kingdom of God. What then could Jesus possibly give that would make His leaving expedient? The answer comes from Jesus in the 16th Chapter and the 7th verse. He declared that after I'm gone I'm going to send back the Comforter—The Holy Ghost.

What is the Holy Ghost? First, I've got to clean up your question. The Holy Ghost is not a "what." What you really want to ask me is[,] who is the Holy Ghost? Why don't we just get to the bottom line? The Holy Ghost is (you may not be ready for this) not magic—not Casper—not a strange thought—not vibrations, but the Holy Ghost is God. I couldn't possibly defend such a *statement but all I can tell* you *is I believe in the* Word *and the* Word says *the Holy* Ghost is God. Hold your finger in St. John 16 and flip your Bible open to Acts the 5th chapter, 3rd and 4th verses, Let's read it together. "But Peter said to Ananias why has Satan filled thine heart to lie to the Holy Ghost and to keep back part of the price of the land? While it remained was it not thine own? And after it was spoiled was it not in thine own power? Why has thou conceived this thing in thine heart? Thou hast not lied unto men, but unto God. Why has Satan filled thine heart to lie to the Holy Ghost? Thou has not lied to men but to God." The Holy Ghost is God. Keep turning, let us turn to 2nd Corinthians 3rd chapter 17th and 18th verses: "Now the Lord is that spirit and where the spirit of the Lord is, there is liberty but we all with open faith beholding as in a glass the

glory of the Lord are changed unto the same image from glory to glory, even as by the Spirit of the Lord." Who is the Holy Ghost? The Holy Ghost is God, so says the word of God. The Word said it. I believe it and that settles it. God, in sending Jesus, performed a Kenosis. He emptied himself and then wrapped himself in human form and dwelt amongst us. But at the time of the Ascension, that part of God that walked amongst us, had to go back to the Father. But once man got used to being in relationship with man, then God had to fix it so that when Jesus had to leave, the flesh would be able to be with man at all times. So God sent a part of himself back without flesh, God is the Holy Ghost.

If it had not been for the Holy Ghost, men of all generations would have been deprived of a Divine relationship after the crucifixion. Matthew, Mark, Luke and John would have had something on me if it had not been for the Holy Ghost. Because you see—they had the opportunity to walk and to talk with the Lord. But when the Lord was crucified, that would've meant that all men through all ages would've been deprived of the Divine Relationship. But because of the Holy Ghost, Matthew, Mark and Luke ain't got nothing on me. I got the Holy Spirit. He who has lived to hear, let him hear, you see I know the Holy Ghost is God because the Holy Ghost acts just like Him.

What God intends for man, and it can be seen from Genesis to Revelation, is carried out through the Holy Ghost. Now, let me say this to you about the Holy Spirit. The Holy Ghost is subordinate to God the Son because God the Father and God the Son send the Holy Ghost. He is subordinate but He is not inferior. He is one in the God-head. He functions as a servant of The Trinity. His activity is mostly confined to the age of the Church.

If you want to see the Holy Ghost, he is in the midst.

How does the Holy Ghost function? First of all if we turn back to St. John 16, we'll see that He functions just the way God had always functioned. The first thing that is said is that the Holy Ghost convinces and convicts men of their sins. If you don't know of the Holy Ghost you could be doing wrong and going to Hell and not even know you are heading that way. There was a crowd of folk who persecuted Jesus, and they crucified Him and they didn't even know what they were doing, but on the day of Pentecost, Acts 2:37 says that when a man of God preached they were pricked in their hearts because the Holy Ghost convicted them of their sins. The Holy Ghost will convict you of your sins—not only that the Holy Ghost will taint your righteousness, not your righteousness but of Jesus' righteousness. I know that Jesus is the righteous God because of the Holy Ghost. If you don't have the Holy Ghost you'll think that Jesus is nothing but a God man. If doing that. If they are having trouble with Jesus turn around and ask for the Holy Ghost, for if you don't have the Holy Ghost you'll think that Jesus is nothing but a God man, but if you know Jesus, then you've got the Holy Ghost.

Jesus said to Peter one day, flesh and blood didn't reveal that to you. Folks around here are saying I can't deal with you—I can't deal with no man who's supposed to be God. For some reason that is a heavy transition for our minds to make and that's why when you're trying to witness to somebody they can tell you I can't deal with a historical character who was supposed to have been at the beginning and who is supposed to be at the end. I can't deal with a man who you said died but yes today He is still alive. I can't deal with a man who says He is born of a woman and yet in the next text you say He died, and then when we witness we try to convince them of Jesus. Stop[. The] Holy Ghost can show them the sign. That's not all He does. He also convicts and convinces of judgment so that we might know that this stuff that we are doing we're not getting away with, so that we might know that the Eternal God is coming back again, so that you might know He is coming like a thief in the night, so that we might know that one day He is coming to judge the quick and the dead, so that He might know that there is going to be a Judgment Day.

The Holy Ghost is here to convince us that the judgment of the Lord is at hand, but there is something else about the Holy Ghost that I love—the Holy Ghost loves to hang out around humanity, the Holy Ghost can't be locked up in a Church—but the Holy Ghost will go where you go—walk where you walk, stand where you stand. The Holy Ghost is God. He is not substance, a vapor, an imagination or a figment. No, He is God, a Divine personality.

Let me tell you three things about the personality—God, the Holy Ghost. The first thing you might want to know about the personality of God, the Holy Ghost is that the Brother is intelligent—the Man has all knowledge. In St. John 15:13 it says that when He comes He has all proof, in other words He has all knowledge. He's smart enough to tell you how to save your soul, to make you whole. Not only by personality is He intelligent, but that is not all you need to know about. The Holy Ghost can do no wrong. The Holy Ghost knows how to walk, knows how to talk—He moralizes. The thing that you ought to know about Him is that the Holy Ghost is courageous. He's not afraid of anything.

The world that crucified Jesus, anybody in their right mind would have been afraid to come to a world like this but the Holy Ghost has courage. The Holy Ghost has so much courage He will walk through the valley of the shadow of death. The Holy Ghost will hang out in a bar. He'll walk with prostitutes. The Holy Ghost has courage. He'll go to the Pentagon and He'll stay in the White House. The Holy Ghost will see through the power 'cause He's got courage.

I believe in God, the Holy Ghost because I remember my life before I got the Holy Ghost. I can remember Church when I didn't have the Holy Ghost—I used to come every Sunday. I'd sit back there with the children. Before Church I'd go to the store and get a bag of "Good and Plenty" and a bag of potato chips and I'd sit there waiting for the show to start. I'd peel the potato chips open so quietly nobody knew what I was doing. After I've eaten my belly full I'd lay my head over and go to sleep and wait for the circus to start. and sure enough every Sunday the circus would start. My father would get excited and things started happening. Sister Carrie Garrett used to get up back there and walk seats. Rev. Tapps used to clap and walk in front of the Church like he still does. Rev. Johnson used to sit right there and make his way to the corner and I used to laugh with a bunch of my friends. But one day the power of the Holy Ghost got me. It sure did. Let me tell you how He acts and why I'm so glad that there is a Holy Ghost then I'm through. Ole Peter believed in Jesus and he knew who Jesus was. He heard Jesus preach and he heard Jesus teach. Jesus healed but whatever Jesus did He couldn't get next to Peter. Peter kept trying, Peter stayed weak, hooked on water. Then he doubted the Lord, cut off a man's ear and in the last week of the Lord, Peter cried, "Take Him now". That's alright Peter[;] you denounce Me now[,] but Peter in a few days I've got another part of me, a part you've never seen before and when He comes He'll lead us too.

And one day after Jesus had preached, one day after Jesus had ascended they were in Church praying the same ole way, singing the same ole songs, preaching the same ole words, but then Holy, Holy! fell on Peter. I'm glad I believe in the Ghost because one day He touched my soul, the Holy Ghost filled me up, made me whole, shook my dungeon, loved my heart, Oh Lord the Holy Ghost, I love Him, I love Him, I love Him.

Two years ago, I was down in El Salvador at a world religious conference and everybody in that Church was speaking Spanish, there was a crowd from Guadeloupe and everything in the service was in Spanish—Hallelujah—those South Americans started getting happy in Spanish, the choir was singing in Spanish and I was sitting next to a so-called Christian from Harlem. He turned to me and said[,] Brother Bryant, isn't this ridiculous? They're wasting our time. We're sitting here and we don't know a thing that's going on. They're preaching in Spanish and they're singing in Spanish—I wish I had stayed home, but before I could say me too, I forgot to tell you one thing, the Holy Ghost is a Divine translator. Something broke through that Spanish and slapped me. I cried Hallelujah and a Spanish man was right next to him crying Hallelujah. I believe in God, the Holy Ghost.

ROBERT FRANKLIN
(1954–)

Church of God in Christ

Robert Michael Franklin Jr. represents a new genre of Pentecostal intellectuals who remain in the movement but extend their influence throughout the wider church as well as the broader society. He was born in Chicago where he was raised as a member of a local Church of God in Christ congregation. He left that city to attend Morehouse College in Atlanta, Georgia, and from there went on to receive his Master of Divinity from Harvard Divinity School, returning to his hometown to pursue a PhD from the University of Chicago Divinity School. While back in Chicago, he served on the faculty of that university and as the assistant pastor of Saint Paul Church of God in Christ.

Franklin has also served on the faculties Harvard Divinity School, Colgate-Rochester Divinity School, and at Emory University's Candler School of Theology. He has published manuscripts and numerous articles centered on the ethical concerns of the Black Church and the African American community. In 2007, he became the tenth president of his alma mater, Morehouse College, the prestigious historically black men's college.

The Gospel of Bling[4]

I am convinced that the single greatest threat to the historical legacy and core values of the contemporary black church tradition is posed by what is known as the "prosperity gospel" movement. That movement, however, is only symptomatic of a larger mission crisis or "mission drift" that has placed the black church in the posture of assimilating into a culture that is hostile to people living on the margins of society, such as people living in poverty, people living with AIDS, homosexuals, and immigrants.

This is not a new challenge. Christians have grappled with their relationship to material goods and opportunities in this world since the first century. But in our era something new and different has emerged. Today, prominent, influential, and attractive preachers and representatives of the church now are advocates for prosperity. Perhaps this could only

occur at a time and in a place where two conditions exist. First, Christianity is the dominant faith tradition; second, the nation permits and rewards extraordinary inequalities of wealth and power.

The gospel of assimilation provides sacred sanction for personal greed, obsessive materialism, and unchecked narcissism. That distorted gospel dares not risk a critique of the culture and systems that thrive in the presence of a morally anemic church. This is more than a concern about the encroachment of the prosperity gospel movement that receives so much negative attention. Rather, this is a more thorough and comprehensive distortion of the religion of Jesus.

To be a successful (different from faithful) pastor in today's world is to confront the ever-present temptation to sell one's soul, compromising one's vocation and ethical responsibilities, in exchange for or access to wealth. One Houston-based minister observed that when the church gets a mortgage, "poor people" become just another church program. Poor

4. Reprinted, Franklin, "The Gospel of Bling," *Sojourners Magazine*.

people were central to Jesus' own self-definition, but they are often relegated to one of many service programs of today's corporate church, simply another item on the services menu.

The tragedy is that one-fourth of the black community lives in poverty while many clergy and churches are distracted and seduced by the lure of material wealth. When churches devote more time to building their local kingdoms and less time to nurturing and uplifting poor people, they are struggling with a mission crisis.

A prosperity field trip. One Sunday, I visited the church of my Atlanta neighbor, the Rev. Creflo Dollar. I had heard about the burgeoning ministry of the World Changers Church and felt I should see for myself.

I found a parking space three blocks from the sanctuary. The hike to the sanctuary was so far that I momentarily forgot where I was headed and began to window shop the stores en route to the church, perhaps unconsciously getting into prosperity mode. I finally arrived and entered the enormous domed sanctuary, taking a seat near the front. Everything was neat and comfortable. The blue carpet and plush pew covers were welcoming. The huge rotating globe and other props on stage subtly reminded one that what happens here is intended for a global television audience.

After the choir sang, Rev. Dollar entered the sanctuary dressed in a business power suit and took his seat. Most black preachers begin their sermons in a conversational way. They acknowledge the presence of special guests and familiar faces and invite people to relax and laugh before they begin the journey toward an encounter with the holy. But this was a bit different, perhaps because the stage lights and television cameras were operating. Dispensing with all of the "old school" black church conventions, he went right to the text for the day.

The first 15 minutes of his message were encouraging and impressive. I heard evidence of a critical thinker who had done his homework and given careful attention to various scholarly sources for the selected biblical text. Then, out of nowhere, he began to testify about a friend who had recently given him a second Rolls Royce. He continued, "Now, that's not the Rolls that you all gave me years ago. See, so don't get mad. This was a gift from a friend." I wonder if anyone else wondered, "Why does he need one Rolls Royce? But, two?"

More amazing was that the congregation seemed to affirm this testimony of personal indulgence and excess. No one seemed to have the power to hold the preacher accountable for exceeding his proper allowance as a representative of Jesus. I do not know Rev. Dollar personally and I will reserve judgment about his motives and character, but it appears he has followed the script for how a successful and affluent corporate executive behaves. He does not seem to have entertained the possibility of rewriting that script and offering to other ministers and followers a new paradigm of socially responsible affluence.

If most black preachers—and other preachers for that matter—are preoccupied with pursuing the "bling-bling" life of conspicuous consumption, then poor people are in big trouble, because it indicates that the hearts of their chief advocates are "drunk with the wine of the world," to use James Weldon Johnson's phrase, and incapable of speaking truth to power.

Given the distorting influence of the prosperity movement on authentic Christianity, I should say more about the phenomenon.

We should distinguish between three realities: First, the "gospel of prosperity." Second, the "prosperity gospel." And third, radical Christian stewardship that may include the ownership of material goods.

The Gospel of Prosperity: "Greed Is Good"

The "gospel of prosperity" refers to the cultural ideology that suggests that the accumulation of material possessions, wealth, and prosperity are morally neutral goods that are necessary for human happiness. I characterize it as an ideology rather than merely an idea because it functions like a powerful, unconscious force that does not revise its position in the face of counterevidence. For instance, its advocates would not admit that possessing material goods in excess may actually induce unhappiness. As an ideology, its believers insist upon its correctness, deny the legitimacy of other perspectives, and pursue wealth without concern for long-term consequences. Prosperity becomes an intrinsic good and an end in itself.

Most examples of this vulgar form of material worship do not pretend to be religious, certainly not Christian. Rather, they are elements of what might be called America's largest quasi-religious tradition, namely the religion of capitalism. The gospel of prosperity has been a guiding ideology or myth embodied in the Horatio Alger story (among others), where people acquire wealth through the heroic exercise of risk-taking, ingenuity, high energy, inordinate self-confidence,

and tireless effort. That's the gospel of prosperity that underwrites American capitalism. The gospel of prosperity is a competitor to authentic Christianity (and other faith traditions) and ruthlessly seeks to establish its preeminence in the culture.

The Prosperity Gospel of the Spiritual Entrepreneurs

The "prosperity gospel" asserts that Christian faith is an investment that yields material abundance. Rev. Dollar fits in this category, along with scores of other televangelists who live and instruct others on how to "think and grow rich." Wealth is outward proof of an inner grace and righteousness. Salvation is both spiritual and material. And although the "prosperity gospel" may not be as vulgar an expression of greed as the "gospel of prosperity," both are corrosive and threatening to American churches, which are constantly tempted to focus on their own institutional wellbeing at the expense of serving the vulnerable.

The prosperity gospel may be even more insidious and dangerous because it subverts particular elements of the Jesus story and of classical biblical Christianity in order to instill a new attitude toward capitalism and riches. It often deliberately suppresses, ignores, and/or deletes language about radical sacrifice for the sake of God's kingdom. In other words, it excludes a core message of the Jesus story, namely, that which is symbolized by the cross. That symbol is an enemy to the underlying confidence people invest in material prosperity at the expense of trusting God. "Cross talk" insists that believers share their material prosperity rather than hoard it. At times the call to share wealth may be so radical that a person is compelled to give it all away in order to serve and please God.

I refer to the clergy who operate from this orientation as "spiritual entrepreneurs" who know how to produce, package, market, and distribute user-friendly spirituality for the masses. The spiritual product lines they market rarely make stringent ethical demands upon their listeners. Instead, they proffer a gospel of health, wealth, and success designed to help others become more affluent. When these leaders serve as pastors of congregations, they function like "entrepreneurial ecclesiastical executives" at the helm of corporate organizations. Such congregations and leaders may be changing who they are and are called to be, distorting the meaning of church as a community of holy awareness, care, interdependence, sharing, moral deliberation, and action.

Prophetic Stewardship

A third view of faith and money is "prophetic stewardship." I use the word *prophetic* to emphasize that this model represents something of a negative judgment on its alternatives, the secular gospel of prosperity and the pseudo-religious prosperity gospel. It seeks to displace them with a more radical version of stewardship and shared prosperity. Here it is understood that the Christian gospel includes many goods—spiritual, social, psychological, physical, and material. But none of them, apart from the spiritual good of salvation, is promised without qualification. Again, the cross and a disciple's faithful embrace of it may require one to practice what theologian Jacquelyn Grant has called an "ethic of renunciation," in which we may have to

sacrifice physical well-being, psychological comfort, social support, and material goods for the sake of saving our souls. Is this the meaning of Matthew 6:33, "But, seek ye first the kingdom of God and his righteousness and all these things shall be added to you"?

Prophetic stewardship invites reflection upon the meaning of the values found in passages such as Matthew 6:19–20. There, Jesus engages in "cross talk" as he declares "do not store up for yourselves treasures on earth where moth and rust destroy and where thieves break in and steal, but store up for yourselves treasures in heaven." Acts 2:44–45 indicates that "All the believers were together and had everything in common; selling their possessions and goods, they gave to anyone as he had need." When people had a life-changing encounter with Jesus, it also reshaped their attitude toward their possessions.

Prophetic stewardship is the most adequate and authentic expression of a Christian orientation to money. Consequently, Christians should aspire to understand, accept, and practice prophetic stewardship. Such stewardship both encourages Christians to live in a simple but comfortable manner (leaving a small footprint on the earth) and publicly works to change the culture's prevailing habits of greed. This public move is what makes it prophetic. That is, prosperity per se should never become a prominent theme or mark of the faithful Christian life. It should never compete with the cross for center stage. Material acquisition should always be incidental to one's vocation and one must always be prepared to make radical sacrifices for the sake of one's soul and/or the good of the reign of God.

Against the background of the prosperity gospel movement and the seductions of spiritual leaders is the more chilling report that many churches located in high poverty neighborhoods are not responding to local needs effectively. R. Drew Smith, a senior fellow at the Leadership Center of Morehouse College, undertook research in four cities on the relationship between churches and low income residents. His 2003 report, *Beyond the Boundaries: Low-Income Residents, Faith-Based Organizations and Neighborhood Coalition Building*, states the following conclusions:

Two-thirds of the housing complex residents surveyed report having little or no contact with faith-based organizations in the previous year; many congregations report having programs of potential value to neighborhood residents but indicate that church members take advantage of these programs more frequently than non-members; and, roughly two-thirds of the congregations report that most of their members live more than one mile from their place of worship.

Smith and others underscore the social isolation of low-income, urban residents from the jobs, social services, and poverty-alleviating networks in their metro areas. And he points to the potential of churches to bridge that distance and help to connect people and their communities.

I hope that the disconnect between churches and their local neighborhoods will become an issue that evokes conversation about how congregations that do little for local residents can revise their ministries to serve them more effectively. And I hope that the same community that criticizes inactive churches will acknowledge and reward those that are active and faithful to their mission.

Why are churches so susceptible to misreading or misplacing their moral compasses? The work that Jesus left for the church is clearly set forth in the New Testament, and the people he wanted us to assist and empower are clearly identified. Moreover, Jesus provided the means for doing effective ministry before he departed. So what's the problem? I would submit that leadership, its quality, performance, and education, are essential.

The irony is that many black preachers stylistically present themselves to the world as large, powerful, and accomplished individuals. How many of today's denominational leaders, local pastors, or founders of the new megachurches have risked their access to important people or revenue streams in order to achieve goals in the arena of social justice, such as dismantling penalties against the working poor, expanding health-care coverage, or dramatically improving the wellbeing of children?

We must invite and challenge leaders to do the right things, to do them more effectively, and in a collaborative manner. Further, we should reward institutions and leaders that meet our expectations and ignore those who are unresponsive or deliberately clueless. Moreover, we should actively isolate, stigmatize, and discourage those who are harmful to our communities. This must never be done in a mean-spirited way, but we must not permit leaders who exploit people to think that the community approves of such poor stewardship. The community deserves prophetic stewards.

chapter nine

Theological Challenges of African American Pentecostalism into the Twenty-First Century

BENNIE GOODWIN
(1933–)

Church of God in Christ

Bennie E. Goodwin's two passions revolve around education and social justice. He earned a bachelor of arts degree in music education from Barrington College; a master of religious education degree from Gordon-Conwell Theological Seminary; a master of arts in religion degree from Pittsburgh Theological Seminary; a master's in education and a PhD from the University of Pittsburgh. His dissertation, which he later published, was on the civil rights legacy of Dr. Martin Luther King Jr.

Goodwin has served as a visiting professor at religious institutions and theological seminaries throughout the United States and Europe.

He has pastored three churches, held memberships in the National Association for the Advancement of Colored People and the Southern Christian Leadership Conference, and was vice president of the National Black Evangelical Association. In 1972, he was involved in founding Goodpatrick Ministries, a publishing company that operated until 2004, producing numerous works of Goodwin, along with several other authors.

Social Implications of Pentecostal Power[1]

One of the most noticeable qualities of Pentecostals is the particular emphasis on the immediate presence and power of God, But outside of Pentecostal churches, millions continue in their bound conditions, chained to alcohol and drugs, Millions more are victims of poverty, hunger and disease. They are held down by personal and systemic prejudice, oppression and exploitation, The dilemma revolves around the difficulty of making the power effectual in solving these problems. The question facing Pentecostals is: How can the power that is continually experienced within the church fellowship be brought to bear on the problems God's children are continually experiencing outside of the church?

Jesus himself stressed this power potential when he told his disciples to go to Jerusalem and wait until they were endowed with "power from on high." (Lk 24:49) Again, in Acts 1:8, he said, "You shall receive power after the Holy Ghost is come upon you." When that Pentecostal event took place, it represented a new awareness of God's power breaking dramatically into history.

The Pentecostal experience is an experience of power in response to a faith-request (Lk 11:13). It is a personal experience in a social setting; a mystical experience in a cultural context; a transforming experience that changed cowards into bold men and a cursing fisherman into an eloquent preacher. The Pentecostal experience is a supra-rational experience. It is not illogical, but it defies logical explanation and is not dependent upon rational understanding or explanation for its validity. It is a psycho-pneumatic-somatic experience. It cannot be accounted for in exclusively rational terms.

The poet said it like this:

1. This article was originally published as "Social Implications of Pentecostal Power," *Spirit: A Journal of Issues Incident to Black Pentecostalism* 1/1 (1977) 31–35.

I was shackled by a heavy burden
Beneath a load of sin and shame
Then the hand of Jesus touched me
And now I am no longer the same.

Someone must have interrupted him and said, "Brother, that sounds good, but tell us what happened." The poet continued:

He touched me, He touched me,
And oh the joy that filled my soul.
Something happened, and now I know,
He touched me and made me whole.

A Black bard caught the feeling and tried to express the inexpressible like this:

Something within me that holdeth the reins;[2]
Something within me that banishes pain,
Something within me that I cannot explain;
All that I know, there is something within.

There is power in the Pentecostal event. There is power in the Pentecostal experience. There is also power in the Pentecostal expression. There is something beautifully powerful and powerfully beautiful that takes place in Pentecostal worship. There is something beautiful about the lifting of the hands in praise, the free movement of the body, the joyous music, the new speech behavior, the casting out of demons, the healing of sick bodies, the new sense of love, faith and hope. Tremendous power is released and transferred during Pentecostal worship.

Often individuals who have no intentions of making commitments to God are miraculously and permanently affected as they are caught up in the contagion of a Pentecostal worship experience. There is

2. [Ed.] The original has "reigns."

also a wholesome, life-preserving power in the Pentecostal ethic. Holiness of body, mind and spirit liberates a person from certain time-consuming, mind-degrading, body-deteriorating, spirit-stifling behaviors. Commitment to a holy life frees that person to put at the disposal of God, for the service of people, the best that he or she can do and be. The Pentecostal ethic says, "Do not permit anything into your body, your mind or your spirit that will contaminate you or handicap you and thereby make you unavailable to God." Those who are committed to the Pentecostal ethic say with the poet:

I want to live so God can use me
Anytime and anywhere

The Pentecostal ethic, in conjunction with the Pentecostal experience and expression makes for a positive power-potential that is almost beyond comprehension. At this point I hear some questions being raised. The questions sound like this. If all of this power is available in Pentecostalism then why do two billion people go to bed hungry every night! Why is it that in America, where Pentecostalism has been active for over seventy years, there are 500,000 people addicted to non-prescribed drugs?

Why are there nine million people addicted to alcohol? Why did it take the leadership of a Black Baptist preacher to break down legal racial segregation and discrimination? Why have white Pentecostals voluntarily and deliberately been living in separation from their Black brothers and sisters?

Why is it that one out of three marriages ends in divorce and 30,000 wives run away from home every year? Why are many of our largest cities rapidly becoming increasingly unsafe for human habitation? Why have almost one million people died in war since 1900? Why? Why? Why? Why all of these personal, social, economic and political problems, when we Pentecostals have all of this power? How do we connect the power with the problem?

Jesus, the original Dr. Christian Education, has the answer. He said, "the kingdom of God," the headquarters of God's authority and power, "is in you." Paul, who carried on the Christian education program that Jesus had begun, reiterated the answer. He said that God "is able to do exceeding abundantly, above all that we ask or think, according to the power that works in us." (Ephesians 3:20) Again he said in Colossians 1:27, "Christ in you, that is the glorious hope."

When things were dark and Israel had reached an all-time low in its social. economic, political and religious life, God said to Jeremiah, "Don't weep anymore. Get up! Run to and fro in the streets of Jerusalem (San Francisco, Atlanta, New York, Los Angeles, Detroit, Houston and Chicago) and find me a man." (Jeremiah 5:1) Find me a person, an individual.

God sees all of these problems and he has the power, the Pentecostal power, to do something about them. But he needs a person. When he finds a person— young or old, weak or strong, educated or uneducated, Black, white, red, yellow or brown, Jew or Gentile, Pentecostal or non-Pentecostal—when he finds that person who is willing to be the connecting link, he uses him to bring together the power and the problem.

He found William Seymour and started the Azusa Street revival. He found C. H. Mason and founded the Church of God in Christ. He found E. N. Bell and began the Assemblies of God.

He found B. T. Washington and started Tuskegee Institute. He found Dr.

Jonas Salk and revealed to him the polio vaccine secret. He found Dr. Martin Luther King, Jr. and through him championed the defeat of legal segregation.

He found Richard Allen and started the African Methodist Episcopal Church. He found Dave Wilkerson and started Teen Challenge. And God is still looking for people through whom he can bring together the power and the problem.

Some of the problems are psychological; therefore the church and Pentecostal educational institutions must produce Pentecostal psychologists, psychiatrists and personal counselors. We must produce Pentecostal-empowered persons who can write literature and conduct classes, seminars and conferences that will assist people with their financial problems, sex problems, child-raising problems, their mental, physical and psychosomatic problems.

Some of the problems are social; therefore the church and Pentecostal educational institutions must produce Pentecostal-empowered social scientists, sociologists, social engineers and social educators to become the vehicles through which God can deal with the society's social ills.

Some of the problems are political; therefore the church and Pentecostal educational institutions must encourage and prepare Pentecostal-empowered persons to become mayors, representatives, senators and political leaders at every level of political life.

The times in which we live demand more than people jumping around in church, lifting their hands and saying, "Praise the Lord" in an unknown tongue. The times demand that we speak with power to the powerful in a known tongue. The times demand that we discover where the power is trying to express itself is us, and that we develop that expression. We must take our places among the powerful and devote the God-given Pentecostal power within us to the liberation of the poor, the brokenhearted, the oppressed, the blind and the bruised. Through the Christian Education processes of worship, study, evangelism, fellowship and service, we must constantly seek to bring to bear upon the problems of people, the liberating energy of Pentecostal power.

I want to suggest some issues we Pentecostal scholars address specifically and immediately.

1. Pentecostal scholars must tell their story and proclaim their message in writing. There is a definite dearth of scholarly writing by and about Pentecostals generally and by and about Black Pentecostals particularly.

2. White Pentecostal educators must open the doors of their schools to non-white teachers, students, administrators and board members. With the exception of the Quakers and certain "liberal" denominations, white Christians, including evangelicals and Pentecostals, have been as racist in their attitudes and policies as the rest of white America. If present-day white Pentecostal educators wish to have their righteousness exceed that of their non-Pentecostal white counterparts, this wish should be reflected in the racial composition of their schools.

3. Black and white Pentecostal educators must carry on a continual dialogue. Fellowship will have a positive effect on both Black and white Pentecostals, particularly in terms of mutual understanding and appreciation. The experiences of fellowship and dialogue may be as important to racial understanding and appreciation as the baptism of the Holy Spirit.

4. Pentecostal educators must not become institution-bound. We must go ourselves, and encourage our students to go out into the "world." We must take them into the prisons, hospitals, "skid-rows," and mental institutions, as well as into the office buildings and state houses where the Pentecostal witness needs to be heard and lived.

5. We must keep our Pentecostal minds open to learn from non-Pentecostals and non-charismatic groups. We must not only seek to share our Christian perspective and experience with those who differ from us, but we must allow them to share their perspective and experience with us, in order that all of us may be mutually enriched.

6. Finally, we must be open to God and to the different expressions of the Holy Spirit's power and presence. We must remember that the Spirit is not fully contained in Pentecostalism, the charismatic movement, or any other "ism" or movement. The Holy Spirit is God; and God is bigger than all of us, all of our ideas about him, all of our denominations, all of our religions, all of our worlds, and all of our universes.

He is so big, so comprehensive in his person and varieties of expressions that we must constantly keep ourselves open to him and his Spirit so that when he speaks, we may hear; and when he moves to bring together his power with our problems, we may move with him. Bringing together the power and the problem will not be easy and it has never been. Not because God's power is unavailable, but because the problems seem so overwhelming, the oppositions seem so persistent. and because we are a part of the problem. Even within the limitations of these handicaps, we must continue to work with the assurance that we do not work alone.

Pentecostal and Charismatic Churches of North America

(PCCNA)
(1994–)

In 1949 the Pentecostal Fellowship of North America was created as an umbrella organization to ostensibly represent the face of American Pentecostalism. In truth, the group represented only one sector of the multifarious movement: white Trinitarian Pentecostals—black and oneness Pentecostals were excluded. In 1994, forty-four years after its formation and twenty after the height of the Civil Rights movement, dissolution of the body and formulation PCCNA as a racially inclusive organization were hailed by some as the turning point in race relations for the North American Pentecostal movement. That organization meeting, dubbed the "Memphis Miracle," unfolded in that Southern metropolis with leaders from the major white Trinitarian Pentecostal bodies (including the Assemblies of God, the Church of God [Cleveland, Tennessee], the Pentecostal Holiness Church, the Church of God of Prophecy, the International Church of the Foursquare Gospel), and major black denominations (such as the Church of God in Christ, the United Holy Church, the Fire Baptized Holiness Church) as well as from several smaller bodies from each side. The leaders elected to serve the body represented both races. Important to note is that Oneness bodies remain excluded from the organization, and leaders of denominations representing other minority groups have voiced their disappointment in not being formally invited to participate. Notwithstanding these limitations, though the organization has no legislative authority, cooperative efforts such as the Racial Reconciliation Manifesto have provided a platform for continued dialogue.

Racial Reconciliation Manifesto

PCCNA[3]

Challenged by the reality of our racial division, we have been drawn by the Holy Spirit to Memphis, Tennessee, October 17–19, 1994, in order to become true "Pentecostal Partners" and to develop together "A Reconciliation Strategy for 21st Century Ministry. We desire to covenant together in the ongoing task of racial reconciliation by committing ourselves to the following agenda:

I.   I pledge in concert with my brothers and sisters of many hues to oppose racism prophetically in all its various manifestations within and without the Body of Christ and to be vigilant in the struggle with all my God-given might.

II. I am committed personally to treat those in the Fellowship who are not of my race or ethnicity, regardless of color, with love and respect as my sisters and brothers in Christ. I am further committed to work against all forms of personal and institutional racism, including those which are revealed within the very structures of our environment.

III. With complete bold and courageous honesty, we mutually confess that racism is sin and as a blight in the Fellowship must be condemned for having hindered the maturation of spiritual development and mutual

3. Used by permission of the Pentecostal/Charismatic Churches of North America.

209

sharing among Pentecostal-Charismatic believers for decades.

IV. We openly confess our shortcomings and our participation in the sin of racism by our silence, denial and blindness. We admit the harm it has brought to generations born and unborn. We strongly contend that the past does not always completely determine the future. New horizons are emerging. God wants to do a new thing through His people.

V. We admit that there is no single solution to racism in the Fellowship. We pray and are open to tough love and radical repentance with deep sensitivity to the Holy Spirit as Liberator.

VI. Together we will work to affirm one another's strengths and acknowledge our own weaknesses and inadequacies, recognizing that all of us only "see in a mirror dimly" what God desires to do in this world. Together, we affirm the wholeness of the Body of Christ as fully inclusive of Christians regardless of color. We, therefore, commit ourselves "to love one another with mutual affection, outdoing one another in showing honor" (Romans 12:10).

VII. We commit ourselves not only to pray but also to work for genuine and visible manifestations of Christian unity.

VIII. We hereby commit ourselves not only to the task of making prophetic denouncement of racism in word and creed, but to live by acting in deed. We will fully support and encourage those among us who are attempting change.

IX. We pledge that we will return to our various constituencies and appeal to them for logistical support and intervention as necessary in opposing racism. We will seek partnerships and exchange pulpits with persons of a different hue, not in a paternalistic sense, but in the Spirit of our Blessed Lord who prayed that we might be one (Jn 17:21).

X. We commit ourselves to leaving our comfort zones, laying aside our warring, racial allegiances, respecting the full humanity of all, live with an openness to authentic liberation which is a product of Divine Creation, until the shackles fall and all bondage ceases.

XI. At the beginning of the twentieth century, the Azusa Street Mission was a model of preaching and living the Gospel message in the world. We desire to drink deeply from the well of Pentecost as it was embodied in that mission. We, therefore, pledge our commitment to embrace the essential commitments of that mission in evangelism and mission, in justice and holiness, in spiritual renewal and empowerment, and in the reconciliation of all Christians regardless of race or gender as we move into the new millennium.

Manifesto Committee

Bishop Ithiel Clemmons
Leonard Lovett
Cecil M. Robeck, Jr.
Harold D. Hunter

GEORGE MCKINNEY
(1932–)

Church of God in Christ

George Dallas McKinney, the son of sharecroppers in Jonesboro, Arkansas, grew to become one of the most educated leaders in the largest African American Pentecostal body in the world. McKinney received his BA from Arkansas State College, studied social work at the University of Michigan, received his MA from Oberlin College School of Theology and a PhD from California Graduate School of Theology. McKinney and his wife, Jean, founded St. Stephen's Cathedral Church of God in Christ in 1962 in San Diego, California. In 1985 McKinney was elected as bishop of the Southern California Second Jurisdiction, and six years later was elevated to the General Board of the denomination.

McKinney has been an ardent social activist, championing such causes as the church's involvement in the civil rights movement and the ordination of women within the denomination a stance he supported by ordaining a number of women to full standing within his jurisdiction. He has authored eight books, including the *New Slavemasters* and *Cross the Line: Reclaiming the Inner City for God*, and has received numerous honors in religion and community service. His work promoting racial reconciliation within the body of Christ and broader society earned him a 2001 Man of the Year Award from the National Association of Evangelicals.

A God of Justice[4]

A key verse that surfaces in our discussion of the issue of justice is Micah 6:8, "He has told you, O mortal, what is good; and what does the LORD require of you, but to do justice, and to love kindly, and to walk humbly with your God?" Consider also the wisdom and the justice literature from the Psalms, particularly Psalm 82:2–4, "How long will you judge unjustly and show partiality to the wicked? Give justice to the weak and the orphan; maintain the right of the lowly and the destitute. Rescue the weak and the needy; deliver them from the hand of the wicked." Please notice the demands for justice. Both of these texts, along with others, show that we must take aggressive action in the cause of justice. Notice too, Ecclesiastes 5:8, "If you see in a province the oppression of the poor and the violation of justice and right, do not be amazed at the matter; for the high official is watched by a higher, and there are yet higher ones over them." Isaiah 1:17 reads, "Learn to do good; seek justice, rescue the oppressed, defend the orphan, plead for the widow." Justice is a theological concept like righteousness, faithfulness and holiness; all well known attributes of God. Justice loses its meaning when separated from God. A cultural concept of justice will change with public opinion and the prevailing political philosophy. To understand the biblical concept of justice we must understand and answer the questions, "Who is the owner of everything," and "Who owns what?"

These questions are answered in Psalm 24:1. A working definition of justice is that justice is God's demand that we be accountable stewards of whatever

4. "A God of Justice," *Reconciliation: Official Journal of the Pentecostal/Charismatic Churches of North America (PCCNA)* 1 (Summer 1998) 4–5.

we have received from God. The preacher serves justice when preaching the whole gospel to the whole person. The teacher does justice when teaching the truth about history, values and life. The judge performs justice when judging without regard to the person or pocketbook of the one who stands before him or her.

The Sin of Referral

The evangelical Christian has long ignored many contemporary justice issues. We have frequently committed the sin of referring justice issues to some other institution. The Church has referred the justice issue of hunger to government welfare programs. We have referred the justice issue of racism to the legislatures and to the courts. We have referred the justice issue of the education of poor and minority children in the inner cities to a bankrupt and overburdened educational institution. Yes, we have referred the issue of economic justice to government and big business. We have referred the issue of environmental justice, the pollution of our air, the water and the stockpiling of toxic waste materials to insensitive government agencies. We must repent of the sin of referral and recover our rightful role as the salt of the earth, change agents and preservatives of the earth; as the light of the world, giving life and illuminating the dirty and scandalous behavior of those who don't know God.

A careful review of recent, and not so recent, church history reveals that the Church has too often come down on the wrong side of justice or has remained silent. Perhaps this is because to stand for justice may cost one's life. It may ultimately lead to a crucifixion. Time and time again the Church has missed great opportunities to make a clear witness for God and for justice.

Yet in those times the Church's silence and inaction have brought shame upon the family of God. Nevertheless, God has always raised up faithful witnesses who are willing to die for the cause of justice and God's glory. When the State Church in Germany entered into complicity with the evil Nazi regime, the "Confessing Church" rose to the challenge. Dietrich Bonhoeffer and Martin Niemoeller stood their ground on Scripture and opposed the injustice that was inflicted upon the Jews in the Holocaust. Many were martyred rather than compromise. Further, the Church was not only silent, but it participated and profited from the global African slave trade. Yet there are lonely voices crying out for justice during those centuries of trafficking in human flesh.

The dehumanizing process violated every biblical principle related to God's creation and redemptive plan through Jesus Christ. The voices that cried out for justice were isolated and frequently silenced. These voices included the slaves who were converted to the Christian faith and identified with the God of justice; spiritual giants like William Wilberforce of England, John Brown, Nat Turner and the Quaker movement. During the more-than-one-hundred years of segregation, lynching and discrimination in the United States, the evangelical Church has not used its moral and spiritual influence to bring about change. Rather the Church resisted change, was married to the status quo and attempted to justify injustice by perverting Scripture. As I reflect on my involvement in the Civil Rights Movement, I think the most painful criticisms were those received from fellow Christians who did not understand that we were being beaten, jailed and enduring all of the suffering for the cause of biblical justice. Justice does not merely make suggestions. Justice demands aggressive action. To refuse to obey justice is rebellion, a sin against God who established justice

The Christian Response to Unjust Policies

When a believing community becomes aware of unjust public policies based upon unjust laws, justice demands that we work to change the law and the public policy. A California law known as Proposition 209 went into effect in 1997. It had the net effect of closing the door of opportunity to black citizens who need tax-supported higher education. In the fall of 1997, 196 black students applied for admission to the medical school of the University of California at San Diego. Because of Proposition 209, which said that no longer would any consideration be given to anyone on the basis of race or past discriminatory actions, not one of these 196 applicants was admitted. Not one! What they were saying was, "Blacks need not apply. They do not qualify." At Irving Medical School and the medical schools of the University of California at Berkeley and at San Diego, not one black was admitted. It's a justice issue. The same is true with the law schools. Only one black was admitted to a state-supported law school in the whole of California. It's a justice issue.

Twenty-six states are now preparing to adopt the same kind of law in an attempt to turn back the gains of the Civil Rights Movement—gains that were made at tremendous cost, including death. Justice demands that we protest and act to change this unjust law that denies tax payers access to tax-supported higher education.

Public policies that allow low income housing to be built and maintained on known toxic waste sites must be dismantled. About a year ago, a group of us traveled to Washington, D.C., and met with Vice-President Al Gore regarding this injustice. We had with us a black pastor from Dallas who testified that he, his wife and their seven children did not know that the low income housing in which they lived was built over a toxic waste site. Now it's too late. All of the children are affected with cancer or some other debilitating disease or deformity. The husband and wife, only in their late fifties, are dying from cancer. In their community, the cancer rate is twenty or thirty times higher than in the rest of the city. The tragedy of the situation was that the city of Dallas was aware that the location was a toxic dump, but no appropriate action was taken. The church, when it is aware of these circumstances, must bring pressure to bear upon those in power, demanding that justice be served to those who are defenseless.

God is a God of justice. Scripture contains many passages that speak to the issue of justice and how the people of God are expected to treat others justly. While it is the case that the world around us frequently acts in unjust ways, and at times, even codifies and legalizes such things, the Church is called by the gospel of Jesus Christ to stand apart from the world and offer love, justice and reconciliation. To be sure, sometimes the Church has failed. Yet a survey of Christian history also provides us with examples when the Church rose to the occasion to guarantee justice for those around it. When it is aware of these circumstances, the Church must be ready to bring pressure to bear upon those in power. It must demand that justice be served to those who are defenseless. Unless it does, it falls short of the expectations that God has for God's people.

JAMES A. FORBES JR.
(1935–)

Original United Holy Church of America

In 1989, James Alexander Forbes Jr. became the first African American and the only Pentecostal to serve as Senior Minister of the renowned Riverside Church, the interdenominational (American Baptist and United Church of Christ) congregation in New York City. In doing so, he followed in the footsteps of such notable pastors as Harry Emerson Fosdick and William Sloane Coffin. Though Forbes served that congregation for eighteen years, his roots lay deep in the black Pentecostal church, and he was first ordained a minister in the Original United Holy Church of America, and pastored several United Holy Church congregations before being called to Riverside. His father, James A. Forbes Sr., was a bishop in the United Holy Church and led the group that broke away to form the Original United Holy Church.

Forbes attended Howard University in Washington DC, where he earned a BS degree in chemistry in 1957. After being called to the ministry in 1962, he earned a master of divinity degree from Union Theological Seminary, and a doctor of ministry degree from Colgate Rochester Divinity School. Like several other theologically trained Pentecostals before him, Forbes eventually sought credentials outside of the Pentecostal movement and was ordained in the American Baptist Churches.

Shall We Call This Dream Progressive Pentecostalism?[5]

Mature Pentecostals know that the Lord saves, sanctifies, and baptizes with the Holy Ghost. We know the power of the Holy Ghost as a source of personal deliverance and fulfillment. In our services we frequently report on the mighty working of the Spirit, concluding with the affirmation, "He's done so much for me, I just can't tell it all." Miracle stories are told with great rejoicing and a shout of victory may go forth in response to "living proof" that God is on the side of the "despised few."

Every Pentecostal congregation has its own case studies of deliverance. Each sincere member has a story of liberation. It is generally known that those persons who are attracted to Pentecostal churches out of loneliness, lostness, meaninglessness, or identity crises, find special fulfillment in the warm and enthusiastic fellowship of the saints. In Pentecostal congregations one's personhood is affirmed by persons and also honored by God with a most vivid sense of his presence through the Holy Spirit. One only needs to listen to testimony after testimony to know that the Pentecostal experience has helped to restore a sense of worth, identity, and God-relatedness to those who expose themselves to its influence. The list of personal benefits includes such diverse things as feeling joy and peace, healing, freedom from bad habits. finding employment, and motivation to help others, These testimonies are given as evidence of the liberation that comes in one's life when the Spirit is present.

What can we say about the impact of Pentecostalism in areas other than

5. This article first appeared in the *Spirit: A Journal of Issues Incidental to Black Pentecostalism* 1/1 (1977) 12–15.

the personal fulfillment or deliverance of Pentecostal members, congregations, or organizations? I believe we have also been a source of spiritual leavening in the wider church family, We have influenced worship forms, styles of leadership, codes of ethics, Biblical interpretations, and theological formulations. Some of our congregations have even constructed apartments, rest homes, schools, businesses, and provided other community services, But it seems honest to acknowledge that. generally speaking, most of our energy has been expended in efforts to liberate and edify ourselves and promote our own organizations,

We have come this far by faith, leaning on the Lord and relying on the power of the Holy Ghost. But suppose that same Spirit which has sustained us through years of struggle should now summon the Pentecostal movement for a fresh assignment? Could it be that the special manifestation of Spirit in our midst was designed to prepare us for a spiritual mission beyond the confines of our accustomed focus and fields of activity? I hear a call to do "greater works"! I have a Pentecostal dream which maintains the rich heritage from our past, personal deliverance and empowerment, but calls us forth to broader perspectives of the work of the

I dream of a Pentecostal movement which is ready and willing to offer itself to God to be used as an instrument of spiritual renewal in the church and the world. It will shift from being a spiritual welfare agency toward being a spiritual warfare movement. The members will be convinced that the greatest need of our time is spiritual renewal. But they will be aware that the resistance to spiritual renewal is great: "For we wrestle not with flesh and blood, but with principalities and powers."

To pursue its revitalizing mission, the movement will have to enter into warfare against the entrenched forces of evil. It will be fully aware that it is only by the power of God that victory will he achieved in the struggle. Remembering the last words of Jesus, who said, "Ye shall receive power after that the Holy Ghost is come upon you; and ye shall be witnesses unto me," the movement will reemphasize this power concept. Its battle cry will be "Holy Ghost power." Its slogan will be, "The greatest power available to those who are dedicated to the work of God is Holy Ghost power." And its goals (set for each member) will be: to receive power, to use power effectively, and to empower others.

In adopting the battle cry, the movement will be declaring all-out war against the devil and his forces of evil. The battle will be undertaken with the firm conviction that Christ has won the victory, although the world does not really know it. We will bring the power of Christ to bear upon every vestige of demonic power. Armed with Holy Ghost power, every member will dedicate himself or herself to the battle with all there is within. Where the Holy Spirit is at work in the church or the world, there we will gather to celebrate the victory of Christ and the triumphant manifestation of His power over all evil. Wherever there are evidences of demonic activities, in whatever forms they occur, we will go forth to witness that Holy Ghost power is at work through natural and supernatural means to bring these conditions under the redemptive power of the resurrected Christ.

Where there is the demonic influence of sin, there we will proclaim power for salvation and forgiveness through grace. Where there is sickness, we will proclaim deliverance and healing through both medically scientific and spiritual means. Where there exists sickness of the mind and spirit, we will offer counseling and exercise spiritual gifts, including the casting out of demons.

Where there is the demonic force of poverty, we will proclaim renewal and enrichment for both spiritual and temporal needs, feeding the poor, offering personal charity, and setting up social service agencies. Where there are demonic influences of racial, class and religious injustices, we will influence social, economic and political structures. Where there exists community strife, ignorance and war, we will offer peace and wisdom as gifts of God through both human effort and divine intervention.

The victory of Christ must be clearly perceived on the local level if our witness is to be felt. Where there are conditions of boundness, the Holy Ghost power within the saints must be brought to bear upon these conditions. Each member must be willing to dedicate his or her natural gifts and talents to the Holy Spirit's work of fully realizing the victory of Christ. There will be the expectation of spiritual gifts by which one can fight the forces of evil and promote the cause of the kingdom. The program of the church should be designed to make these emphases real. The church will welcome the aid of agencies and any temporal resource which can fait fully serve these God-given objectives.

I call this movement "Progressive Pentecostalism." It is Pentecostal because it is based on a firm reliance on the power of the Holy Ghost as essential in the life of each believer who desires to be a powerful witness for God, and because it affirms that all Christians should experience the Baptism of the Holy Ghost in preparation

for a life of service. It is called progressive to underscore the following emphases:

1. This dream calls us to *progress* beyond institutional or denominational narrowness and isolation. The task to which we are called is bigger than anyone group can handle singlehandedly.

2. This dream calls us to *progress* beyond the belief that the Holy Ghost only manifests Himself in one or two ways, or only in supernatural ways. Every aspect of human or divine activity which brings us closer to the realization of the Kingdom of God is the concern of the Holy Ghost.

3. This dream calls us to *progress* beyond the belief that the Holy Ghost is only at work in our churches or only in the organized church.

4. This dream calls us to *progress* beyond the view that the Holy Ghost is only concerned about the souls of individuals, or "spiritual things" in the narrow sense of the word. Anything which affects our attainment of abundant life and liberation is a spiritual matter and on the Holy Ghost's agenda.

5. This dream calls us to affirm our spiritual experiences of the past, but then to *progress* beyond the belief that the Holy Spirit is limited to traditional patterns of the past.

This dream inspires me to believe that the Holy Ghost is moving in new and exciting ways in our time, throughout Christendom and even beyond the borders of the church. The Holy Ghost is manifesting himself in varied ways and sundry places, sometimes in ways we have known before and sometimes in ways that are strange to us. He is moving in small groups and large organizations. He is moving in the shadows of sacred places and in the structures of secular institutions. We know that He is moving to bring to full fruition that victory which was won by Christ on Calvary. But we are not always sure of how or when or where he shall manifest his presence. For he works according to the mystery of his own plan and purpose. We are called to stand ready and open to progress with him wherever he shall lead us, and to be used of him according to his sovereign will.

Shall we call this dream "Progressive Pentecostalism"? Or does it make a great deal of difference what we call it? What is crucial is that those who hear the Spirit's call to a broader vision of Pentecostal power must get ready to move now, under the guidance and the progressive thrust of the Holy Ghost.

JAMES S. TINNEY
(1942–1988)

Church of God in Christ

During his lifetime James Tinney was an outspoken advocate for the blackness of Pentecostal spirituality. Moreover, Tinney consistently attacked one of the most controversial issues within the black church head on—its failure to deal with the issue of homosexuality within its ranks. Tinney, who was born in Kansas City, Missouri, began preaching at fourteen and became an ordained minister at eighteen. During the 1960s, he pastored churches in Arkansas and Missouri and was assistant editor of the *Kansas City Call*. In 1970s, Tinney moved to Washington DC, completed a PhD in political science at Howard University, and served as editor of the *Washington Afro-American* newspaper and as a speechwriter for politicians and government officials. One of his contributions to Pentecostal scholarship was the founding of *Spirit: A Journal of Issues Incident to Black Pentecostalism*. The journal, which was published for three years, provided and opportunity for young Pentecostal scholars to contribute their voices to the intellectual discussion.

Tinney was eventually excommunicated from the Church of God in Christ for his public stance promoting the church's acceptance of homosexuality as a lifestyle. He died at age forty-six from complications related to AIDS. His untimely death was seen by many Pentecostals as a vindication of their stand opposing homosexuality.

Homosexuality as a Pentecostal Phenomenon[6]

Few things excite so much interest as the topic of sex; and yet on fewer issues has the church been more silent. Perhaps this is because it has been assumed that Christians—Pentecostal Christians particularly—are unanimous in their belief that all sex outside of marriage is sinful and to be avoided by a simple act of will. Whether or not unanimity of belief on this matter has characterized Pentecostals, unanimity of practice surely has not. An official of a leading evangelical denomination once privately ruminated, "More of our ministers' licenses have been recalled, and more of our members have been made 'to eat humble pie', for alleged sexual transgressions than for doctrinal departures."

If other evangelical church leaders are hesitant to acknowledge or examine traditional responses to sexual "sins" among believers, they become almost paranoid when the subject involves homosexuality. For a multitude of personal, family, social, economic and career-vested reasons, ministers and bishops consistently avoid admitting that many professed (and otherwise exemplary) Christians are not only homosexuals by inclination, but also by practice, whether frequently or infrequently.[7] To suggest that many

6. [Ed.] This article originally appeared under the title, "Homosexuality as a Pentecostal Phenomenon," *Spirit: A Journal of Issues Incident to Black Pentecostalism* 1/2 (1977) 45–59.

7. Current scholarship, both religious and secular, insists that a distinction be made between the inclination or disposition to homosexuality (the desire for sexual fulfillment with a person of the same sex, whether exclusively or not), and the practice of homosexuality (the actual performance of such sexual acts). Pentecostals generally have followed evangelicalism in conceding that no guilt attaches to the condition

Holiness or Pentecostal claimants also fit this description seems to many to border on some kind of blasphemy. Indeed, one can imagine that some would even take offense at. The suggestion that homosexuality could ever be a "Pentecostal phenomenon," i.e., a perceptible fact or event occurring also among the members of Pentecostal churches. Perhaps as an introduction, one testimony will suffice:

"My life has been that of a Pentecostal witness. As a teenager, I led souls to the Lord through witnessing campaigns and found it possible to walk with God as Enoch. I've been a homosexual for five years, since the age of 15; and have prayed and fasted, been anointed and sought God to make a change in my sexual preference until I was exhausted. Each time I drew closer to God without one iota of difference in my condition."[8]

Hopefully a dispassionate article such as this will better enable some to admit that homosexuality is also a *Pentecostal* phenomenon; that the issues at hand are related to the churches' negligence in formulating an *adequate* theology of human sexuality itself. (One is mistaken, however, in assuming that merely having the problem or developing such a theology will solve things. Such naivety is characteristic of those churchpersons who refuse to integrate and synthesize interdisciplinary and cross-cultural data with Biblical principles.) Hopefully also, this article will better promote a distinctively Black Pentecostal perspective which avoids the peculiarly Western and white Puritan assertion that sexual "sins" are preeminently worthy of condemnation. A distinctively Black Pentecostal perspective would also view this and any other sexual category in full recognition of the implications for African Pentecostalism as well—where literally thousands of groups permit polygamy, though not always as the "highest good."[9]

of homosexuality itself, but only to the actual practice. Even here opinions differ, depending upon how one thinks any sin affects the life of salvation of a believer. Does any single sin break one's relationship with God? Or does only unconfessed sin? Or does only continually- repeated sinning? Or does only continually-repeated sinning of which one is ignorant or not able to control?

8. Quoted by Gordon Lindsay in, "The New America [sic] Horror," *Christ for the Nations* (July 1971) 7. If one thinks born-again believers do not agonize over problems of homosexuality, he would do well to read anonymous testimonies in Roberta, *Gay Liberation* (Tustin, Cal.: PTL., 1975), Kent Philpott, *The Third Sex: Six Homosexuals Tell Their Stories* (Plainfield: Logos, 1975), or Alex Davidson, *The Returns of Love: A Contemporary Christian View of Homosexuality* (London: Intervarsity, 1970). The Davidson book is probably the best first-hand account ever published by evangelicals, showing the struggle of a believer in reconciling his homosexuality with his faith.

9. This writer is not inclined to accept the notion that categorization can be made listing some sins as less sinful or less deserving of judgment than others. Nevertheless, many fundamentalist theologians (who reject any approval of homosexuality) do believe sins can be ranked in degree of condemnation. They usually place homosexuality as a greater evil than fornication or adultery on the basis that it is a sin "against nature" or natural law-a concept now outdated. Others say that by the fundamentalists' own standards, homosexual practices are really a lesser evil than fornication or adultery since: (1) there is no violation of a marital bond, (2) there is no violation of the hymen, (3) there is no risk of pregnancy, (4) true inverts will never marry, (5) a society which disallows marital bonds to homosexuals leaves sex as their only means of expressing ultimate love and consequently frees them from the obligations and prerequisites which marriage entails. On this same basis, lateral polygamy (which Africans practice) may be seen as a lesser evil than successive polygamy (which Americans practice in the name of divorce) since: (1) the mate is not left uncared for or unattended, (2) the mate is not left with unmet sexual needs or forced to seek other men as partners, (3) the children are not deprived of home or lather: (4)

For purposes of clarity, this treatment is divided into three areas: the Pentecostal attachment (Why is it a problem?), the Pentecostal application (How have we responded?), and the Pentecostal approach (How should we approach the matter?). What is at issue here is not the question of homosexuality *per se*, or even of civil rights for homosexuals,[10] but of the lives and salvation of thousands of professing believers who claim to be Spirit-filled yet who cannot (for whatever reasons) cease to practice homosexual acts. Is there room within Pentecostal theology to accommodate such persons?

The Attachment

Whatever one seeks to make of it, there has existed in the minds of many historians a curious affinity between Pentecostal churches and homosexuals. Professed homosexuals themselves have claimed that there are larger numbers of gays within Pentecostal churches than within other denominations, and this claim has circulated freely among homosexual gatherings, although always with the admission that "straights" in these churches are usually unaware of the large presence.[11]

Some non-professing observers or non-homosexuals have noted a supposed disproportionate number of overt or flauntingly effeminate persons (thought to be homosexuals) in Black Pentecostalism.

Gospel music, and especially the Holiness church, attracts [sic] many homosexuals and lesbians. Now bisexuality is much more common, or at least more public, among poor Blacks and Puerto Ricans than among middle-class whites . . . many flamingly overt homosexuals flit through the Sanctified churches."[12]

Let it be said from the outset, that such blanket, universal statement is certainly do not apply to all churches of this faith. Furthermore, one must emphasize that no scientific studies have been made to determine if, in fact, Pentecostal churches do attract unusually larger percentages of gays, or even overtly effeminate persons. White social scientists have always preferred to think that Blacks have countenanced different spiritual practices more so than have whites; but here again, no scientific studies have been made to prove the point.[13] As far as sexual attitudes among Blacks and whites are concerned, some research has been attempted. It suggests, however, that while general tolerance of homosexuality may be greater among poorer Blacks, such is probably attributable to income rather than racial differentials. On the other hand, among Blacks affiliated with churches, "Blacks

---

the relationship has the approval of civil law.

10. There is nothing in the scripture to condone such discriminatory and oppressive opposition to civil and human rights for homosexuals (or anyone) as portrayed by Anita Bryant recently. Scripture does in some instances, however, speak to the spiritual causes or effects of homosexuality. (Some scholars differentiate between perversion, which Bible writers knew: and inversion, which Bible writers clearly did not know.) This article does not make any attempt to discuss particular passages of scripture or to discuss the belief that homosexual practices can be amorally or morally justifiable. Clearly, the multitude of Pentecostals are far from even considering that proposition.

11. "Homosexuals Convene in Kansas City,"

Christian Century (Nov. 5, 1969) 1436.

12. Tony Heilbut, *The Gospel Sound* (New York: Simon & Schuster, 1971), 211, 213.

13. While no scientific studies have been based on the general population, some differences in homosexuality as practiced among Blacks and whites in prison have been documented at least tentatively. See the chapter on "Racial Factors in Prison Homosexuality," in Peter C. Buffum, *Homosexuality in Prisons* (Washington, DC: U.S. Department of Justice, 1972) 22–24.

unquestioningly accepted the puritanical denunciation of homosexuality . . . and the Bible has provided a religious basis for Black abhorrence of homosexuality which transverses age groups."[14]

It is useless to debate without empirical validation the question of whether Pentecostal churches attract disproportionate numbers of overt gays. What is significant, is the fact that many persons do believe such is the case. As sociologists and others have pointed out, implications or consequences may be the same whether they result from mere belief or from actual fact. If enough persons act as if a thing is true, for all practical purposes it becomes true, at least existentially if not statistically,

Furthermore, the track record of Pentecostalism is such that there have been curious appearances of homosexuality even in "high places." Charles F. Parham, the man many white Pentecostals prefer to call their "founder," was widely thought to have been a homosexual. Fundamentalist writer and evangelist R. A. Torrey called Pentecostalism a movement "founded by a Sodomite." [15]And Alma White, leader of the Pillar of Fire movement, called both W. J. Seymour, the Black father of Pentecostalism, and Parham "rulers of spiritual Sodom" on the false supposition of "guilt by association."[16] Synan believes that Seymour's total rejection of Parham's sexual ethics was one of the causes for his rejection of Parham's leadership."[17] In

addition, the Apostolic movement within Pentecostalism has also borne the burden of similar rumors about Henry Prentice, the Black man who brought the Pentecostal message from Azusa Street in Los Angeles to Indianapolis."[18] Even in modern times, it is significant perhaps that the only nationwide denomination of gays, the Universal Fellowship of Metropolitan Community Churches, has Pentecostal leanings, Its founder, Troy Perry, as well as many of its members, claim to be both practicing Pentecostals and practicing homosexuals."[19]

One does not have to accept any special relationship between Pentecostalism and homosexuals, in spite of the foregoing illustrations. Nevertheless, it is legitimate to ask, What aspects of Pentecostalism appeal to homosexuals? Why has Pentecostalism any attraction for homosexuals, given the fact that this faith publicly denounces "free-sex" life-styles? Of course,

charge often made and repeatedly denied by Parham."

18. Prentice brought the Pentecostal message to G. T. Haywood in Indianapolis. Haywood became the seminal figure for the apostolic belief that there is only one person in the Godhead, not three, and that Jesus is God. It should be emphatically stated that both Seymour and Haywood were men of pure reputation. Of Haywood. it was said he lived "a life of purity that the world cannot dely." See James L. Tyson. *Before I Sleep* (Indianapolis: Pentecostal Publications, 1976) 100.

19. Not all MCC members are homosexuals, but the church is self-described as having a special ministry to gays. Church literature supports the idea that homosexual practices are not inherently sinful. Troy Perry was formerly a minister in the Church of God of Prophecy, a Pentecostal denomination headquartered in Cleveland, Tenn. For further study see Troy Perry, *The Lord Is My Shepherd and He Knows I'm Gay* (Los Angeles: Nash, 1972), Tom Swicegood, *Our God Too* (New York: Pyramid, 1972), Ronald Enroth and Gerald Jamison, *The Gay Church* (Grand Rapids: Eerdmans, 1974).

14. Jon L. Clayborne, "Blacks and Gay Liberation," *Gay Academic Union Journal* (Spring, 1977) 55.

15. R. A. Torrey, *The Holy Spirit* (New York: n. p., 1927).

16. Vinson Synan, *The Holiness-Pentecostal Movement* (Grand Rapids: Eerdmans, 1971) 143.

17. Ibid., 112. "One probable reason why Seymour rejected his authority was the reports that Parham was a practicing homosexual, a

the "spiritual" answers are well-known. Non-Pentecostals assert that the religion is not God-inspired, but given to heathen rituals which often included sexual libertinism.[20] Pentecostals, on the other hand, might counter by saying that God directs gays to the faith since it offers the only hope for real "deliverance." In actuality, one should look for other reasons which might be empirically based.

From the following, one may select possible reasons why homosexuals might be attracted to Pentecostalism. (1) The emphasis on guilt and damnation may correspond to or satisfy the need for psychological self-punishment which some psychiatrists have attributed to gays.[21] (2) The emphasis on continence before marriage may lessen the homosexual's fears that church women may expect or require sexual intimacy as a part of a friendship. (3) The promise of forgiveness, and more particularly the promise of "deliverance," held out by the church to gays could be a welcoming attraction to those gays desirous of changing their condition. (4) The personal attention given to the seeker at a Pentecostal altar, including the close physical contacts, may appeal to a homosexual's deep-seated need and desire for love, particularly from other males. (5) The intimacy sometimes associated with the brotherhood of male believers, including the "holy kiss" and frequent embracing, may offer special appeal either for its own value or as a sublimation of sexual desires. (6) The emotional catharsis associated with repentance, salvation, and speaking in tongues may temporarily conceal or diminish the feelings of guilt some homosexuals seem overburdened with. (7) The opportunities for participation which are extended to every worshipper, particularly in public speaking, music and leadership development, even at early ages, perhaps coincide with creative or artistic impulses or talents often thought characteristic particularly of gays. (8) The sexual symbolism in the holy dance may either be an attraction to gays in its own right; or it may offer an opportunity to redirect or sublimate sexual energies.[22] (9) The restrictions placed upon Pentecostal women in dress and administrative position may relate to the punishment of women which some psychiatrists say male homosexuals subconsciously desire."[23] (10) Both homosexuality and Pentecostalism are viewed by some sociologists as forms of rebellion against the status quo or the dominant values of society; for Blacks or persons of low- income, the need for rebellion in "safe" forms such as these may play a role. (11) Contrariwise, since many male homosexuals and especially those most exclusively inverted tend to be passive in overt personality traits, they may find special appeal in a religion which emphasizes non-violence and non-resistance; for Blacks, both homosexuality and Pentecostalism (insofar as it propagates white middle-class values) may be a symbol of accommodation to the dominant society. (12) Homosexuality and Pentecostalism may both be viewed by some as the only refuges for those who lack the super-male stereotype often necessary for survival in the streets. (13) To

20. H. J. Stolee, *Speaking in Tongues* (Minneapolis: Augsburg, 1963) 11–20.

21. Edmund Bergler, *Homosexuality: Disease or Way of Life?* (New York: Collier, 1962) 14–15, 28–29.

22. This is closely related to the way both religionists and psychologists hove viewed the effect of music and dancing on the libido. Inconsistently, Pentecostals have condemned secular dancing while promoting religious dancing.

23. Bergler, *Homosexuality: Disease or Way of Life?*, 15–16.

the extent that Blackness, homosexuality, and Pentecostalism all represent minorities, other mutual factors may be at work.

The Application

It would be easy for Pentecostals to "write off" their responsibility for the presence of homosexuals in their churches. Some have as a matter of course, simply viewed the congregation as a microcosm of general society-all the problems rampant "out there" in the streets are represented in that part of the congregation which is transient, i.e., not joined to the church in membership or salvation. Such dismissal of the church's role in fostering or neglecting homosexuality represents evasion of the issues. The church must indeed bear at least a portion of the responsibility for the presence of homosexuals in its membership, it in no other way than its failure to do more than it has to constructively meet the issue. Guilt by default is guilt nevertheless.

Evidence suggests that Pentecostalism has assuredly contributed to the problems homosexuals face in at least three ways.

(1) The movement has failed to give the gay person any sense of acceptance, forgiveness or assurance of his relationship with God. The truth of the matter is Black Pentecostalism particularly has failed to communicate such assurance to all its members— not just gays. The lack of positive preaching, the emphasis on condemnation and negativism, and the failure to develop any doctrine of assurance or witness of the Spirit (other than speaking in tongues) has led to spiritual uncertainty among most members. White fundamentalists, for all their shortcomings, seem to have more of a sense of personal acceptance by God than do Black Pentecostals.

(2) The movement has failed to develop an empirically realistic doctrine of sanctification which explains the recurring presence of sins in the lives of most believers, even the Holy Ghost-fined ones. This has left members to fend [or themselves in their battles with "besetting sins." For those members with chronic and unyielding sin problems, such as many homosexuals, this early and easily leads to hopelessness—a situation which aggravates the original problem, leading to a furious circle of ills. Members may be able to recite "holiness or hell," but they are given little practical advice (other than the stock answer of "prayer and fasting") for attaining the desired goal. It is sad to admit. but for many or even most, the possibility of hell looms larger on the horizon than the possibility of achieving or maintaining holiness.

(3) Closely related is the failure of the movement to come to grips with an empirically realistic doctrine of divine healing. Many are quick to accuse homosexuals of being "sick" individuals (despite disclaimers by the American Psychiatric Association),[24] yet they are not willing to grant them the same spiritual status they give other physically sick believers who for one reason or another do not find healing. Furthermore, while new or recurring bouts with physical illness are not viewed as evidence of back-

24. "Homosexuality Dropped as Mental Disorder," *American Psychological Association Monitor* 5:2, 1.

sliding, lapses in celibacy by homo-sexuals are not viewed with the same indulgence.

In all practical effects, what Pente-costalism has done has been to create a new category of sin and/or sickness which does not fit the customary molds of holi-ness and/or healing. Homosexuality, for official Pentecostal dam, has become the new sin and/or sickness "unto death." It has replaced anti-Pentecostalism as the new, modern "blasphemy of the Holy Ghost."[25] Such pessimism can do nothing but confirm gays in their rejection of the gospel; and the movement must certainly bear some of the eternal responsibility.

To say, however, that Pentecostalism has contributed to the problem, is not to ignore the various attempts (however crude or uninformed) that some min-isters have made to aid the homosexual. How have Pentecostals traditionally handled the issue? At least six ways will be mentioned here. First. there has been outright condemnation of all gays and gay activities from the pulpits. The most frequent response one encounters in the churches of this persuasion is a warning that all persons who commit such acts are damned.

When Paul wrote of the judgment of God upon the "effeminate," he was talking about homosexuals. He said that such will not inherit the kingdom of God.[26]

Second, the churches have confused the distinctions which exist between perversion and inversion. Pentecostal-ism acts as if it "knows only one kind of homosexual behavior—perversion. To the perplexing problem of inversion it has only indirect relevance.[27] Succinctly stated, perversion is a deliberate choice of behavior made willingly and gleefully, often in willful disregard for the will of God or in rebellion against it. Inversion, though, refers to an indeliberate homo-sexual orientation, a non-consenting and irreversible desire for a person of the same sex—a condition that is not willfully chosen in conscious and deliberate rebel-lion against God's will.

Inversion as a constitutional con-dition is a phenomenon which lies to-tally outside the Biblical perspective and considerations. Until recent findings of medical science and research came to light, inversion lay outside Christian [and Pentecostal] tradition and theological consideration altogether."[28]

Third, Pentecostal churches have often attempted to rush homosexually-inclined or inverted persons into quick marriages within the church. Partially, this stems from an old Black Pentecos-tal prohibition against courtship, which extended to a negation of long engage-ments. Partly also, it represents a mis-guided belief that the homosexual person needs only some kind of an outlet for his pent-up sexual energies—if he can be hurried into a heterosexual release, it is believed he will experience a lessening of homosexual interests. Of course, this position mistakenly identifies homosexu-ality with either conscious conditioning

25. Pentecostalism has long been divided on the definition of the unpardonable sin, blasphe-my against the Holy Ghost, sickness unto death and the sin unto death. Most have held these to be various terms for the same non-forgivable, evil act. Further, older generation Pentecostals usually defined this act to be the apostasy and denial of the reality of Pentecostalism on the part of a former tongues-speaker.

26. Lloyd Christiansen, "Should the Church Accept Homosexuals?" *The Pentecostal Evangel* (Feb 21, 1971) 19.

27. Anthony Kosnik et al., *Human Sexuality: New Directions in American Catholic Thought* (New York: Paulist Press, 1977) 200.

28. Ibid., 196.

or the strength of the sexual urge, rather than with the direction and the object of the urge. Many pastors have discovered too late, as a result, that marriage for homosexually-inclined individuals only adds more problems to the gay person's emotional life, that it sometimes hastens the person's "coming out" into full-fledged gay involvements, and that it is a perfect prescription for another inevitable divorce statistic.

"The homosexual already has a sexual neurosis by his attitude toward the opposite sex, a neurosis that is intra-psychic as well as social . . . the internal difficulties that both members of the union suffer are not eliminated by the marriage."[29]

The myth, perhaps the worst of all, [is that homosexuals simply require willpower to correct their condition, or an experience of heterosexual intercourse of heterosexual marriage.] A pastoral minister should never encourage a homosexual to contract a heterosexual marriage; in fact. such action should be positively discouraged."[30]

Fourth, the movement has often handled homosexuality as demon possession subject to exorcism. Gordon Lindsay, theologian for the deliverance and healing movement once popular within Pentecostalism, unapologetically states, "The real explanation to this [homosexuality] is the fact of demon possession. At one time their consciences revolted against this sin but the demon influence has changed their whole outlook."[31] Black Pentecostalism and the modern charismatic re-

newal movement have also emphasized exorcism of homosexual demons as the remedy. Contrary to the expected pattern for someone who is supposed to be demon-possessed, many practicing gay Pentecostal youths have willfully sought and undergone laying on of hands and exorcism in a self-chosen attempt to rid themselves of their "problem," though without positive results."[32]

In general. Pentecostalism has handled this subject the same way it has, at various times in the past, handled other subjects relating to personal ethics or science. (Wearing neckties, attending movies, buying televisions, and a host of other items, were all once roundly condemned although such condemnation by the churches did not seem to hinder the spiritual vitality of everyone who persisted in the new practices.) The movement has suffered (and still does) from a strongly anti-change mentality. There is a persistent temptation for the church to defy what it does not understand. This fear of that which is not understood (homosexuality is a good example) is bolstered by a super-spiritual hypocrisy which encourages the church to think it has the answers when all the physicians, psychologists, psychiatrists, biologists, and sociologists clearly admit that they do not.

If the Pentecostal movement has been correct in these approaches to gays, what then have been the results? What successes have Pentecostals had in exorcising, "curing," or "delivering" homosexuals? Without controversy, Pentecostals will admit that the successes in reorienting gays have been very few, if any at all. Homosexuality does not readily yield

29. John F. Harvey, "Pastoral Responses to Gay World Questions," in Dwight Oberholtzer, ed., *Is Gay Good?* (Philadelphia: Westminster, 1971) 131.

30. Kosnick et al., 213.

31. Lindsay, "The New America [*sic*] Horror," 7.

32. Troy Perry recounts his numerous attempts to find "deliverance" by means of exorcism at the hands of classical Pentecostal ministers, in his book, cited above.

even to Pentecostal analysis or treatment. While some of the more sensational evangelists claim to have "witnessed" (whatever that means) the "deliverance" or "cure" of gays; and while all Pentecostals alike clearly assert that God can "deliver" or "cure" gays; not a single, solitary case exists where a believer has been freed from homosexual inversion. The most any Pentecostal ministry has been able to claim, is that it has enabled some [usually always unidentified) person to live for a short period of time without succumbing to, i.e., yielding to or participating in, overt homosexual activities. Even in these few instances, no clear testimony or name is released, respectfully because the failure rate of resistance to inverted gay desires is so short-lived."[33]

Pentecostals are thus being patently dishonest when they use the terms "cured" or "delivered" or "freed" in reference to homosexuality. If all that Pentecostal experiences can offer is an indeterminate but conditional period of time when one is supposedly "enabled" to keep from giving in to his still-retained desires to commit a homosexual act, then Pentecostalism offers no more than willpower or positive-thinking approaches (which are certainly not unique to Pentecostalism at all). To continue to use such terms as "deliverance" and "cure" in reference to constant volitional suppression of one's own self and own desires is intellectually dishonest, theologically absurd, and terribly misleading to both the gays and the other members of our churches. Such careless mishandling of terminology not only robs these words of their potential Significance, it also may lead others to be wary of these terms when similarly used in reference to "freedom" from guilt and condemnation and eternal punishment (the essence of the gospel). If observers are led to doubt promises of healing and "deliverance," then they may also doubt promises of forgiveness and grace and eternal life.

The persistent Pentecostal use of such terms in reference to homosexuality, may, on the other hand, sometimes be a case of ignorance. Most do not understand important distinctions, such as between perversion and inversion; between the person who plays the dominant role only, and the person who habitually and preferentially plays the passive role; between actions and conditions; between homosexual experimentation and homosexual orientation; between non-exclusive homosexuality and exclusive homosexuality. (In each of the above sets, the former mayor may not be subject to change; the latter is not.) Neither do most understand the differences between altering life-styles and altering total behavior; between adjusting to non-exclusive alternatives, and constantly combating exclusively-directed urges; between creating new responses and eliminating old desires completely. (In each of these sets, the former represents the partial modifications which can

33. Which brings us once again to the issue of how many sins or lapses is one permitted while testifying to being "saved" or "delivered," without losing his relationship with God! Pentecostal doctrine, for all its enormous claims, seems to be able to give "overcoming power" only for short durations of time—which is certainly not "overcoming power" at all. Not a single saint, as far as can be determined, exists in any single Pentecostal or Holiness church anywhere who can claim not to have sinned since the day he was "sanctified" or "Holy Ghost filled." Sanctification or the Holy Ghost baptism then cannot be said to empower one to live without sin, except in a limited potential and theoretical sense, and then only for a short period of time. It is doubtful if the length of "overcoming" time, even regarding conscious transgressions, is longer for Pentecostal saints than for true Christians (who do not profess sanctification or Pentecost) in other evangelical churches.

sometimes be achieved, at least temporarily, even without religion; the latter have not been achieved even with Pentecostal fullness.)

No empirical proof exists that any person, under the influence of Pentecostalism or otherwise, has ever been completely changed from exclusive inversion to exclusive heterosexuality. Even non-exclusive readjustment is practically non-existent.

The rate of recovery is so slight as to call seriously into question the legitimacy of referring at all to an apparent cure. This seems particularly true if "cure" is taken to mean the adoption or attainment of a psychological attitude unaffected and uninfluenced by the individual's prior homosexual actions. To speak of [this] . . . is to describe the unreal."[34]

It matters not what theory of cause one attributes to the incidence or phenomenon of homosexuality. For all practical purposes, it is useless to argue whether a person is born an invert or becomes one as the result of childhood family tensions or other environmental or psychological or sociological factors. "The fact that homosexuality is [may be] an acquired characteristic does not by any means imply that it can be sloughed off later" even through will-power or radical religious commitment." The doctrine of the "freedom of the will" which Pentecostals share with some other evangelicals is veritably deficient.

From psychological forces operative long before responsible choice is made, the molding of life has occurred in such manner that the sexual propensities have been reversed, perhaps indeed in varying degrees for different individuals, but

34. Michael F. Valente, *Sex: The Radical View of a Catholic Theologian* (New York: Stein & Day, 1960) 41.

in such manner that now a homosexual "condition" truly exists, and homosexual activity becomes an expression of one's "nature."[35]

Even the Teen Challenge ministries of Dave Wilkerson, which have had such tremendous successes with "deliverance" of youths from drug addiction, have admitted that homosexuality poses an entirely different and usually insurmountable obstacle. Other Pentecostal and evangelical ministries to homosexuals, such as Sanctuary House in Virginia, have been founded on the premise that God not only can, but does, and promises to "cure" or "deliver" from homosexuality.[36] But these ministries are silently undergoing real crises at present, since their faith has not yielded faithfulness among those supposedly "delivered." Other Pentecostal approaches such as "Pastor Dave" in Saskatchewan, Canada, simply play word games with the terms "homosexual" and "gay;" so that a believer is told that once he is saved he is no longer to accept the classification or identity of himself as "a homosexual" or as "a gay." But denying that one is an invert in the face of continuing desires, produces only greater psychological distress among the truly repentant.

If, in fact, any person has ever been ridded of inversion, such should be

35. Oberholtzer, *Is Gay Good?* 9.

36. Pentecostal laymen have often confused these propositions. The question has never been, "Can God?" The questions are rather, "Does God?", and more especially, "Does God usually or always?" God can perform miracles, but he seldom chooses to do so. Further, a distinction must be made between healing and miracles. Pentecostal theology holds that healing (from an acquired "illness") is provided in the atonement and promised by faith; miracles (changing natural states or conditions) are not provided in the atonement or promised to all by faith. but are the result of the sovereignty of God and subject to His will in unusual circumstances.

attributed to the miraculous power of God. But miracles are not promised to everyone on the same faith conditions as are forgiveness and the gift of the Holy Ghost. While God certainly can deliver from homosexuality and blindness and mental retardation (and a host of other "hard cases"), He does not usually do so.

To close the discussion at this point would be to leave questions unanswered, as well as a generally pessimistic tone. It is therefore fitting to ask, How can Pentecostals better approach homosexuality? Both doctrinal and practical suggestions are in order.

The Approach

Doctrinally, Pentecostalism can accommodate the possibility of homosexuals as true believers without any major[37] alterations in key points of faith. Specifically, no changes in the doctrines of sin and sanctification need occur in order to accept homosexuals within the household of faith. No lowering of the "standard" of sin or sanctification is needed in order to make this adjustment. Pentecostals need not *justify* homosexuality in order to see that God justifies through faith the homosexual person. Ministers may still preach the sinfulness of homosexuality and homosexual acts; no acceptance of MCC or "gay theology" is required, i.e., one does not *have* to view homosexuality as "good" or *even* a simple amoral difference. Like all other sinful deeds and thoughts and

motives, homosexuality may be seen as a universal effect or sign of the fallen state of mankind generally—certainly "missing the mark," "corning short of the glory," and less than God's perfect plan of heterosexual marriage and procreation."[38] At the same time, however, carefulness must be taken to ensure that homosexuality is not regarded as greater than other sins."[39]

In turn, ministers may still preach the possibility of holiness, sanctification, or Christian perfection (under whatever terms are used by each denomination). One does not *have* to discard belief in the possibility of a holy heart or *even* a holy life in order to admit that few Pentecostals have actually attained or obtained "[40] this ideal. In fact, the rediscovery of the

37. Obviously some subjective judgments are involved here, since what some consider "major" others may consider "minor" points. Holiness churches may be considered as emphasizing major doctrines of sin and sanctification; Pentecostal churches may be considered as emphasizing major doctrines of the Holy Ghost and spiritual gifts. Some denominations share both emphases and traditions.

38. While in the viewpoint of gay liberationists such description of homosexuality as sin may be utterly unacceptable, it will be a progressive step forward for Pentecostals to view it as no greater sin than any other transgression.

39. While all sin deserves eternal death, Christ's atonement clearly cancels out that penalty of death for all who accept Him. Homosexuality is provided a covering in the blood even as every other sin is. While in the eyes of God, all sin merits death, in terms of practical effects (as far as mankind is concerned) social sins are "worse" than personal sins; while even among personal sins, Jesus stressed sinful motives (the interior life) more than he did sinful actions. If Pentecostals begin to emphasize these things, a needful corrective will he applied to the entire movement and many additional misplaced emphases will also be corrected.

40. Apostolics and the Deliverance wing of Black Pentecostalism view sanctification as an ongoing process, to be attained through personal, spiritual effort and growth. As such they may most easily accept homosexuals or other "imperfect" saints into the fold. Wesleyan Pentecostals, on the other hand, have traditionally viewed sanctification as a crisis experience obtainable by faith subsequent to justification. They will have more difficulty adjusting to this acceptance since to do so will require admitting that entire sanctification may not be a prerequisite for the Pentecostal baptism, but may actually come much later than the filling of the Holy Ghost.

Biblical categories of "carnal Christians," "babes in Christ," and unprofitable Pentecostal gift"; without love (as stressed by Paul in his Corinthian letters among other places) may lead to a more intensely honest appraisal of Pentecostal spirituality generally.

Accepting the possibility that a person may be a Spirit-baptized Christian believer and still beset by recurring problems with homosexuality, will not damage the Pentecostal thrust, if gay activities or lapses are *viewed* as either sin or sickness. Considered as simply one of many kinds of continuing sins or sicknesses in the believer, homosexuality can be understood and accepted (though not necessarily approved) by the Pentecostal *movement*. Although it has not often been realized, (and even less often preached), Pentecostal theology, whether Baptistic or Wesleyan,[41] makes allowances far imperfections continuing in the lives of the saints. Unfortunately, this is one of the "best kept." secrets in Pentecostalism.

How does Pentecostalism make allowance for imperfections? It does so in several ways, depending upon the particular definition of sin emphasized in each definition. (There is no uniquely Pentecostal doctrine of harmartiology. Pentecostals have never formulated a distinctive theology of their own except with reference to one doctrine: speaking in tongues as the initial evidence of the

Baptism of the Holy Ghost. Every other doctrine has a non-Pentecostal historical origin; some Pentecostal groups' doctrinal differences are traceable to the former affiliations of their founders.)

(1) Some Pentecostal churches accept a Calvinistic definition of sin as "any deviation from the perfect will of God, in word or thought or deed, whether done intentionally or unintentionally." By this standard. a Christian can be "sanctified" in his position or status in Christ, while still "being sanctified by degrees" in actual day-to-day experience as he continues to draw closer to God. He is positionally sanctified; while experientially still being sanctified; i.e., not quite yet perfect. Almost all Pentecostal churches which emphasize sanctification as a progressive experience, accept this doctrine of sin, in the same sense, the Pentecostal experience may give one the potential power *over* sin, but. in actual experience that. potential is not always appropriated or utilized, Hence, the Corinthian church, probably one of the most. thoroughly Pentecostal ones in Paul's time, still had problems with fornication, and lack of love, and carnal divisions and jealousies among its constituents."[42]

(2) Some Pentecostal churches accept an Arminian definition of sin as "any willful transgression of a known law of God." By this standard, it is easier to claim entire sanctification or complete freedom from sinning since the standard has in essence been adjusted to make perfect obedience easier and surer. As long as a

---

41. "Baptistic" refers to those churches, including Apostolic and Deliverance. which view sanctification as a progressive experience, as do Baptists. "Wesleyan" refers to those churches. primarily with roots in the early Holiness movement, which view sanctification as an instantaneous experience. (See above note [Ed., n. 40]) The first historian to use the term "Baptistic" in this sense was Klaude Kendrick, *The Promise Fulfilled: A History of the Modern Pentecostal Movement* (Springfield[, MO]: Gospel Publishing House, 1961) 75, 145.

42. An excellent discussion by a Holiness theologian of the various doctrines of sin, including Calvinism, is contained in Richard S. Taylor, *A Right Conception of Sin* (Kansas City: Beacon Hill, 1960). Key scripture references for the Calvinistic approach include: Rom 3:23–31; 7:15–23; 8:26–39; 14:1; I Cor 3:1–3; 5:1, 5; 13:1–13; 14:1–12; Eph 4:1–4; Phil 1:12: I Jn 1:8.

Pentecostal believer does not willfully choose to disobey God in rebellion by doing something he personally has been convicted against doing, he may claim (under this definition) to be free from sinning. Thus if a person has no personal conviction of wrongdoing, or has not "seen the light" on a particular issue, or is subject to conditions (whether psychological or social or physical] over which he has no control or no freedom of will, he has not properly and scripturally-speaking "sinned." In this sense, the Pentecostal experience may "lead one into more truth." but it does not ensure that all believers arrive at all the truth at the same period in time, Hence, the need for Paul to continually instruct, and correct, the early church in his numerous writings?[43]

(3) Some Pentecostal churches accept a Wesleyan definition of sin as "any violation of the law of *love*." By this standard, the unbeliever is judged by the written commandments of Scripture; whereas the believer is judged under a different standard known as the "perfect law of *love*." According to this view, a Christian is sanctified or "made perfect in *love*" when he trusts Christ to purify his inward being of all unloving tempers and motives. This is an instantaneous experience. And a sanctified or perfect Christian is one who is pure in heart, while he may still be less than ideal in actions or character. Thus a person may commit a multitude of infractions of the commandments, but if he does so, he is not held guilty for his actions, so long as his motives remained pure in their *love* for God and man. A man may, in this view, be mistakenly wrong, without being *Sinfully* wrong, In this sense, the Pentecostal experience is unrelated to sanctification. (Wesley himself never identified entire sanctification or Christian perfection as being the baptism in the Holy Ghost.) It is not power over sin, but power to be a more effective witness—a Pentecostal witness, endued with convincing signs and proofs—which is the purpose of the fullness of the Holy Ghost."[44]

(4) If homosexuality is viewed as sickness rather than sin, then there is another Pentecostal approach. The failure to find "healing" from homosexuality may be viewed as the result of a lack of faith, a postponement of God's will, or a "thorn in the flesh." In other words, the failure to find "healing" from this physical or psychological "infirmity" should not be viewed as affecting one's salvation, any more than the failure to find a cure for cancer or any other humanly-difficult disease. One may enter heaven with a sick body, but not with an unrepentant spirit.

Practically speaking, Pentecostalism should attempt to minister to homosexuals in the following ways: (I) By encouraging them to feel comfortable in the church, rather than forcing them outside where a whole alternative "gay lifestyle"

---

43. An excellent treatment by a Holiness theologian of the various doctrinal schools vs. Arminianism is contained in W. T. Purkhiser, *Conflicting Concepts of Holiness* (Kansas City: Beacon Hill, 1961). Key scripture references for the Arminian position include: Jn 16:13, 17:7; Jas 4:17; and I Jn 1:7, 2:27, and 3:21.

44 The primary source for this viewpoint is, of course, John Wesley, *A Plain Account of Christian Perfection* (reprinted, Kansas City: Beacon Hill, 1966). Other excellent articles are: Irwin L. Brown, "The Relation of Knowledge to the Experience of Holiness," in Kenneth Geiger. Further Insights into Holiness (Kansas City: Beacon Hill, 1963): and Roy S. Nicholson, "Holiness and the Human Element" in Geiger's insights into Holiness, a companion volume. For crucial scripture references for this position see Wesley's famous "Thirty Texts" in *Plain Account*, and the following: Matt 22:37–40; Jn 17:26; Rom 5:13, 20; 6:14–17; 7:1–6; 8:2; Heb 4:9–10; and 1 Jn 2:5; 4:12, 17–18.

may result. Because the Christian is concerned about sin, he will not seek by his reactions or responses to drive another person from one sin to twenty. (2) By encouraging the homosexual to become a truly loving individual and a witness for Christ, thus lessening the tendency toward promiscuity and reckless indifference to other Christian standards. After all, private sin is not as damaging to the cause of Christ as is public sin. (3) By encouraging the person to see God at work in his life, despite his homosexuality and despite his failure to understand it, so that faith may grow together with a calm reliance upon God's promises to bring him finally into his eternal kingdom. The Holy Ghost, it is true, is not like a spoiled child who picks up his toys and runs home when he doesn't get his way. Rather the Comforter "abides" to "reprove of sin, righteousness and judgment."

This is the moment when it would be more honest and moral for the Christian to adopt an ethic of distress, admitting to himself and his God that his actions beyond this point are not Christian or ethical. In adopting an ethic of distress, the Christian seeks no ethical justification for what he feels he must do.[45]

The difference is analogous to the distinction between the redeemed sinner and the unredeemed sinner. One recognizes that, despite his participation in it, the world is unjust, and he must be committed to its liberation. The other believes that the world is in good hands, and he enjoys his participation in it. This distinction is crucial.[46]

45. Major J. Jones, *Christian Ethics for Black Theology* (Nashville: Abingdon, 1974) 176.

46. James H. Cone, *God of the Oppressed* (New York: Seabury, 1975) 220.

Afterword

Prayer for Freedom from Race Prejudice

ROBERT CLARENCE LAWSON (1883–1961)

Church of Our Lord Jesus Christ of the Apostolic Faith

God, who has made man in thine own likeness, and who doth love all that Thou hast made, suffer us not because of difference of race, color, or condition to separate ourselves from others, and thereby from thee. But teach us the unity of thy family and universality of thy love. As a Son, being born of a Hebrew mother who had the blood of many nations in her veins, you ministered first to thy brethren of Israel. But you also rejoiced in the faith of a Syro-Phoenician woman, and a Roman soldier, and suffered your cross to be carried by an Ethiopian. Teach us also Savior, while loving and serving our own, to enter into the communion of the whole human family: and forbid that from pride of birth, color, achievement and hardness of heart, we should despise any for whom You died nor injure or grieve any in whom You live.

We pray in Jesus' precious name. *Amen*

Bibliography

Allen, Earline, editor. *Go Tell My Brethren: Overcoming Changes and Challenges Facing Women in Ministry in the Church of God in Christ*. Hazel Crest, IL: Faithday, 2005.

Allen, W. F. "The Ring Shout." *The Nation*, May 30, 1867. Reprinted in *Afro-American Folk-Songs: A Study in Racial and National Music*, edited by Edward Henry Krehbiel, 33. New York: Ungar 1962.

Bright, C. F. "Stick to the Church of God." *Church of God Evangel* 15/13 (March 29, 1924) 2.

Brown, Hallie Q., compiler. *Homespun Heroines and Other Women of Distinction*. Schomburg Library of Nineteenth-Century Black Women Writers. New York: Oxford University Press, 1988,

Bryant, John R. "I Believe in the Holy Ghost." In *The Preaching of Bishop John Bryant*. Edited by Mankekolo Mahlangu-Ngcobo. Baltimore: Victory, 1992.

Christian, William. *Poor Pilgrim's Work in the Name of the Father, Son and Holy Ghost*. Texarkana: Joe Erlich Print, 1896.

Collier-Thomas, Bettye, editor. *Daughters of Thunder: Black Women Preachers and Their Sermons, 1850–1979*. San Francisco: Jossey-Bass, 1998.

Cotton, Emma. "The Inside Story of the Outpouring of the Holy Spirit—Azusa Street—April 1906." *Message of the Apostolic Faith* 1/1 (April 1936) 1–3.

Dabney, E. J. *What It Means to Pray Through*. Philadelphia: Dabney, 1945.

Farrow, Lucy. "The Work In Virginia." *Apostolic Faith* 1/2 (October 1906) 3.

Field, Jim. "History and Philosophy of Community Organization." Paper presented to the SCUPE Congress on Urban Ministry, March 17–21, 2001, Chicago, Illinois.

Foote, Julia. *A Brand Plucked from the Fire: An Autobiographical Sketch by Mrs Julia A Foote*. New York: Higgens, 1879.

Franklin, Robert M. "The Gospel of Bling." *Sojourners Magazine* 36/1 (January 2007) 18–23.

Gaines, Adrienne. "Revive Us, Precious Lord." *Charisma and Christian Life* 28/11 (May 2003) 39.

Garlington, Joseph L. *Right or Reconciled? God's Heart for Reconciliation!* Shippensburg, PA: Destiny-Image, 1998.

General Assembly of the Church of God. "Resolution on Human Rights," 67–68. Cleveland, TN: Church of God Publishing House, 1964.

———. "Resolution on Racism and Ethnic Disparity." Cleveland, TN: Church of God Publishing House, 1991.

General Presbytery of the Assemblies of God. *Statement of the General Presbytery Regarding Social Concern*. Springfield, MO: General Presbytery of the Assemblies of God, 1968.

Golder, Morris E. *"The Principles of Our Doctrine": What We Believe*. Indianapolis: Grace Apostolic Church, n.d.

Goodwin, Bennie E. "Social Implications of Pentecostal Power." *Spirit: A Journal of Issues Incident to Black Pentecostalism* 1/1 (1977) 31–35.

Goodwin, Randolph. "Can a Woman Preach or Teach the Gospel of Christ." Online: http://theholytemplechurch.org/pdf/CAN_A_WOMAN_PREACH_OR_TEACH_THE_GOSPEL_OF_CHRIST.pdf/.

Harrison, Bob, with Jim Montgomery. *When God Was Black*. Grand Rapids: Zondervan, 1971.

Haywood, Garfield T. *Before the Foundation of the World: A Revelation of the Ages*. Indianapolis: Christ Temple, 1923.

————. *The Birth of the Spirit in the Days of the Apostles*. Portland, OR: Apostolic Book Publishers, n.d.

Horn, Rosa Artimis. "Is Jesus God the Father or Is He the Son of God?" Sermon delivered on WNYX Radio, New York, NY, n.d.

————. "Was a Woman Called to Preach?" Sermon delivered on WNYX Radio, New York, NY, n.d.

Hurston, Zora Neale. *The Sanctified Church*. New York: Marlowe, 1981.

Hutchins, Julia. "Sister Hutchins Testimony." *Apostolic Faith* 1/2 (October 1906) 1.

Jones, Charles Price. *The Gift of the Holy Spirit in the Book of Acts*. Jackson, MS: Truth Publishing Co., 1910.

Kosnik Anthony et al., *Human Sexuality: New Directions in American Catholic Thought* New York: Paulist, 1977.

Lawson, Robert C. *The Anthropology of Jesus Christ Our Kinsman*. Piqua, OH: Ohio Ministries, 1925.

Lewis, Meharry H., compiler and annotator. *Mary Magdalene Lewis Tate: Collected Letters and Manuscripts*. Nashville: New and Living Way, 2003.

Mason, Charles Harrison. "Tennessee Evangelist Witnesses." *Apostolic Faith* 1/6 (February–March 1907) 7.

Mason, Mary. *The History and Life Work of Bishop C. H. Mason and His Co-laborers*. Memphis: Church of God in Christ, 1924.

Moore, Jennie Evans. "Music from Heaven." *Apostolic Faith* 1/8 (May 1907) 3.

O'Quinn, Doretha A. *Silent Voices, Powerful Messages: The Historical Influence and Contribution of the African-American Experience in the Foursquare Gospel Movement*. Los Angeles: International Church of the Foursquare Gospel, 2002.

Pentecostal and Charismatic Churches of North America. *Racial Reconciliation Manifesto*. N.p.: PCCNA, 1994.

Ramsey, Jerry. *The Ordination of Women: Right or Wrong?* Gloster, MS: Old Path In-reach Ministries, n.d.

Rawick, George P., editor. *The American Slave: A Composite Autobiography*. Vol. 16. Contributions to Afro-American and African Studies 11. Westport CT: Greenwood, 1972.

Richardson, James C. *With Water and Spirit: A History of Black Apostolic Denominations in the U.S.* Washington, DC: Spirit Press, 1980.

Robinson, Blondell. "A Personal View on the Ordination of Women." In *Go Tell My Brethren: Overcoming Changes and Challenges Facing Women in Ministry in the Church of God in Christ*, edited by Earline Allen, 81–84. Hazel Crest, IL: Faithday, 2005.

Robinson, Ida. "The Economic Depression." *Latter Day Messenger* (May 23, 1935) 2.

Seymour, William J. *The Doctrines and Disciplines of the Azusa Street Mission of Los Angeles, CA*. Los Angeles: Azusa Mission, 1915.

Smith, Amanda Berry. *An Autobiography: The Story of the Lord's Dealings with Mrs. Amanda Smith the Colored Evangelist; Containing an Account of Her Life Work of Faith, and Her Travels in America, England, Ireland, Scotland, India, and Africa, as an Independent Missionary*. Chicago: Meyers & Brother, 1893.

Stevens, Shirley. *A New Testament View of Women*. Nashville: Broadman, 1980.

Tate, Mary Magdalene Lewis. "A Letter from Mother Tate Concerning Baptism." In *Mary Magdalene Lewis Tate: Collected Letters and Manuscripts*, compiled and annotated by Meharry H. Lewis, 34. Nashville: New and Living Way, 2003.

————. "A Special Message from Mother to Her Children." In *Mary Magdalene Lewis Tate: Collected Letters and Manuscripts*, compiled and annotated by Meharry H. Lewis, 36. Nashville : New and Living Way, 2003.

Tinney, James S. "Homosexuality as a Pentecostal Phenomenon." *Spirit: A Journal of Issues Incident to Black Pentecostalism* 1/2 (1977) 45–59.

Wiley, Ophelia. "Sermon on a Dress." *Apostolic Faith* 1/2 (October 1906) 2.

Credits

CHAPTER 1
Excerpts from *The Sanctified Church* are used with permission from the Zora Neale Hurston Trust.

"Is It Right for the Saints of God to Dance?" by Charles Harrison Mason, was previously published in *History and Formative Years of the Church of God in Christ with Excerpts from the Life and Work of Its Founder* (Memphis: Church of God in Christ Publishing House, 1969).

CHAPTER 2
All works are in the public domain.

CHAPTER 3
All works are in the public domain.

CHAPTER 4
"A Special Letter from Mother to Her Children," by Mary Magdalene Lewis Tate, was previously published in *Mary Lena Lewis Tate: Collected Letters and Manuscripts*, compiled and annotated by Meharry H. Lewis (Nashville: New and Living Way Publishing House, 2003). Used by permission.

"Elder Mason Tells of Receiving the Holy Ghost," by Charles Harrison Mason, was previously published in *The History and Life Work of Elder C. H. Mason, Chief Apostle, and His Co-Workers*, by C. H. Mason and Mary Mason, 1924.

Excerpt from *The Basis of Union* ("Who We Are") and the excerpts called "Sanctification" and "Baptism of the Holy Spirit" were previously published in *Introducing the Fire Baptized Holiness Church of God of the Americas: A Study Manual*, edited by Patrick L. Frazier (Wilmington, NC: The Fire Baptized Holiness Church of God of the Americas, 1990).

"Jesus Christ: The Surprising Contemporary," by Herbert Daughtry, was previously published in *Jesus Christ: African in Origin, Revolutionary and Redeeming in Action* (New York: House of the Lord Church, 1985).

CHAPTER 5

"Water Baptism" and "Jehovah of the Old Testament Is Jesus of the New Testament," by James C. Richardson Jr., were previously published in *With Water and Spirit: A History of Black Apostolic Denominations in the United States* (Washington DC: Spirit, 1980).

"A Letter from Mother Tate Concerning Baptism in the Name of 'Jesus Only,'" by Magdalena Lewis Tate, was previously published in *Mary Lena Lewis Tate: Collected Letters and Manuscripts*, compiled and annotated by Meharry H. Lewis (Nashville: New and Living Way Publishing House, 2003). Used by permission.

CHAPTER 6

"Stick with the Church of God," by Crawford F. Bright, was previously published in *The Church of God Evangel* (March 29, 1924) 2, and is reprinted courtesy of the Dixon Pentecostal Research Center, Cleveland, Tennessee.

"Let Their Works Speak for Them and the Strength of Their Faith Live On in Us," by Doretha A. O'Quinn, was previously published in *Silent Voices, Powerful Messages: The Historical Influence and Contribution of the African-American Experience in the Foursquare Gospel Movement* (Los Angeles: International Church of the Foursquare Gospel, 2002). Used by permission.

"Resolution on Human Rights" was previously published in *Minutes of the 50th Church of God General Assembly* (Cleveland, TN: Church of God Publishing House, 1964). Copyright Pathway Press. Used by permission of the Church of God Publishing House/Pathway Press.

"Resolution on Racism and Ethnic Disparity" was previously published in *Minutes of the 68th Church of God General Assembly* (Cleveland, TN: Church of God Publishing House, 2000). Copyright Pathway Press. Used by permission of the Church of God Publishing House/Pathway Press.

CHAPTER 7

"My Covenant Ends" and "God's Approval and Manifestation," by Elizabeth J. Dabney, were previously published in *What It Means to Pray Through* (Memphis: Church of God in Christ Publishing Board, 1991).

"Closing Argument," by Earline Allen, was previously published in *Go Tell My Brethren: Overcoming Changes and Challenges Facing Women in Ministry in the Church of God in Christ*, edited by Earline Allen (Hazel Crest, IL: Faithday Press, 2005).

"Personal Views on the Ordination of Women in the Church of God in Christ," by BLondell Robinson, was previously published in *Go Tell My Brethren: Overcoming Changes and Challenges Facing Women in Ministry in the Church of God in Christ*, edited by Earline Allen (Hazel Crest, IL: Faithday Press, 2005).

"The Ordination of Women and Those Who Support Them," and "Summary," by Jerry Ramsey III were previously published in *The Ordination of Women: Right or Wrong?* (N.p.: Old Path In-Reach Ministries, n.d.).

"Can a Woman Preach or Teach the Gospel of Christ?", by Randolph G. Goodwin, was previously published in *Should Women Preach?* (N.p.: Holy Temple Church of Our Lord Jesus Christ of the Apostolic Faith, n.d.).

CHAPTER 8
Material from *Right or Reconciled?: God's Heart for Reconciliation*, by Joseph L. Garlington, is used by permission of Destiny Image Publishers, 167 Walnut Bottom Road, Shippensburg, PA 17257, http://www.destinyimage.com/.

"I Believe in the Holy Ghost," by John Richard Bryant, is used by permission of the author.

CHAPTER 9
"Social Implications of Pentecostal Power," by Bennie E. Goodwin, was previously published in *Spirit: A Journal of Issues Incident to Black Pentecostalism* 1/1 (1977) 31–35.

"Racial Reconciliation Manifesto" (1994), by Ithiel Clemmons et al., is used by permission of the Pentecostal/Charismatic Churches of North America.

"A God of Justice," by George D. McKinney, was previously published in *Reconciliation: Official Journal of the Pentecostal/Charismatic Churches of North America (PCCNA)* 1 (Summer 1998) 4–5.

"Shall We Call This Dream Progressive Pentecostalism?", by James A. Forbes, was previously published in *Spirit: A Journal of Issues Incidental to Black Pentecostalism* 1/1 (1977) 12–15. Used by permission of the author.

"Homosexuality as a Pentecostal Phenomenon," by James S. Tinney, was previously published in *Spirit: A Journal of Issues Incident to Black Pentecostalism* 1/2 (1977) 45–59. It is republished here with the permission of the Moorland-Spingarn Research Center at Howard University, which houses the James S. Tinney Papers.

Index

Index